Singapore Food

Wendy Hutton

Singapore Food

Wendy Hutton

TIMES BOOKS INTERNATIONAL
Singapore • Kuala Lumpur

FOR PETER
WHO NOT ONLY DESIGNED AND EDITED THIS
BOOK, BUT LITERALLY ATE HIS WAY THROUGH
IT MANY TIMES.

Editor's Note: Three of the "Quartet of Cooks" are real people; the fourth – Mrs Tan
– is a composite portrait of a number of Nonya ladies interviewed by the author,
and does not refer to a specific Mrs Tan. The illustrations on page 2 and pages 24 to
41 are not pictures of the women referred to by name in the text of the book.

Photographs: Reg Morrison

© 1989 Wendy Hutton
(Published by Times Books International,
an imprint of Times Editions Pte Ltd)
Times Centre
1 New Industrial Road
Singapore 1953

2nd Floor
Wisma Hong Leong Yamaha
50 Jalan Penchala
46050 Petaling Jaya
Selangor Darul Ehsan
Malaysia

First published in Australia by Ure Smith
This edition reprinted in 1992

Printed in Singapore

ISBN 981 204 305 5

Preface

When I first sampled Singapore food in 1967, my delight was matched by frustration at not being able to cook more of it myself. I longed to be able to reproduce the magnificent Indian vegetarian dishes served on a banana leaf, to prepare richly spiced Malay curries and to cook Singapore's famous chilli crab. But I couldn't identify the majority of mysterious foodstuffs in the market, and didn't know how to cope with the tasks so simple for a Singapore cook. Was I supposed to boil hundred-year eggs? How did I prepare a bird's nest for soup? Should I soak dried fish before cooking it?

Patient effort eventually paid off. I gradually learned the names and uses of the tantalising goodies available. Generous friends let me watch them cook, and shared their family recipes. Chinese kitchen hands laughed good-naturedly as I peered into bubbling pots in restaurant kitchens, and my Indian spice merchant fed my children on rock sugar as he lit the daily incense stick and advised me on the combination of spices for various dishes.

I found to my delight that once I had learned the basic ingredients and methods, I could easily follow recipes and turn out delicious local food. When my husband told me he thought I prepared a certain local dish better than a well-known restaurant, I took it as flattery. But when Singaporean friends started saying that I cooked *rendang*, *dosay* or paper-wrapped chicken just as well as they did, I became convinced that there is no reason why any enthusiastic Western cook cannot prepare authentic Asian food in her own kitchen, either in Singapore or elsewhere.

I would like to share my years of culinary adventure with cooks everywhere. Increasing numbers of Westerners are learning the delights of Asian food. Those who have yet to visit Singapore and fall in love with the food will be able to do so from a distance, and foreigners lucky enough to have enjoyed a morning bowl of noodles at the edge of a bustling market in Chinatown, or to have sat out under the stars eating *satay*, will be able to relive their memories with this book. I also hope that Singapore girls who are learning to cook — now that the days of *amahs* and resident mothers-in-law are fast disappearing — will find this book helpful.

Wendy Hutton

5

Contents

Four cooks (facing title page) representing the Nonya, Chinese, Indian and Malay culinary traditions of Singapore. The satay man (opposite) fans his charcoal into life and cooks his ever-popular morsels with great flair.

Introduction

'Chah pah boey?' 'Sudah makan?' 'Sapittacha?'

Food is almost a national obsession in Singapore. When you meet a friend, you don't ask 'How are you?' but 'Have you eaten?' The reason becomes apparent the moment you begin to experience the endlessly varied culinary delights of Singapore. One of the first outsiders to sample the local food was Stamford Raffles; when he stepped ashore in 1819 to negotiate the purchase of the island as a British trading base, he was showered with juicy red *rambutan* and other fruits by the local Malays. Raffles' reaction to his first meal in Singapore was not recorded but, ever since, the response to its cuisine has been so enthusiastic that Singapore is now recognised as an unrivalled centre for Asian food.

Singapore is unique in Southeast Asia, not only socially and economically, but gastronomically as well. Three great cultures and their cuisines — Chinese, Malay and Indian — meet, mingle and flourish. Over the past century and half, they have influenced each other to varying degrees, resulting in food that is as ancient in style as the spice combinations described in a three-thousand-year-old Sanskrit document, or as modern as today's instant noodles.

The food of a country provides a fascinating insight into the very soul of its people, and it has always puzzled me that social historians tend to ignore such an obvious subject when studying a culture. Because the background of the different peoples who migrated to Singapore is such an interesting topic, as well as being vitally important to the food as it is today, I have discussed this at considerable length.

Most cookbooks are concerned primarily with recipes. You will find, however, that *Singapore Food* differs considerably. It is divided into three parts.

Part 1, 'The Background', gives a feeling of the people of Singapore and their food. It discusses briefly their original cuisines and then goes on to examine the ways in which the different racial groups have influenced each other's food. In the latter section of Part 1, 'A Quartet of Cooks', we meet four cooks, each of whom gives us an insight into her life-style, attitudes towards food, and the basic cooking techniques that are representative of the Chinese, Malay, Indian and Nonya households in Singapore today.

Part 2, 'A Singapore Kitchen', is basically the 'how to do it' section of the book. Here the major ingredients vital to all ethnic groups are discussed in detail, and the glossary is, I hope, exhaustive in its presentation of every ingredient you may ever need to know about for Singapore cooking. I feel this section is essential to the successful use of the recipes presented in Part 3, for unless you have a thorough understanding of the ingredients, of how to prepare certain basic items, how to grind spices, how to store various ingredients, what to use as substitutes, and so on, you cannot hope to produce authentic Singapore food.

The latter half of Part 2 discusses the basic utensils and cooking techniques used. It also give suggestions on where to buy ingredients; advises on how to plan menus; and presents several sample menus for sit-down dinners, buffets, barbecues and cocktail parties. It also tells how to present the food and the type of tableware you will need.

Part 3, 'Recipes', presents the best of Singapore food in 234 recipes, every one of which I have tested. These are grouped by type of dish, namely soups; rice, noodles and breads; vegetables; seafoods; poultry; meat; eggs, *sambals*, accompaniments, snacks and 'miscellaneous'; and desserts, cakes and drinks. Each recipe section has a brief introduction, and the ethnic origin of every recipe is given. When using the recipes, be sure to refer to the glossary or the index if any clarification about ingredients or substitutes is necessary.

It is worth emphasising that although these recipes have all been collected and tested in Singapore over the years, they are not beyond the reach of enthusiastic cooks in Western countries. I had the opportunity to observe this during a brief sojourn in Australia, where I found that very nearly all of the ingredients and utensils used in Singapore were available. Those ingredients that I could not find I was able to replace with acceptable substitutes; and in the absence of an *amah*'s help in the kitchen, I learned to develop methods of preparation that were easier than some of the traditional ones. I had no difficulty keeping my family happy with a steady stream of authentic Singaporean dishes.

Modern Singapore, founded as a free-trade entrepôt, received its lifeblood through hardworking immigrants whose cultures and culinary traditions still survive.

Weights & Measures

I cannot recall having seen a set of kitchen scales or a graduated liquid measure in a Singapore home. Ask a Chinese cook how much water she uses in a certain dish and she may reply 'about one rice bowl' (that is, roughly 1 ¼ cups or 10 oz). The Malay cook who once measured flour with an old-fashioned round cigarette tin now shakes 'just enough' into her mixing bowl. An Indian cook will take a handful of this, a pinch of that, and keep on tasting and adding until the result pleases her. *Agak agak* or cooking to taste is very much a way of life in the kitchens of Singapore.

Obviously, if you have not grown up with a cuisine you cannot rely on experience to be your guide. I would suggest following the amounts given in the recipes in this book the first time you try them; the next time, if you'd like to alter the flavour, you can adjust the amounts according to your taste — adding a little more sugar, using a few less chillies, and so on.

Singapore markets and stores have, in the past, used two measuring systems: the *kati* (605 g or 1 ¼ lb); and the Imperial system of ounces, pounds and pints. Since mid-1974, Singapore, like many other countries previously using the Imperial system, has been converting to the metric system of kilograms, grams, litres and millilitres. Like cooks everywhere, Singaporeans have been slow to change. They may buy packaged goods using the metric system (since this is now the law), but in the market place, the fish seller and the vegetable man will still quote the price per *kati*.

Measures used in this book: All weight, volume and liquid measures specified in the recipes give you the option of following metric or Imperial measures (e.g. 500 g lean beef *or* 1 lb lean beef). However, it is most important that you do not mix them — although the proportions of metric to Imperial remain constant, they are not exact equivalents, and the metric yield of cup or weighed measures is approximately 10% greater than the Imperial yield. Therefore, use *either* metric weights and measures *or* Imperial weights and measures, but do NOT use a mixture of the two. Linear conversions (i.e., from millimetres or centimetres to inches) are reasonably accurate as given, but exact linear measurements are not critical.

The following tables are extracted from conversion equivalents adopted by the Cookery Sector Committee of the Metric Conversion Board (Australia).

Watching the murtabak *man fling a ball of dough into an almost-transparent sheet is nearly as good as eating the result (recipe page 102).*

CONVERSION EQUIVALENTS

IMPERIAL				METRIC	
Liquid Measures		Cup Measures		Cup Measures	Liquid Measures
1 fl oz			=		30 ml
2 fl oz		¼ cup	=	¼ cup	
		⅓ cup	=	⅓ cup	
3 fl oz			=		100 ml
4 fl oz (¼ pint US)		½ cup	=	½ cup	125 ml
5 fl oz (¼ pint Imp.)			=		150 ml
6 fl oz		¾ cup	=	¾ cup	185 ml
8 fl oz (½ pint US)		1 cup	=	1 cup	250 ml
10 fl oz (½ pint Imp.)		1¼ cups	=	1¼ cups	
12 fl oz		1½ cups	=	1½ cups	
14 fl oz		1¾ cups	=	1¾ cups	
16 fl oz (1 pint US)		2 cups	=	2 cups	500 ml
20 fl oz (1 pint Imp.)		2½ cups	=	2½ cups	

Mass (Weight)		Mass (Weight)
½ oz		15 grams (g)
1 oz	=	30 g
2 oz	=	60 g
3 oz	=	90 g
4 oz (¼ lb)	=	125 g
6 oz	=	185 g
8 oz (½ lb)	=	250 g
12 oz (¾ lb)	=	375 g
16 oz (1 lb)	=	500 g (0.5 kg)
24 oz (1½ lb)	=	750 g
32 oz (2 lb)	=	1000 g (1 kg)
3 lb	=	1500 g (1.5 kg)
4 lb	=	2000 g (2 kg)

For those of you more accustomed to the old Singapore system of weighing in *tahils* or *katis*, the following table gives the approximate metric equivalents.

1 *tahil*	=	40 g
2 *tahils*	=	80 g
4 *tahils* (¼ *kati*)	=	150 g
8 *tahils* (½ *kati*)	=	300 g
12 *tahils* (¾ *kati*)	=	450 g
16 *tahils* (1 *kati*)	=	600 g

Measuring cups and spoons: The metric weights and metric fluid measures used throughout this book refer to those of The Standards Association of Australia (AS 1325 1972). A good set of gram/kilogram scales, a graduated Australian Standard measuring cup and a set of Australian Standard measuring spoons will be most helpful; these are available at leading hardware and kitchenware stores.

- The Australian Standard measuring cup has a capacity of 250 millilitres (250 ml).
- The Australian Standard tablespoon has a capacity of 20 millilitres (20 ml).
- The Australian Standard teaspoon has a capacity of 5 millilitres (5 ml).

The British Standard metric measuring cup (250 ml) and spoons (20 ml and 5 ml) are the same as those of the Australian Standard. The New Zealand Standard metric measuring cup (250 ml) and teaspoon (5 ml) are also the same, but the tablespoon has a capacity of only 15 ml; therefore all tablespoon measures specified in the recipes should be taken generously in New Zealand.

Unless otherwise specified, all spoon measurements given in this book are level spoonfuls.

A special note to North American readers: Canadian or North American readers using American Standard measures can easily follow the quantities specified in the recipes by using the American Standard cup, tablespoon and teaspoon in conjunction with ounce or pound (Imperial) quantities as listed.

Note that the American (Imperial) and metric quantities listed are in proportion, but they are *not* exact conversions (the metric yield is approximately 10% greater), so do not attempt to use a mixture of the two.

If you wish to follow the specified metric measures, you can do so with American Standard spoons and a gram/kilogram scale; for measuring liquid or dry cup quantities you will also need a cup or jug clearly graduated in millilitres (ml) and litres (l).

¼	metric cup	=	60 ml			
½	metric cup	=	125 ml			
¾	metric cup	=	185 ml			
1	**metric cup**	=	**250 ml**	=	**¼ litre**	
2	metric cups	=	500 ml	=	½ litre	
3	metric cups	=	750 ml	=	¾ litre	
4	metric cups	=	1,000 ml	=	1 litre	

The American teaspoon has exactly the same capacity as the metric teaspoon specified in this book:

1 metric teaspoon = 5 ml = 1 American teaspoon

The American tablespoon is fractionally smaller than the metric tablespoon specified in this book. Therefore, use an American tablespoon *plus* one teaspoon for metric quantities.

A Culinary Crossroad

IN THE BEGINNING

Sitting at the tip of the Malay peninsula, between the South China Sea and the Indian Ocean, the island of Singapore has always been at the crossroads of Asia. For two thousand years or more, ships have passed by on missions of trade or conquest: the northeast monsoon winds carried Chinese junks laden with precious silks and brocades, pearls and superbly glazed porcelain, vast jars filled with tea, pickled ginger and other foodstuffs; Arab and Indian traders borne on the southwest monsoon passed with cargoes of glass and precious metals and cotton cloth, with ebony and opium and perfume, and with spices such as cardamom, fennel and pepper.

In the fifth century AD, Chinese Buddhist scholars on their way to the seat of the powerful Srivijaya empire in Sumatra noted that Singapore (then known as Temasek, or 'Sea Town') was part of that far-flung realm. By the thirteenth century, the island had been renamed Singa Pura, meaning 'Lion City', and was part of the Javanese Maja-pahit empire. But as Indian Muslim traders spread the word of Allah in the ports of Malacca and Java, Singa Pura became the victim of a Java-nese-Siamese power struggle and fell, utterly destroyed, early in the fifteenth century.

The jungle reclaimed Singa Pura, leaving monkeys, tigers, brilliantly plumaged birds and the occasional sea gypsy or pirate to watch the passing of a new kind of ship as the Portuguese and Dutch began their scramble for the treasure of the Indonesian Spice Islands. Singa Pura slumbered on. The warm waters bathing the shores of the small island teemed with fish. Trees hung heavy with headily perfumed *durian*, furry red *rambutan* and other luscious fruits. Wild pigs rooted through the undergrowth, bruising clumps of lemon-scented grass. The steamy heat of the jungle was cooled by sudden heavy downpours or refreshing sea breezes. Crocodiles slithered in the swamps on the west of the island and, over it all, vividly coloured butterflies floated lazily as in a dream.

AND THEN THEY CAME

The Lion City was awakened from its four-hundred-year slumber by the kiss of a prince disguised as an East India Company official. When Sir Stamford Raffles proclaimed Singapore as the site for 'a great

This detail from an engraving made in 1828 shows the growth that had taken place at the mouth of the Singapore River since 1819.

15

commercial empire' in 1819, the hundred or so Malays living around the mouth of the Singapore River and the few Chinese growing pepper and gambier were to see an abrupt change in their peaceful isle.

The magic words 'free trade' began the rush. Chinese traders from nearby Malacca and faraway Manila were soon joined by their countrymen direct from southern China in the search for a new life and profits. The seafaring Buginese from Celebes, maintaining their centuries-old reputation as daring sailors and traders, were followed by Javanese and Sumatrans, while traders from India, known in the region for more than two thousand years, were unable to resist the lure of Singapore.

Just five years after Raffles had stepped ashore, the racial mixture that makes modern Singapore such a fascinating blend was already established: of the ten thousand people counted in the 1824 census, 45 percent were Malays, 30 percent Chinese, 17 percent Buginese and 7 percent Indians; the rest were a mixture of Europeans, Americans and Arabs. Singapore became a vast emporium for the magical goods of the Orient, many of them destined to sail on graceful Indiamen to the cold lands of the north. There were porcelain, ivory, gold, tin, and silver thread; precious woods such as ebony and sandalwood; bolts of silk, cotton and *batik* textiles; Birds of Paradise whose feathers would adorn the fashionable ladies of Europe. For the kitchens of the well-to-do there were tea, sago, sugar, and the fabled spices — pepper, nutmeg, cloves, coriander and cassia.

Early Singapore flourished under the administration of the British and the industry of the Chinese, who quickly became the dominant group, making up half the population by 1840 and three-quarters of it by the turn of the century. In the first few decades, Singapore was plagued by piracy and lawlessness; brothels, gambling and opium dens abounded, and gang warfare often burst into open battles. During the 1870s, tin suddenly increased in importance with the development in the USA of food canning, and thousands of Chinese coolies laboured in the tin mines of neighbouring Malaya. Later they were joined by others who were attracted by another profitable new commodity, rubber. Singapore became the headquarters for financiers and shippers, and the centre through which Chinese migrant labour entered.

The migrants arrived without women and were generally forced to work without pay in the first few years to pay off their passage. Until the 1930s, Chinese women were very much in the minority. In 1880, for example, there were only seven women to every ninety-three Chinese men. A number of early Chinese traders solved the problem by marrying Malay wives, leading to the formation of a separate ethnic group known as Straits Chinese.

The Chinese migrants did not form one homogeneous group. Although they came almost exclusively from southern China, they were from different provinces and spoke distinctly different languages. Even their food and eating habits differed. The majority were Hokkiens from Amoy and the surrounding countryside in southern Fukien; next in importance were the Teochews from east Kwangtung and the Cantonese from south Kwangtung; smaller groups of Hailam people came from the island of Hainan; and there were also numbers of Hakkas, Hokchius and Hokchias.

The various Malayan peoples of Singapore had more in common than the Chinese migrants. They were bound by a common faith, Islam, by the Malay language, and by centuries of contact. Territorial boundaries in the Malay peninsula and the islands of what is now Indonesia had always been fluid as different sultanates and kingdoms rose to power, held sway, and fell. At various times, groups of people from one area would migrate to another island or state — a large number of Minangkabaus from western Sumatra, for example, moved to the

Malay state of Negri Sembilan during the nineteenth century. In the new colony of Singapore, Malays from nearby Johore mixed amicably with those from other Malay states as well as with Sumatrans, Javanese, Buginese from far-off Makassar, people from the huge island of Borneo or from the small Rhiau islands to the south. Most of them continued to work as fishermen or farmers, leaving trade and commerce to the soon-dominant Chinese.

Traders were the cornerstone of the Indian community in Singapore, although the majority of Indians prior to 1860 came as soldiers or convicts. Large numbers of indentured labourers were later brought out to work as rubber tappers, while there were a number of small traders and clerks. The slender, dark-skinned Tamils from Madras state (now known as Tamil Nadu) make up just over half of Singapore's Indian population today, with the Malayalee people from Kerala in the southwest of India forming the next largest group. There are also Sri Lankans (Ceylonese), Pakistanis, Punjabis, Bengalis, Eurasians, and even a few Parsis, Zoroastrians who originated from Persia, all adding to the cultural contribution of the vast Indian subcontinent.

The days of gin slings and *stengahs* on spacious verandahs have long since passed from the Singapore scene, and most of the 'old hands' have retired to their cottages in Surrey. Yet the British influence lingers, lately joined by the hamburger and Coca-Cola culture. Over the past one hundred and fifty years, this incredible mixture of people has lived in Singapore, remaining largely within their own ethnic community yet unconsciously influencing each other and their food.

Chinese coolies, like these working in a Singapore dockyard, came to the settlement in an attempt to escape the harsh poverty of China and to make their fortune.

The Chinese immigrant's aspiration was to become a towkay, *a wealthy businessman, blessed with as many sons as possible.*

A MEETING OF STYLES

The Chinese immigrants who arrived by the boatload with little apart from the clothes on their backs were to continue the traditions of their home region. The Hokkiens, Teochews, Cantonese, Hainanese and others joined clan associations that helped them find their feet and kept alive the customs, language, deities and cuisine of each district.

Today, it is possible to eat your way around China in Singapore's restaurants. From the mild sophisticated cuisine of Peking with its occasional Mongolian dishes, you can move to the seafoods of the Shanghai region. Heading farther south you meet the heavier pork stews of the Teochews and Hokkiens, and sample the imaginative beancurd creations of the Hakkas and the chicken rice favourite of the Hainanese before letting yourself be wooed and won by the internationally acclaimed cuisine of Canton. Moving west, you can sting your tastebuds into new life with the chilli-hot, garlic-laden dishes of Szechuan and Hunan.

But the food served in restaurants is not necessarily representative of home-cooked food. In their homes, the Singapore Chinese still prepare basically the same food as their grandparents did in the southern Chinese provinces of Kwangtung and Fukien. To the non-Chinese, it seems difficult and even unnecessary to distinguish between the food of the different regions of China. Internationally, Cantonese is the best-known cuisine, for the majority of Chinese who migrated to the West during the late nineteenth and early twentieth centuries came from Kwangtung province, but Cantonese food is only one of many schools of Chinese cooking.

There are, however, many universal elements. To all Chinese, 'meat' is synonymous with pork. Lamb has never been popular (except among the Mongolians), and one criticism made of the 'long-nosed, red-haired barbarians' was that they smelled of 'milk and mutton'. Beef is eaten by those who are not strict Buddhists, although only in small amounts because an excess is believed to be bad for the body. Poultry and fish are next in importance to pork, while vegetables achieve the level of *haute cuisine*. Being from the south, Singapore's Chinese immigrants brought with them a cuisine centred on rice, although some of the wheat-based dishes of northern China, such as steamed dumplings (*pow*) and a wide variety of noodles, have a definite place in their diet.

While continuing to eat much the same food as their ancestors, the Singapore Chinese have modified their food in ways that reveal their long association with other racial groups in the island. Chinese 'cook-boys' (usually the Hainanese, who developed an unrivalled reputation in this field) working for colonial employers laboured to reproduce English food, and picked up a few tricks along the way. Experts in seasoning, they quickly realised the potential of tomato sauce, Worcestershire sauce, and spiced fruit sauces such as HP, and soon used them to flavour Chinese-style pork ribs or fish, and to make dipping sauces for fried chicken. In time, too, Chinese families discovered the convenience of a number of Western foods. Today, few have the time, extra relatives or servants to prepare traditional rice porridge for breakfast; the Western solution of a slice or two of bread usually provides the answer.

Life alongside the chilli-loving Malays and Indians has resulted in the Chinese liking a touch of heat. Chinese noodle dishes in Singapore are invariably accompanied by a side-dish of pickled green chillies; red chilli paste is smeared inside *popiah* (a type of spring roll) or tossed with fried noodles; a dish of red chillies pounded with ginger and garlic will be served with chicken rice, or with steamed crab and prawns. Malay-style curries are served on occasion in many Chinese homes, especially on the second day of the Chinese New Year celebrations (the first day is reserved for all the Chinese traditional favourites).

Nonya cakes made with glutinous rice flour and coconut milk, the result of a fusion of Chinese and Malay cooking, have become firm favourites among the Singapore Chinese, whose own culinary tradition has never been particularly strong on cakes or desserts. Today's Chinese have also enthusiastically adopted Japanese instant noodles as a tasty snack — though they usually prefer to replace the somewhat synthetic-tasting seasoning with their own creations.

The Chinese Singaporean may dine out on steak and salad; he'll tuck into Sumatran *nasi Padang* or Malay *satay*; he'll lunch on Kerala-style fish-head curry or Punjabi mutton chops and *chapati*. But for dinner at home, there'll probably be steamed fish, crisp fried chicken or braised pork ribs, stir-fried vegetables and clear soup.

The gentle, conservative lifestyle of **the Malays** has given them a reputation for being traditionalists, yet their cuisine shows anything but a resistance to change. What is today regarded as Malay food is the result of centuries of outside influence.

Until adequate roads were constructed during the twentieth century, most Malays lived along the peninsular or island coasts, or at the edge of the wide brown rivers that provided their only means of transport. For more than a thousand years, the coastal Malays (like their cousins in Sumatra and the northern coastal ports of Java) dealt with foreign traders and were inevitably influenced by them. Many of the seasonings that are now essential to the Malay cuisine were brought by Arabs and Indians: fragrant root ginger, pepper, pungent lemony cardamom and headily sweet fennel.

Islam was adopted by the Malays during the fourteenth century, not from Arabs (who had by then stopped trading in the area on a large scale) but from Indian Muslim merchants from the state of Gujarat. The Malays absorbed a tradition of Middle Eastern dishes with Indian overtones, such as *nasi biryani* (rice stirred in oil and simmered with 'Arab' spices, onions, raisins and nuts) and *ayam korma*, a mild chicken curry using Arab seasonings; even the famous Malay *satay* is a spicy form of the Middle Eastern *kebab*.

In more recent times, Singapore's Malays borrowed from Indian and Sri Lankan (Ceylonese) cooks. The Malay housewife will often buy a ready-mixed curry paste for her fish curry from a southern Indian vendor, and most Malay *kampungs* have the Indian *karuvapillai* (curry-leaf) tree for seasoning. Malay cooks often whip up *roti paratha*, the flaky unleavened bread that Indians enjoy with curries, although many Malays prefer to sprinkle it with sugar and eat it as a snack.

For more generations than anyone can accurately tell, the Malay peoples of the Indonesian archipelago and the Malay Peninsula have been migrating and intermarrying, and their cuisines have blended as a result; thus, the food of the Singapore Malays is very similar to that of Indonesia. The Chinese have also helped add variety to Malay food, with soya sauce (called *kicup*, and pronounced 'keechup', giving us the English 'ketchup'), noodles and beansprouts being the most important contributions. From the West, Malays have adopted bread (so much quicker and easier for breakfast than steamed glutinous rice with a savoury filling) and the ubiquitous tomato sauce.

Because Malays have traditionally lived near the water, the abundance of fish, prawns, crab, squid and all kinds of seafood naturally made these star items in the daily diet. Fish is still the main source of protein for the Malays of modern Singapore, with chicken second in importance. Although beef is enjoyed on occasion, mutton and lamb are eaten less frequently and pork is strictly forbidden because all Malays are Muslim.

Rice is the staple of the Malays, though tapioca, sweet potatoes, yams and other tubers that flourish in the tropical climate are cheap and popular. A typical Malay meal consists of plenty of rice with fish, vegetables, sometimes poultry or meat or eggs, with little savoury side-dishes called *sambal*.

Until 1867, Singapore was administered by the East India Company and was regarded as part of India. If you ate in an Indian home today, you might think that Singapore was still part of India, for alone among the people of Singapore, **the Indians** continue to cook and eat almost exactly as their forefathers did, with very little evidence of a century and a half of contact with the Malays, Chinese and Europeans. The only notable exceptions are the use of tomato sauce by some cooks; the Indian hawker's version of fried noodles, a dish unknown on the subcontinent; and an adaptation of *rujak*, a Malay-Indonesian fruit and vegetable salad.

Their lives bound by ancient religious and cultural observations, Singapore's Indians have been slow to change any aspect of their life-style, although twentieth-century pressures have forced on many the change to high-rise living. Children no longer help gather fruit or tend the family vegetable patch to help supply the table; nor do they milk the cow or buffalo for milk to make yoghurt, creamy desserts and rich sweetmeats (the fruit and vegetables come from the market, and milk is bought from tin and brass containers or old drink bottles strapped onto a vendor's bicycle). But the dietary restrictions remain unchanged. Hindus are forbidden to eat beef and Muslims do not touch pork. Thousands of southern Indians shun meat and seafood altogether, and a few who are members of the strict Jain sect will not even eat eggs.

The Tamils of southeast India brought their unusual vegetables, such as snake gourd and drumsticks (long tree-grown seedpods), to supplement the familiar tropical vegetables and fruit they found growing in their new home. They retain their superb vegetarian cuisine, creating endlessly varied dishes from all kinds of lentils, dried beans, vegetables and such fruits as unripe jackfruit and cooking bananas or plantains.

Part of the Chinese district of Singapore in 1837 shows how the migrants clung to their traditional styles of architecture and clothing — and, of course, their food.

Indians from the lush green coast of Kerala in the southwest happily turn Singapore's plentiful seafood into excellent fish-head and crab curries for which they are renowned, while Indian and Pakistani Muslims specialise in fiery hot mutton curries, rice *pilau* and *biryani*, and delicious breads.

Singapore boasts a number of rather classy restaurants serving the milder, more sophisticated dishes of northern India and Kashmir, although there are relatively few people from this region in Singapore. Northern cuisine is lavish in its use of *ghee* (clarified butter), and reflects the Persian influence introduced by the sixteenth-century Mughal emperors in the use of almonds, pistachios, raisins and other fruits.

The majestic bearded Sikhs continue the food habits of their homeland in the Punjab, making the best *chapati* (unleavened bread, which they often eat with a bowl of yoghurt and a few whole green chillies), and creating robust *kebab* and mutton dishes. Smaller groups, such as people from Sri Lanka (Ceylon) and the Parsis (refugees from Persia who found a home in India over a thousand years ago) still follow their culinary traditions.

The disdainful, suspicious attitude of the early **British** colonials towards 'native' food astonishes us today, and one can't help feeling sorry for them, knowing what they missed. Perhaps fear of the unfamiliar was reinforced by a desire to 'show the flag', to uphold tradition and to avoid 'going native', despite the discomfort this sometimes entailed. For example, the colonials clung to their heavy constricting clothes, designed for a northern climate, when it would have been cooler and more comfortable to adopt the Malayan wraparound *sarong*, especially for evening relaxation (Major William Farquhar, the first Resident of Singapore, was a notable exception who scandalised the European community by wearing a *sarong* at home).

In Singapore, the Victorian British continued to eat heavy meals, many of them poorly prepared by cooks who did not understand

The settlement and the mouth of the river in 1846, as seen from Government Hill. The somewhat fanciful rendition of Singapore's inhabitants includes Europeans, a couple of Indian or possibly Malay women playing with a baby, three Malay men, a party of Chinese coolies, and a number of men in Arab dress.

English cooking. How much better it would have been if *mem* had requested her cook to prepare Chinese food. Perhaps the attitudes of Major James Low, writing in Singapore in 1841, were shared by most Europeans: 'Chinese cooks … distribute viands which, however tempting to their own class, could hardly be ventured on by others since the materials of which they are composed may, for ought anybody knows to the contrary, be the flesh of dogs, lizards, and rats, all of which come within the scope of the Chinese cook's oracle.'

The British who had done service in India allowed some variety in their diet, eating occasional curries and an English version of a southern Indian soup, which became known as mulligatawny. The eating of curry and rice eventually became more widespread among the colonials in Singapore, and the Indian word for the midday meal, *tiffin*, became synonymous with curry. Today, you may still be invited for Sunday 'curry tiffin' in the homes of long-term European residents in Singapore, though the number of side-dishes — chutneys, pineapple chunks, salted egg, peanuts and chopped bananas — will be greater than that found in an Indian or Malay home.

A number of Asian dishes were modified to suit Western tastes. Ironically, some of these have, over the years, become favourites with local cooks. One example is the Indian savoury stuffed pancake known as *samosa*, which underwent modifications and became a 'curry puff' to suit English tastes; today, curry puffs are sold everywhere in Singapore and are eaten by people who have never heard of *samosa*. Local cooks have also borrowed such English seasonings as tomato sauce and spiced fruit sauces, while modern Western foods such as bread, hamburgers and steaks are familiar to many Singaporeans.

The British merchants of early Singapore often lived in great style, their 'country' houses surrounded by lush jungle. Gharries returning home at night were usually preceded by runners with flaming torches to keep away tigers.

The culinary traditions of **the Eurasians** in Singapore are usually ignored in discussions of local food. Perhaps this is partly because Eurasian cooks are often reluctant to pass on their recipes; perhaps it is because the Eurasian community encompasses such a wide variety of people and cuisines. Strictly speaking, the term 'Eurasian' refers to anyone with both European and Asian blood, though in Singapore it is generally used to mean people of Portuguese and Indian or Sri Lankan (Ceylonese) origin. Their food is an astonishing blend of East and West: European olive oil combined with chillies and spices; sherry or wine in curries; cakes of Dutch origin that have come via Sri Lanka. Many of the dishes, not surprisingly, are similar to the food found in Goa, a Portuguese enclave in India until 1961. Singapore Eurasian cooking is delicious and excitingly different, and deserves to be more widely known.

A Nonya or Straits-born Chinese woman and her Chinese husband. The Straits Chinese in Malacca, Penang and Singapore had adopted the Malay language and many Malay customs, and made a unique contribution to Singapore's culture.

Is there such a thing, then, as a truly Singaporean cuisine? The answer is a qualified 'yes'. It is a unique cuisine, neither wholly Malay, Chinese, Indian nor European, which evolved in Singapore and which is sadly disappearing. This is the food of **the Nonyas**, the Straits Chinese women whose cooking is perhaps the most creative (and arguably the most delicious) to be found in Singapore.

The development of Nonya cuisine is a romantic story. Long before the large-scale immigration of Chinese towards the end of the nineteenth century and the beginning of the twentieth, a number of Chinese traders settled in Malacca, and later in Penang and Singapore. Because of the dearth of Chinese women, these men took Malay wives, and their language, customs and food eventually became a fascinating mixture of Chinese and Malay.

The children of these mixed marriages were known as *Peranakan* or Straits Chinese. Within one or two generations the Straits Chinese men were no longer marrying Malay women, but took their brides from other Straits Chinese families; while the *nonyas*, or Straits Chinese women, often married Chinese men who had come straight from China. Thus, today, the Straits Chinese are racially almost pure Chinese. From the beginning, they identified themselves more strongly with the development of Singapore than later migrants from China, and were invariably pro-government and Western oriented.

As modern Singapore strives to minimise the differences between the various ethnic groups, the Straits Chinese are becoming absorbed. A Nonya mother will no longer react in horror if her son or daughter decides to marry someone who is not also Straits Chinese. Although the young Nonya housewife may have learned a few favourite recipes from her mother, the chances are that she will cook largely to please her husband, and this may mean serving mostly Hokkien or Cantonese food.

Nonya food uses basically Malay methods of preparation and is therefore often time-consuming, another factor contributing to its slow demise. Many typically Chinese ingredients such as pork and dried mushrooms take on a totally new flavour when cooked by Nonyas with coconut milk, *asam* (the sour acidic fruit of the tamarind tree), *blacan* (pungent dried shrimp paste), hot red chillies and the aromatic roots and leaves so essential in a Nonya kitchen.

A Quartet of Cooks

MADAM FU:
AT HOME WITH THE KITCHEN GOD

'Come to my eldest brother's house for dinner next Tuesday night,' Jok En suggested. I accepted immediately, not only because I would be among friends, but because Jok En and good food were inseparable. We had been eating out together for more than a year, starting in Kuala Lumpur where we had met, and continuing in Singapore where we now both worked. It was through Jok En, a young Chinese of Cantonese-Hainanese origin, that I really discovered Singapore food.

Together, we had set fire to our mouths eating fish-head curry at a well-known Indian restaurant, and had perched on bamboo stools among the coolies along the banks of the Singapore River, sucking at braised ducks' feet. We'd eaten raw fish salad to commemorate Chinese New Year in a Cantonese district where wealthy men discreetly housed their lady friends, and had committed the dreadful sin of asking for a meat curry the first time we unwittingly entered a Hindu vegetarian restaurant. After poking through the jewellery in dusty old pawnshops, we'd dashed to the nearest *satay* seller or bought slices of freshly barbecued sweet dried pork to chew on.

Jok En was the second daughter in a family of six children. Since her father had died several years earlier, the eldest brother had become the head of the household, but her mother, Madam Fu, continued to live with the youngest son in her old house in a village.

On the appointed evening, I eagerly approached the home of Eldest Brother. My arrival was heralded by the staccato gunfire of exploding crackers flung in my path. Giggling somewhat guiltily, three little boys came out from behind a bush and chorused *'Kong Hee Fatt Choy,* aunty' — Prosperity and a Happy New Year! These words were being said all over Singapore that evening, for it was the beginning of Chinese New Year, the biggest, brightest and noisiest feast in the Chinese calendar. Like millions of Chinese around the world, Jok En and the rest of the Fu clan were getting together for the traditional family reunion dinner.

The small living room of the flat (one of thousands built by the government to house almost half the population of Singapore) overflowed with brothers, sisters, nieces and nephews. Presiding over it all was the granny of the family, Madam Fu. Small red paper packets or *ang pow* containing gifts of money were handed to the children, who

Home-style Chinese food requires only the most simple of kitchens: a stout chopping block and cleaver, a metal kuali or wok, a clay cooking pot and a brazier. An altar to the Kitchen God is purely optional.

laughingly executed the traditional forehead-to-floor *kow tow* to their elders. Madam Fu pretended to grumble at the lack of genuine respect among the younger generation, but her crinkling eyes and widely smiling mouth gave her away. The younger children nibbled on salted black melon seeds while incense sticks were lit and placed in front of a small, red-painted altar. Honour was being paid to Tsao Wang, the Kitchen God, who was about to depart on his annual trip to Heaven to report on the family's conduct during the past year.

The noise of frying food and the clatter of pans in the kitchen warned us that dinner was not far off. New Year, like all Chinese festivals, provides an excellent excuse for a banquet. Good food brings happiness, and on happy occasions such as this no expense is spared. Even without the excuse of special festivals — such as *Cheng Beng* (All Souls' Day) when honour is paid to the dead and food is set out on their graves, or the Moon Festival when the large moon-shaped cakes stuffed with eggs, nuts, fruit and spices are even more popular than the traditional coloured paper lanterns — a group of friends or relatives will get together for the sole purpose of enjoying a ten-course dinner.

There was no room for a large round banquet table in the Fu's flat, nor were there servants to ensure a steady flow of dishes from the kitchen. Instead, several large platters were set together on the serving table, and everyone helped themselves before finding an empty chair or a quiet corner.

Platters of golden, crisply fried chicken and spiced braised duck, fragrant with star anise and cinnamon, sent us reaching for chopsticks. Fingers grasped huge prawns, their pink shells touched with brown soya sauce in which they had been cooked. Large dried black mushrooms, as dark as midnight and as smooth as velvet, glistened in a clay cooking pot. An exquisite combination of tiny golden corncobs (so small they could be eaten whole), vivid green snow peas and crisp white water chestnuts sat beside another dish known as *chap chye*. Who would credit that this mixed vegetable dish containing such quaintly named ingredients as 'golden needles' (dried lily buds) and 'cloud ear fungus' had undergone a transformation and finished up in the West as 'choy suey'!

Everything I sampled was superb, but the mushrooms, bursting with juices, seemed the most delicious dish of all. Madam Fu, who had cooked the mushrooms, grinned with pleasure — what cook doesn't love to have her food praised? — and explained that because of their umbrella-like shape, mushrooms were thought to represent family unity: 'They cover the family and hold it together, so we must always serve them on festive occasions.' I thought that the taste alone would justify their presence.

The following week, I set off with Jok En to her mother's home for a lesson in cooking black mushrooms. The house was at the back of a *kampung* (village) in Changi, right opposite the grim gaol where hundreds of British and Australian soldiers were interned during World War II. To reach the house, we passed the village shops that straggled along the main road (the provision shop, the bicycle repairer, the seamstress, and the fat-bellied Indian *mee* seller whose checked *sarong* was held up by a vivid maroon belt with yellow leather pockets), then followed a narrow lane past huts overflowing with children, plastic furniture, the sound of television and the quacking of a few grubby ducks.

Madam Fu's old-fashioned wooden home squatted under tall coconut palms at the back of the *kampung*. The true centre of the house was the kitchen, a large cement-floored room with a work table in the middle. Unpainted wooden cupboards, old biscuit tins used as storage bins, and cooking utensils were stacked about in a rather haphazard fashion. Heavy blackened iron *woks*, known locally as *kualis*, hung like peasant hats from the walls. A row of traditional cooking pots made of terracotta or pale grey clay sat on the shelf, as beautiful in their utter simplicity as a delicately painted Chinese porcelain teacup.

Madam Fu seemed like an extension of her kitchen. Wearing a loose, pyjama-like *samfoo* and inexpensive plastic slippers, she exemplified the Chinese virtues of thrift and hard work. Born to a peasant family in China more than sixty years earlier, she had come to Singapore as a child. After her marriage, she moved to a tea plantation in the Malayan highlands where she worked as a cook and servant with her husband until the communist insurgency prompted their return to Singapore. Despite almost half a century in *Nanyang* (The Southern Seas), Madam Fu had lost none of her old ways. Illiterate herself, she had had the satisfaction of seeing her children grow up well educated.

My thoughts were interrupted as Madam Fu began to reveal the secrets of her delicious braised mushrooms. 'You must use only the best quality mushrooms for this dish,' she cautioned as she rinsed a couple of handfuls of mushrooms to free them from grit and dust. 'The thinner, cheaper type should be used only if you're adding them to meat or vegetables.'

She put the mushrooms into a bowl of hot water to soak, then minced up several cloves of garlic with a wicked-looking cleaver which moved swiftly across the eight-centimetre-thick chopping block. Selecting a small clay pot, she set it over a charcoal brazier. Although she had a kerosene cooker. Madam Fu insisted on using charcoal for slow-cooked dishes, claiming it greatly improved the flavour.

An assortment of bottles sat on a small table beside the cooking area. Splash! Into the pot went some peanut oil — probably about a table-spoonful, but, like most Chinese cooks, Madam Fu never bothered to measure with a spoon. When the oil was hot, she threw in the minced garlic and stirred until it turned golden, filling the kitchen with a warm, pungent aroma. Then, before the garlic became too brown, she quickly scooped it out and discarded it.

Next, the mushrooms, swollen after their hot-water bath. Madam Fu squeezed them dry, removed their tough stalks (which were kept aside for a soup), and stirred them in the hot garlic-flavoured oil for a few minutes before adding a couple of slices of root ginger and the water in which the mushrooms had soaked.

She picked up two large bottles, their crown seals punched to let the liquid flow through, and shook them over the pot: a brief splash of thick black soya sauce, a longer shake for the light clear soya sauce. The flavours of the two types of soya sauce were quite different, Madam Fu explained, so it was essential not to muddle them up or substitute one for the other when cooking.

About two hours later she removed the clay pot from the brazier, discarded the ginger, and sprinkled a few drops of sesame oil over the mushrooms. The dish was ready. So very simple, really, but the mushrooms were so full of flavour, their texture slightly resistant yet melt-in-the-mouth, that this dish is my favourite among all Chinese vegetable recipes.

Simplicity is, of course, one of the hallmarks of Chinese cooking. Starting with absolutely fresh ingredients, Chinese cooks use relatively few seasonings in any given dish. Rather, it is the balance of ingredients that provides variety. A few dried shrimps or mushrooms, or a few shreds of pork, do wonders for vegetables. The careful combining of textures to provide contrast, such as tender prawns and crisp cashew nuts, adds yet another dimension to Chinese food.

The seasonings kept in Madam Fu's kitchen were typical: bottles of soya sauce, sesame oil, oyster sauce and rice wine were all strategically placed for frequent use. Little jars held salted soya beans (taucheo) and salted black beans (tau see), a spoonful of either guaranteed to liven up any dish. Finely ground white pepper, five-spice powder, and star-shaped whole anise were the only spices that Madam Fu used frequently. She also kept a jar of monosodium glutamate, which she added sparingly to some dishes to accentuate the flavour, and bought other seasonings such as tim cheong (sweet sauce) or nam yee (fermented red beancurd) in small quantities at the market as she needed them.

About the only thing missing in Madam Fu's kitchen was an altar for the Kitchen God. When I commented on this, she pointed to her rice pot, a deep heavy metal pan blackened by years of use. 'That's my kitchen god,' she said. 'I brought that back to Singapore with me from the Cameron Highlands. I've been cooking rice in that pot for almost twenty-five years, ever since Jok En was a baby.'

Although she no longer bothered to follow many ritual observances, such as keeping an altar for the Kitchen God, Madam Fu still adhered to centuries-old attitudes towards food. 'We believe that the food you eat determines the sort of person you are,' she explained. 'Food is so important to us that we have a saying "even the Thunder God won't strike a man when he's eating." Once upon a time, you would never interrupt anyone while they were eating.'

She laughed as she went on to recount the occasion when she had seen a couple of young detectives hovering anxiously near a man they obviously wanted to question. This man was busy eating a bowl of noodles, and the detectives dared not intrude. Realising this, the man ordered another bowl of noodles, then another, then another, appar-

The market stalls lining the streets of Singapore's Chinatown district are full of fascinating ingredients, offering anything from a snake steak to a hundred-year egg, from a live carp to medicinal herbs.

ently hoping the detectives would tire of waiting for him to stop eating and go away. Alas for the man, impatience and duty eventually won out over respect, and the detectives moved in.

Madam Fu, like thousands of Chinese who are not Taoist, still applied the old Taoist concept of balance, or *yin* and *yang*, to food. 'You must never take too much beef,' she warned me, 'for it is very "heaty" and will give you a fever, constipation or ulcers.' Ideally, the body should be in a perfect state of balance, but if too many foods that are said to be 'heaty' are eaten (chocolate, stout, tonic drinks, *durian* fruit), the balance will be disrupted. To counteract an excess of 'heaty' food, the Chinese recommend taking 'cooling' food such as tomatoes, cucumber, lotus root or herbal soups to restore the balance.

Soups, in fact, play a very important role in the diet of most Chinese. 'The Hokkiens don't care so much for soups because they always like to serve wet, soupy food,' Madam Fu said, 'but we Cantonese must have soup with every meal to help wash our rice down — even if it is just boiled pork bones with a few leaves of watercress or *choy sam.*' And when you're feeling run down, soup is the answer. A specially brewed soup (*por*) containing medicinal herbs and perhaps a whole chicken will work wonders. If you're a man, *ginseng* root (often reputed to be an aphrodisiac) is strongly recommended.

Several weeks later, Madam Fu offered to take me around the morning market held in the streets of the old section of Singapore known as Chinatown, where jumbled collections of mobile carts, piles of orange boxes, or even woven mats on the footpath become instant stores.

We made our way slowly, dodging the washing hung from bamboo poles overhead and hundreds of *samfoo*-clad women clutching coin purses, cane shopping baskets and bundles tied with strips of rattan. Marketing is, for these women, a daily affair. Everything that comes into a Chinese kitchen must be absolutely fresh; Chinese cooks turn away in horror from frozen food, which they claim has a 'dead' smell. Some Western housewives, shopping in a Chinese market for the first time, might find the smell of 'live' food rather overpowering!

Madam Fu led me past the fruit stalls — a kaleidoscope of red, orange, yellow, green and brown — to the butcher's shop. Only one type of meat, pork, was sold here, but in every form imaginable: loins of roasted pork with the skin blistered to a deep golden crunchiness; fillets of red-roasted *char siew*; lacy membrane or caul used to wrap home-made sausages or meatballs; dark red pig's liver and alabaster-white back fat; pink and white streaked belly pork and dainty-toed pig's leg; whole piglets weighing a mere two kilos ready for roasting; piles of lean pork suitable for mincing up with a cleaver — who needs anything else but pork?

Frugality is deeply ingrained in the Chinese. These old women are sorting coriander leaves, discarding the wilted portions and keeping the rest for sale. Provision shops, like the tea merchant's, add colour to Chinatown.

Well, if you insist on a change, there's always fish. Madam Fu inspected the live carp swimming in a tank at the side of the road, selected a fish, then haggled over the price. Eventually, she and the vendor agreed, and he then quickly scooped the fish out with a net and wound it with a rattan cord. We set off with the live fish gasping as it dangled from its cord, and I couldn't help thinking of that line from the old song about the Doggie in the Window: 'You can't take a goldfish for a walk.' You *can* take a carp for a walk in Singapore!

A stall set among piles of vegetables — looking so fresh we could almost feel their crispness in our mouths — held an assortment of unfamiliar leaves. Fresh medicinal herbs for soup, Madam Fu told me. If we needed a foreleg of monitor lizard to boil with the herbs, we could visit the 'Python Lady' opposite. With cool nonchalance, she'd cut a chunk of snake steak, prepare a live turtle for soup, or pick up live frogs and, with a sudden blow, break their necks on a wooden board, skin them, and hand us the plump pink legs.

Slightly less esoteric items were sold in the sundry shops of the market. Great brown-glazed Ali Baba jars held all types of salted or fermented beans and pastes, while dried goods hung down from the ceiling: huge bundles of puffed fish maws (tripe) for soup, shark's fins, scallops, flattened waxed ducks and mottled sausages (*lap cheong*). Vats of salted cabbage, piles of fresh root ginger, tiny red onions, garlic, dried mushrooms, lotus seeds, dried red dates ... Madam Fu pointed to various ingredients, one after the other, and told me how she used them.

Wandering out into the street once more, I was moved by the shabby beauty of the three-storey shop-houses with their solid ground-floor archways, their delicate wooden balustrades and curving fanlights. The pastel-coloured paint was faded by monsoon rains and relentless tropical sunshine, and nature seemed set for a take-over, planting little bursts of fern or trees in earth-filled cracks along balconies or roofs.

How much longer would they survive? Even though I would mourn the passing of such lovely surroundings, I could be certain that one thing would not change: the Chinese devotion to good food, in existence for at least two thousand years, would always remain.

FATIMAH: DOING IT THE OLD WAY

The woman who taught me more about Malay cooking than any book or cooking class always claimed she was not a good cook. '*Saya malas*, I'm lazy,' apologised Fatimah with a smile. But of course she was not lazy, and her food — that of the average Malay housewife on a limited budget — was always imaginative and tasty.

Fatimah, dressed in a flowered *batik sarong*, with gold ear studs and long black hair coiled at the back of her neck, became part of our family when we first came to Singapore. Since then, we have shared each other's daily life: children and grandchildren made their appearances, weddings took place, parents visited from Malaysia and New Zealand, and annual festivals came and went.

We were lucky to live in a rambling old bungalow that would have delighted Somerset Maugham, the sort of place where, every evening on the verandah, you could almost hear the ghosts clinking the ice in their pink gins or *stengahs* (whisky water). Behind the house were separate *amah's* quarters where Fatimah lived with her husband, Hamid, and their three youngest children. Every day, I was able to watch Fatimah prepare food for her family, and to call on her for advice and help in my experiments with Malay food. Life became a never-ending cooking adventure.

Before long, our garden began to resemble that of a Malay *kampung* as we planted the fresh herbs and seasonings essential to Malay food. The few stems of lemon grass (*serai*) that we put out near the lawn quickly multiplied and became a thick clump. A root of *lengkuas* soon sent up tall leaves similar to those of a ginger plant. I loved the faint pink tinge and almost medicinal smell of the *lengkuas* root, though the intense yellow colour and earthy pungency of fresh turmeric (*kunyit*) were far more striking.

Bushes of tiny hot bird's-eye chilli splashed the garden with green and red, and attracted birds with cast-iron throats who nonchalantly pecked away at fiery pods that would leave most people gasping. In a corner of the garden, under the *bunga tanjung* tree whose jasmine-scented flowers floated like stars to the ground, grew a clump of *daun pandan*. We used the leaves of this aromatic plant to give flavour and colouring to cakes, drinks, and the occasional curry. I could rarely resist tearing off a leaf and crushing it between my hands each time I passed, revelling in the mysterious smell with its hint of lush jungles. Another leaf I loved grew on the *karuvapillai* or curry-leaf tree. Like many Malay cooks who frequently buy freshly pounded spices from an Indian vendor, Fatimah had acquired the habit of using a sprig of curry leaves in her fish curry.

Hamid planted several types of bananas. Within months, we were enjoying the fruit, cooking the banana flower as a vegetable, and using the leaf as a wrapping for cakes or fish (suddenly, I seemed to have no need for aluminium foil in the kitchen!). The rural atmosphere of our garden increased when Hamid started bringing home feathered additions to the family. Day-old chicks eventually grew into candidates for the curry pot, although we had no success in rearing ducklings.

By this time, our garden had trees, flowers, herbs, poultry, song-birds and children. But that wasn't all, for there always seemed to be something drying outside. Before the days of canning and refrigeration, food was preserved by drying or salting; today, dried foods still form an important part of the Malay diet, and in an exceptionally humid climate like Singapore's most dried foods need a final sunning before being cooked. Our backyard proved a regular temptation for the local cats, with trays of woven bamboo filled with *ikan bilis* (tiny salted dried fish) and *krupuk* (wafers made from prawns or fish) set out to dry. We also dried the scrapings that were carefully removed each day from the bottom of the rice pot. When they were thoroughly dry, we deep fried them in hot oil; puffed and golden, with a sprinkling of salt, they were one of our favourite snacks and cost us nothing.

All these bits and pieces were, of course, only trimmings. The serious shopping was done at the market and the provision shop. Once a month a small delivery truck arrived from the local Chinese *kedai* (general store) with Fatimah's basic supplies: a fifty-kilo bag of rice and several kilos of sugar, kerosene for the stove, cooking oil to be siphoned into Fatimah's containers and stored in the *dapur* (kitchen), and about thirty coconuts still in their husks.

Although I always bought freshly grated coconut from the market on the day I needed it, Fatimah preferred to save a few cents (but expend a great deal of effort) by doing what she'd done for many years: chipping the shell off the coconut with a *parang* and grating the pieces of flesh on a *parut* or small metal grater. She then moistened the grated coconut with water and squeezed it, handful by handful, to make coconut milk.

Hamid, like many Malay and Indian husbands, took care of the daily marketing. A triumphant smile meant that he'd got a real bargain, such as a huge bag of cockles or a couple of dozen small fish that had been reduced for a quick sale at the end of the day. The market at which Hamid shopped was like all Singapore markets, with the pork segregated from the fish, poultry and mutton. Malays and Indian Muslims insist that their food should be *halal* (conforming to dietary restrictions) and animals must be slaughtered in the manner prescribed by Muslim law. For this reason, strict Muslims will not buy frozen poultry or any packaged goods they fear may contain ingredients that are not *halal*, and their food must not be tainted by contact with pork.

Fresh fruit is available all year round in Singapore, so it seemed a mystery to me, initially, that there should be a time known as the *musim buah* or 'fruit season'. But this was the time when special local fruits flooded the markets, overflowing onto pavement stalls. Hamid would come home laden with great bunches of red *rambutan*, smooth green or golden mangoes, little brown *duku* tasting vaguely of grape-fruit, or immense spiky *durian* smelling like the notorious Rochor Road canal but tasting divine. Fatimah's family, like many other Malays I knew, usually ate fruit as a between-meal snack. In the 'fruit season', we absolutely gorged ourselves, often finishing several kilos at one sitting! Not content with that, we dried the stones of the *durian* and *nangka* (jackfruit), boiled them in salty water and ate them as nuts.

As I watched Fatimah prepare her meals day after day, I began to detect a pattern. Naturally, there was always rice — great mounds of it, more than twice the amount I could comfortably eat, filled every plate. The rice was accompanied by *lauk*, the selection of dishes that always includes vegetable, fish, and a *sambal*. There was usually another dish or two, depending on what was cheap and good in the market, and on how much time there was to prepare the meal.

Fatimah either fried her vegetables or cooked them with liquid (generally thin coconut milk). If Hamid had brought home small fish, these were soaked briefly in tamarind water to remove the 'fishy' smell, then rubbed with salt and turmeric powder and fried in oil; or they might be stuffed with a little *sambal* before being fried. Large fish steaks such as *ikan tenggiri* (Spanish mackerel) were cooked with coconut milk and seasonings to make a *gulai*, or prepared as *ikan asam pedas* in a vividly sour hot sauce.

She normally served prawns as a *sambal goreng*. *Sambal goreng*, Fatimah explained, was a dish containing meat, prawns, eggs or vegetables cooked with lots of chillies and coconut milk; a *sambal* was merely any type of condiment, used as Westerners might use mustard, chutney, or tomato sauce.

Fatimah's two basic cooking methods — frying and simmering —

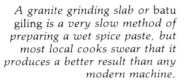

A granite grinding slab or batu giling *is a very slow method of preparing a wet spice paste, but most local cooks swear that it produces a better result than any modern machine.*

met most of her culinary needs. Unlike Chinese cooks, she never steamed fish or chicken, though she used a steamer for sweet or savoury cakes. *Panggang* or roasting over an open fire, a traditional Malay method, has regrettably lost popularity in Singapore. 'My mother always had a fire going in her *dapur*,' Fatimah told me, 'so it was easy for her to roast a fish or a chicken. But I use a kerosene cooker, so if I want to *panggang* food I have to buy the charcoal and make a fire specially. So much *susah* (trouble)!'

Although Fatimah prepared many meat, poultry, fish and prawn dishes that appeared to be curries, she called only one by that name. This puzzled me at first: surely (thinks the Westerner), most Malay food is curry or *satay*, and a curry is Eastern food with a spicy hot sauce? But the word 'curry' comes from the Tamil *kari*, a name for *any* sauce, and Fatimah applied it to only one fish recipe using spices prepared by an Indian. All her other hot or spicy dishes were known as *gulai*, *korma*, *sambal goreng*, *asam pedas*, *masak merah* (literally 'red cooked', usually involving tomatoes and chillies), and so on depending on their origins and seasonings.

Names, of course, are less important than cooking methods. These seemed rather complex at first, but Fatimah taught me that there is a basic pattern in the preparation of most Malay 'curries'. The basis is the *rempah*, the combination of 'wet' and 'dry' spices and seasonings that are ground or pounded just before cooking.

My initial efforts at grinding the whole 'dry' spices such as coriander and cummin were hilarious. After heating the spices gently in a dry pan to make them easier to grind, I perched on a stool about eight centimetres high and, firmly grasping a granite pestle in my hand, pounded away with such gusto that I sent the spice seeds careering around the kitchen. 'Not such big bangs! Gently, gently,' Fatimah advised.

The 'wet' spices were even more troublesome. Crushing up fragrant shallots left my eyes streaming, and even worse were the red chillies that burned my eyes like acid if I leaned too closely over the mortar or splashed up a drop of juice. But I mastered the technique of using the *batu lesong* or mortar and pestle, and graduated to the *batu giling*, a granite slab and roller that is perfect for pulverising large amounts of 'wet' spices such as ginger, *lengkuas*, fresh turmeric root, onions, chillies and garlic. Then, several years later, I discovered the joys of a Magimix, a super-efficient food processor that grinds 'wet' spices infinitely faster and more efficiently than I could by traditional methods, while a little coffee grinder took care of the 'dry' spices.

The second step in the preparation of a 'curry' is to *tumis* or gently fry the ground ingredients in a little oil. '*Sampai wangi*, until they become fragrant.' Fatimah echoed the phrase given in local cookbooks. And it was true. As the spices cooked, a wonderful fragrance filled the kitchen. *Blacan*, the dried shrimp paste with an almost nauseating smell when raw, underwent a transformation and gave off an exciting pungency; the orangey smell of coriander was released; and the aromas of onions and garlic blended with the fresh tang of ginger. It took three to five minutes for the spices to cook. Meat, chicken or prawns were then added and stirred for a few minutes until they were coated with the spices, but if fish were used, it was generally added later to stop it breaking up.

Coconut milk was then added. To prevent it curdling, Fatimah continually stirred it with a coconut-shell ladle, lifting up a scoop of liquid and pouring it back into the pan, a process called *timboh*. When the coconut milk came to the boil and the danger of curdling was over, she left the food to simmer gently until cooked. The *kuali* or deep curving pan, in which she usually cooked, was rarely covered; the amount of liquid used at the beginning always took into account the evaporation occurring during cooking. Sometimes there was one more step, the addition of *pati santan* (thick coconut milk) at the end of cooking, making the 'curry' even thicker and richer in flavour.

Fatimah was quite specific about cooking methods, but exasperatingly vague on the amount of ingredients. She never used a cookbook, but cooked from memory, using the *agak agak* method — a combination of guesswork and experience. 'How many cloves?' I would ask. Unable to tell me exactly, Fatimah took up a pinch of whole cloves, and when the amount *felt* right, put them on the table and counted them.

Whenever Fatimah's grandchildren visited us, it was a happy time for all. The children enjoyed playing with my daughter and son, and we invariably finished up making *kueh* (cakes) or *bubor* (a type of porridge). One favourite was *bubor kacang hijau*, made by boiling green mung peas with water, thin coconut milk and palm sugar. We'd all sit around on the back steps or the verandah, filling ourselves with warm sweet *bubor*, or getting sticky eating flaky *roti paratha*, an Indian fried bread sprinkled with white sugar.

The best food of the year was reserved for *Hari Raya Puasa*, the festival marking the end of the fasting month when Muslims abstain from food and drink between sunrise and sunset. A week or so before the big day, new clothes and shoes were bought for the whole family. Excitement mounted a couple of days before the festival when Fatimah's daughter, Maimoon, and daughter-in-law, Kachar, appeared loaded down with ingredients for making the cakes and biscuits to be eaten during the holiday period.

Using a large pottery container normally reserved for salting eggs, Fatimah, Maimoon and Kachar worked for hours, mixing flour, butter,

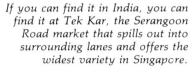

If you can find it in India, you can find it at Tek Kar, the Serangoon Road market that spills out into surrounding lanes and offers the widest variety in Singapore.

sugar and dozens of eggs to make tiny tarts they later filled with fresh pineapple jam; peanut cookies; moist yellow cakes and crisp little morsels that disappeared in one bite.

On the eve of *Hari Raya Puasa*, Fatimah prepared the *lauk*. Her dishes reflected perfectly the diverse cultural influences that the Malays have experienced over the centuries. There was always *rendang daging*, a Sumatran dish combining beef in a very rich coconut-milk sauce. *Ayam korma*, a mild chicken curry of mixed Indian and Middle Eastern origin, was served with a typically Malay prawn curry, spicily hot and sour. The Chinese touch was evident in the beancurd simmered in coconut milk with cabbage and long beans. Java's contribution was the *tempe* (fermented soya bean cake) fried with tiny fresh prawns and peanuts.

Weddings were another occasion for feasting. The rituals of engagement, the receiving of contributions from the groom's parents towards the cost of the wedding, the recording of gifts by officials, the staining of the fingers and toenails of the bride with henna, and all the other wedding practices were deeply rooted in tradition, but the food served varied from one wedding to the next.

One ever-present item, however, was the *bunga telur* or 'egg flower' given to departing guests. In the past, hardboiled eggs were wrapped in green paper to look like a flower or fruit on a stem. Very rarely now do Malays bother spending days creating these lovely 'flowers' that symbolise fertility; instead, little plastic baskets with a gaily coloured plastic flower on top make a cheaper and simple egg container.

Today's *bunga telur* is a perfect symbol of the continuity and change inherent in Malay culture and food, which cherish elements of the past while adapting to the realities of the present.

Provision shops selling spices, lentils and other items for Indian cooking cluster at the bottom of Serangoon Road near the market.

RANI:
SHARING SPICY SECRETS

Being with Rani was rather like living through an Indian movie. There were drama, passion, and flashing of *kajal*-rimmed eyes; there were warmth and tenderness and spontaneous generosity; there were laughter, frivolity and colour as we surrounded ourselves with jasmine, incense and gaudy Indian jewellery.

Like the majority of Singapore's Indian population, Rani was a Tamil whose parents had been born in the southeast Indian state of Madras (now Tamil Nadu). To look at, she was 'typically' Tamil: her thick black hair hung heavily in a single plait, often garlanded with fresh flowers; her incredibly white teeth and soft mobile mouth stood out against smooth, almost black skin; her short, plump body was swathed in a filmy, vividly coloured *sari*, and her wrists were ajangle with dozens of glass, plastic and gold bracelets.

Yet as we grew to be friends, I realised that Rani was typical only in appearance, for she possessed a remarkable degree of independence compared with the majority of Tamil women who lead sheltered, restricted lives. A divorcee whose son lived with her parents, Rani dreamed of the day when she had saved enough money to open a small restaurant. If the restaurant ever eventuates, I'll be its best customer, for Rani was an excellent cook whose experience was not limited to food of her own region — she could prepare a Kerala fish curry with as much ease as a Madras lentil stew or a Mysore mutton curry. Rani preferred the food of central and southern India to that of the north, which has been subject to outside influence over the centuries.

'We think the northerners are rather extravagant in their cooking — just look at how much *ghee* they use! They eat a lot of meat, too. Many

Tamils are strict vegetarians and never touch meat, fish or even eggs. To make up for this, they eat all sorts of lentils and dried beans or peas. My family eat *dhal* every day, but we also eat quite a lot of fish. Sometimes we might have a mutton curry or mutton cutlets, and occasionally a chicken, but we don't eat meat on Fridays because that's the day we pray. We never touch pork — it's not for religious reasons, but I suppose many people apart from Muslims just regard it as unclean.'

Whenever we had the time, Rani and I explored the shops along Serangoon Road, an area sometimes known as 'Little India'. Sellers of *betel* and fragrant garlands of temple flowers sat in tiny booths jammed between stores selling a dazzling array of goods: shiny metal cooking pots and *thali* (food trays) crowded among jars of waving emerald and turquoise peacock feathers; a blue-painted Ganesh, the Elephant God, peered through great twists of false hair, jingling toe rings, bejewelled nose studs, and row upon row of bangles.

The latest Indian love song rose above the roar of the traffic and the babble of voices, while the heady smell of 'Madras Night' incense competed with the slightly acrid tang of spices being ground for *garam masala*. Amid all this noise and colour the flour shop was a dusty, cool oasis where immense sacks of wheat and chickpeas sat waiting to be ground into wholemeal flour (*atta*) or *besan*.

Rani introduced me to her favourite provision store: terracotta cooking pots (*chatties*), sacks of dried chillies and tins of dried beans crowded onto the pavement, while inside sacks of at least eight different types of lentils or *dhal* leaned against several varieties of rice. In front of the shop, round iron discs (*tawa*) used for frying *chapati* hung near wooden boxes filled with whole spices; glass jars arrayed along the shelves revealed a treasure trove of nuts, dried fruits, and other mysterious items whose musical Tamil names still left me in the dark as to their use. Bottles of rose essence, canned goods, cooking oil and tins full of rock sugar were crammed into every corner, leaving little room for customers.

'I always buy my *garam masala* here,' Rani said, and then went on to explain the difference between *garam masala* and *masala*, something that had been puzzling me. A *masala* is similar to the Malay *rempah*, being a combination of dry spices and 'wet' seasonings such as onions, ginger, garlic and chillies. Unlike many Western cooks, who indiscriminately use the same curry powder for every dish, the Indian cook carefully selects her spices to enhance the flavour of the main ingredient. She knows that while cardamom and cloves do wonders for mutton, they'd overpower a vegetable dish; she'll probably include fenugreek in most fish curries, but seldom combine it with other foods. A *masala* may contain as many as a dozen dry spices together with the various 'wet' ingredients.

A *garam masala*, however, is a mixture of about four to six powdered spices kept in the storecupboard and frequently used in a wide variety of dishes. Coriander and cummin are always used in *garam masala*. In the north of India, black pepper, cinnamon, cloves and cardamom will also be included, while in the south, some of these spices are replaced by turmeric and chilli. Rani added *garam masala* to batters and lentil savouries; sprinkled it over yoghurt or added it to *dhal* stew; or sometimes added a spoonful or two to the *masala* specially prepared for a particular meat or fish curry. She claimed she was usually too busy to grind her own *masalas*, so she bought them from the spice seller in the Kandang Kerbau ('buffalo pen') market.

This market (referred to by most Singaporeans as Tek Kar, its Chinese name) offers a stunning selection of fruit, vegetables, dried goods, herbs and seasonings, as well as fresh fish, poultry and meat. 'If you can buy it in India, you can buy it here' might well be the market's motto as it displays dozens of mutton carcasses, tubs full of sour green mangoes, baskets of brilliant purple or palest green aubergine, piles of long skinny snake gourds or trays of tender little okra.

The spice seller sits cross-legged on a high wooden platform, his *dhoti* tucked up around his knees. Like a wizard surrounded by magical potions, he sits among plates of freshly ground spice paste, dozens of jars of powdered spices, a huge tub full of crushed red chillies, bowls of fresh coconut, and sprays of curry leaf.

Twenty cents worth of *masala* for a fish curry? Working rhythmically, he takes a large scoop of this, a dab of that, adds a sprinkle from one jar and a generous dollop from another, piling it all onto a large smooth leaf with a sprig of curry leaves set on top. He wraps it up into a neat bundle and hands it across, the whole operation having taken less than twenty seconds.

Whenever Rani and I shopped in Serangoon Road, I made my inevitable suggestion: 'How about some *dosay*?' Complaining that she was getting too fat, Rani would nevertheless allow herself to be persuaded to join me at my favourite restaurant where the sheer inventiveness of southern Indian vegetarian cooks never ceased to enchant me.

If we wanted a typical breakfast, we would sit downstairs and eat *dosay*, a thin, slightly sour pancake, or *idli*, a steamed bun. Both of these were served with fresh coconut chutney and a dish of watery *dhal*. The *dosay* and *idli* had an elusive tang that I thought might have come from a rice-flour and yoghurt batter. 'They get that taste from *ulundoo*.' Rani corrected me. 'That's the black-skinned lentil I sometimes add to vegetables for extra flavour. To make *dosay* or *idli*, you soak the lentils overnight, then grind them up with a little water and mix with rice flour and water to make a batter which you leave to stand for half a day. If you want to make *vaday*, you add some onions, chilli and ginger to the mixture and fry spoonfuls of it.'

If we felt like eating a more substantial meal at the restaurant, we went upstairs and were presented with four or five vegetable dishes served on a fresh banana leaf with a pile of white rice, sour lime pickle, a chutney, a couple of crisp *poppadums* or fried banana chips, a glass of pepperwater (*rasam*) to aid digestion, and a tiny bowl of yoghurt.

To describe the superb vegetable creations as 'vegetable dishes' is to do them an injustice. Nothing in any Western vegetarian cuisine prepares you for such food. Instead of attempting to create vegetable dishes resembling meat (such as vegetarian meat loaf), Indian cooks glory in the essential quality, texture and flavour of a wide range of vegetables. Fresh vegetables may be combined with lentils for an entirely new taste. Spices — the most popular combination being brown mustard seed, chilli, blackgram *dhal* and curry leaf — change plain old cabbage into a gourmet's delight; the cool sourness of yoghurt or the sweet milky taste of freshly grated coconut transforms sweet potato, cucumber or pineapple.

One Tamil favourite is *pachadi*, a vegetable dish that includes yoghurt, spices and grated coconut. It is similar to the *avial* popular among the Malayalee people of Kerala, and to some of the northern *raitas*. Carrot *pachadi* is a typical example: grated carrot and coconut are mixed with brown mustard seed, onion and red chilli. A spoonful of mustard seed and a broken dried chilli are quickly fried in a little oil, then the carrot and coconut mixture added. Just as the carrot is beginning to soften, the whole lot is put into a bowl and, when it is cool, yoghurt is stirred through. This *pachadi* is an excellent dish in which the fresh taste of the carrot and coconut is retained, and the tingle of spice and chilli balanced by soothing yoghurt.

Fresh chutneys are an essential part of any Indian meal and are almost unlimited in number and variety. Rani sometimes served a

A few hearts of banana palm, some bananas and a bag of orchids: subjects for a still life painting on the edge of the pavement outside a market.

chutney that was fiery hot, another time it would be mouth-puckeringly sour. Mango chutney with raisins had a fruity sweetness, while fresh coconut chutney combined so many different flavours and sensations as to be almost indescribable. Pounded fresh mint mixed with tamarind juice was so similar to mint sauce that I wondered whether the English condiment had been inspired by the Indian chutney. (Incidentally, the word 'chutney' comes from the Indian, *chatni*.)

The most important Indian festival celebrated in Singapore is *Deepavali* (or *Divali*, as it is also called.) This is the Festival of Lights, when hundreds of oil lamps or electric lights are burned to show the souls of the dead their way when they return to earth. It also symbolises the triumph of good over evil. 'We pray for the dead at *Deepavali*,' Rani told me. 'In my house, a curry made with a female chicken is put on banana leaves with two eggs and some *vaday* while we pray, then the eldest man in the family eats the food.'

Deepavali is also a time for giving cakes to friends and relatives. And such cakes! Wonderfully rich *barfi* made from condensed milk with ground almonds or pistachios; heavy *rasgulla*, round balls wallowing in sugar syrup; brilliant yellow twists called *jalebis*, almost unbearably sweet; crunchy dry little sweetmeats flavoured with coconut; *halwa* made from grated carrots boiled in milk and flavoured with *ghee* and sugar. 'I never bother to make these cakes,' said Rani. 'They take so much time that I always buy mine in Serangoon Road.'

Like most of Singapore's Indians, Rani has had to move with the times. It is not always possible to combine life in a busy, competitive urban environment with the old practices of village life. There must be compromise. Fortunately, traditional food and hospitality are still deeply entrenched. As you walk up to an Indian home on the eve of *Deepavali*, your pathway bordered by flickering oil lamps, and are greeted with cakes and warm wishes for the coming year, you feel particularly thankful that some things have not changed.

MRS TAN: IN TOUCH WITH THE PAST

You may see them in the markets near Singapore's Orchard Road or in Katong, these beautiful old ladies in *sarongs* of brightly flowered *batik* held up by silver belts that gleam through transparent embroidered *kebayas* (blouses). The three-pin gold *krosang* that fastens the *kebaya* is Malay in origin, but the jade bracelets and ear studs are unmistakably Chinese. Listen to the voices and you will hear Malay. Look at the faces and you will see the features of a Ming dynasty empress.

Who are they, these women who combine Malay and Chinese in such an intriguing manner? Let my friend, Mrs Tan, explain.

'A lot of Westerners don't know that the Chinese have a long history as travellers. Centuries before Marco Polo made his famous trip, Chinese scholars, traders and monks had voyaged as far west as Afghanistan and south to Sumatra. So you see it's not surprising that the Chinese were among those who helped make Malacca one of the world's great trading centres in the fifteenth century. Some of these Chinese traders decided to remain in Malacca and took Malay wives because, of course, there were no Chinese women there. Did you know that just ninety years ago, there was only one woman for every nine men among the Chinese in Singapore?

'The children of these early Chinese-Malay marriages became known as Straits Chinese or *Peranakan*; we ladies are called *nonyas* and the men *babas*. Over the years, our way of life, our language, food, clothing and customs have become a combination of Chinese and Malay.

'When Singapore was established, many Straits Chinese families moved down here from Malacca and Penang. They were joined by Chinese who had lived in Indonesia for several generations. The reason I and other Nonyas look pure Chinese is that after the first few genera-tions, the girls often married men straight from China, or married men from the Straits Chinese community, so we have scarcely any Malay blood. Nonetheless, our customs are strongly influenced by the Malays and we are quite different from the *sinkehs*, the people who came from China only two or three generations ago.

'I was born here in Singapore many years ago,' (her smile dares me to ask just how many, but I know it's well over seventy) 'and when I was fourteen, I was sent to my grandmother's house in Malacca to learn all the things a young Nonya must know before her marriage.'

Just because the strictly brought-up Straits Chinese girls of half a century ago were not permitted to go to school, this did not mean that they did not receive a rigorous education, Mrs Tan assured me. From a very early age, they were taught how to embroider *kebayas* and the exquisite velvet pouches, belts and slippers that formed part of their trousseau. They learned how to wait at the table, for no *Peranakan* family would treat guests disrespectfully by allowing them to be waited upon by servants. They were shown how to serve coffee and cakes, how to comb hair and fix it with heavy gold pins, and how to behave in a demure fashion that would endear them to their mother-in-law.

But above all, Nonya girls learned how to cook. 'There is such a lot to

The Nonyas are proud of their unique heritage, a combination of Chinese and Malay cultures brilliantly exemplified by their cooking.

learn in Nonya cooking as it is rather complicated and sometimes a lot of hard work, but the flavours are so delicious that we prefer our food to any other. When my grandchildren come around here for dinner, they ask me in advance to cook them Nonya favourites.' Mrs Tan smiled before adding sadly, 'But they seem to be too busy these days to learn how to cook it themselves.'

Just what is Nonya food like? Mrs Tan describes it as a mixture of Chinese and Malay, with Indonesian and Thai overtones. 'The Indonesian influence isn't surprising, since some Singapore *Peranakan* families came here from Java or Sumatra. Many well-known Nonya dishes such as *sayur lodeh* and *ayam buah keluak* are Indonesian in origin. The food of the Penang Nonyas is more similar to Thai food than the dishes I prepare. Of course, Penang is so much closer to Thailand! When I make *laksa*, I use *santan* (coconut milk) for the gravy, whereas a Penang Nonya will follow Thai cooks and make a thin sour pineapple gravy. But we Singapore Nonyas often borrow dishes from our Penang cousins and we all love *mee Siam* or Thai-style noodles.'

The Nonya taste for plenty of fresh coriander leaves, richly perfumed citrus leaf and other fragrant leaves is typical of Thai cooks who rely on fresh herbs and chillies for seasoning their food. Nonyas use less dried spices than the Malays, generally limiting their choice to coriander and cummin, but they cook their food in the same style, pounding the spices and seasonings and frying the resulting *rempah* in oil before adding coconut milk or other liquid.

The Chinese contribution to Nonya food is evident in the many dried ingredients such as mushrooms, other types of fungus, lily buds, fish maws, and seasonings like soya sauce and salty brown soya beans (*taucheo*). The most obvious Chinese ingredient is pork, something the Muslim Malays are forbidden to eat. Although the Straits Chinese adopted Malay customs and ritual observances they did not alter their religion. Anyone who has enjoyed pork *satay*, which is based on the famous Malay dish but is sweeter and juicier, will appreciate the creative genius of Nonya cooks.

How does one sum up a cuisine that is an amalgam of so many styles? The words sophisticated, creative and elusive come to mind, but perhaps the best description is 'fragrant'. To help explain the exciting aromas that make Nonya food irresistible, Mrs Tan set out an array of basic ingredients on her traditional *toh panjang* or 'long table', which stretched away from the formal gaze of an ancestral portrait.

Next to familiar fresh root ginger were a wrinkled yellow root of fresh turmeric and a pinkish ginger-like root called *lengkuas*, all of which Nonyas use more freely than other Singapore cooks. Red shallots, pearly white garlic and candlenuts (*buah keras*) were overshadowed by fire-red chillies and the brilliant green of fresh herbs: *daun kesom*, a particularly pungent, almost bitter herb; slender bulbs of lemon grass (*serai*); long blades of *daun pandan* (fragrant screwpine or pandanus) and leaves of the fragrant lime, *daun limau perut*. Small round green limes with yellow flesh yielding a sweet-smelling but tangy juice that enlivens curries and *sambals* were joined by other items that provide the fruity sourness so loved by Nonyas: pulpy brown dried tamarind (*asam*), and a tiny acidic fruit known as *blimbing*, a relative of the larger golden star fruit. Finally there was *blacan*, the strong-smelling dried shrimp paste that is used generously to give an intense flavour and fragrance to so many Nonya dishes.

As a young girl, Mrs Tan learnt how to deal with all these ingredients, how to pound spices and fresh roots to just the right degree, how to cook grated coconut to a golden brown, catching it just before it turned bitter, how to judge the correct amount of sugar to counteract the sourness of a fish *gulai*.

Now, like most *Peranakans* whose long-established position has ensured a comfortable standard of living, Mrs Tan employs a cook to do all the pounding, chopping and mincing in the kitchen. However, she still supervises everything closely and frequently lends a hand. Time is catching up with her, but by turning to her kitchen and her traditional food, Mrs Tan seems to reassure herself of the old values.

The objects surrounding Mrs Tan as she sits in her best room speak eloquently of a past where intense family loyalty was matched by a willingness to adapt to the customs of the Malays and, later, the British colonial administrators. The Straits Chinese were always the first to learn English, to send their children to school, and to follow Western sports and music.

There is no place for chromium, plastic, or cheap tile flooring in Mrs Tan's home. Beautifully worked antique blackwood chairs inlaid with mother-of-pearl and exuberantly carved cabinets highlighted with red and gold are matched by embroidered satin hangings. A traditional three-tiered lacquered bridal box used by Mrs Tan — and her mother before her — to carry a gift of cakes to her parental home; huge porcelain vases depicting ancient sages under towering mountain peaks; a few choice pieces of camellia-white jade; and a large red wooden plaque with carved gold characters proudly proclaiming the Tan family name, all bear witness to the past.

'We Nonyas devoted ourselves to our family and friends,' reminisced Mrs Tan. 'I used to spend most of my free time with my friends in Katong, which was once the fashionable place to live.' In those mellowed timber or brick bungalows with flower-splashed gardens leading down to the sea, Mrs Tan and her friends would while away the hours playing *mahjong* or Chinese card games. 'Since we moved from Katong, I find it too difficult to visit my friends frequently. It is so far and I don't like to take a taxi there on my own.'

Whenever Nonyas gather together, you will still find their famous cakes — the sort of cakes that instantly appeal to a child's unfettered imagination. Wonderful layered jelly-like confections stained brilliant violet, yellow, green, blue, red and pink. Rolled-up pancakes in cheerful green hiding a filling of sweet brown palm sugar and pure white coconut. Rich heavy golden slabs made from glutinous rice flour and coconut milk. Spicy light *kueh lapis*, layer upon layer of egg-rich batter striated with warm brown cinnamon and cloves.

The fanciful touch shown in Nonya cakes is apparent in other dishes too. Have you ever eaten a flower? Try a Nonya version of *mee Siam* and you can nibble the delicate pink bud of a ginger flower. Or sample *jantung pisang*, the heart of the banana flower cooked with prawns, onion, chilli and coconut milk. The flavour, not unlike that of globe artichokes, is surprisingly delicious.

Through their willingness to adapt and absorb new ways, the Nonyas have created a unique cuisine that is too good to be allowed to fade into oblivion. Yet perhaps a new Singaporean cuisine is even now evolving and, in years to come, a harmonious combination of Malay, Chinese and Indian cuisines will equal the delights of the food of the Nonyas.

PART 2: A SINGAPORE KITCHEN

Basic Ingredients

If you peeped into the kitchen of a Singapore home, you'd probably be able to guess who lived there. Bottles of oyster sauce and rice wine, dried mushrooms and pickled ginger would certainly belong in a Chinese home. A wide variety of spices, jars of candlenuts (*buah keras*) and dried tamarind, and a pile of tiny salted dried fish (*ikan bilis*), and you'd know the cook was a Malay. Brown mustard seed and fresh curry leaves, lentils and wholemeal flour — as Indian as a jewelled nose stud.

But many of Singapore's spices, dried goods, sauces and other ingredients are used by all cooks, regardless of ethnic origin. These essential basic items, ways of handling and storing them, and substitutes, are described in this section. A full description of all other ingredients is given in the glossary (page 53-63), together with the names by which they are known in Singapore and suggestions for substitutes. When using the recipes, please be sure to refer back to this section and to the glossary for any clarification necessary.

CHILLIES

The heat of curries comes from chillies rather than spices. Curries need not be searingly hot to be authentic; in fact, too many chillies tend to mask the flavour of the spices. To the uninitiated, chillies can be very hot. But don't be discouraged, tolerance of hot foods increases. In my first year in Singapore, my heat tolerance increased four-fold, and instead of using four chillies in a meat curry, I'd happily toss in sixteen!

Being a self-confessed chilli addict, I cannot praise too highly the delightful effect of eating chillies. After a hot curry, you experience a superb feeling of wellbeing, a kind of magical all-over glow that perhaps has something to do with the lowering of body temperature (at least, that's what Indians claim!).

Chillies are such an integral part of Southeast Asian food that it's hard to believe that they are not native to the region, having come, like other members of the capsicum family, from America. Be sure not to confuse chillies with mild red sweet peppers or capsicums.

Two sizes of chilli are used in Singapore: the more common is the long chilli (10-15 cm or 4-6 in), while the other variety is the tiny bird's-eye chilli or *chilli padi* (1 cm or ½ in), which is fiery hot. Chillies

1 Lengkuas, 2 pandan *leaf*, 3 *'local' celery*, 4 *curry leaves*, 5 *pink ginger bud*, 6 *fresh coriander leaves*, 7 *Chinese limes*, 8 *fragrant lime leaf*, 9 *ginger*, 10 *shallots*, 11 *garlic*, 12 *fresh turmeric*, 13 *chillies*, 14 daun salam, 15 daun kesom, 16 *coarse chives*, 17 *turmeric leaf.*

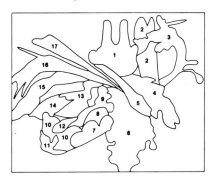

are used either in their unripe green state or when they are a ripe fire-engine red. The flavour and heat intensify with ripeness, so be sure to use the type of chilli specified in the recipes in this book. Dried red chillies, which lack the strong smell of fresh chillies, and give a brighter colour, are often used. Before grinding dried chillies, whether you are using a mortar and pestle or an electric blender, tear each chilli into three or four pieces and soak in hot water for about ten minutes. Squeeze out excess moisture before grinding.

The seeds are the hottest part of the chilli, so if you want to retain the flavour but reduce the heat, slit the chilli down one side and flick out the seeds with the point of a knife. A good shaking will usually dislodge the seeds of dried chillies once the stalk end is removed.

When handling either fresh or dried chillies, take care not to rub your nose or eyes as they'll burn for ages, and be sure to wash your hands thoroughly afterwards. Some cooks, when handling a lot of chillies, first rub their hands with oil to prevent their skin from stinging.

Although both fresh and dried chillies are generally available overseas, you may find it a lot easier to use ready-crushed chilli. Conimex market *sambal ulek* (which they still spell *oelek* in the old manner), a paste of fresh round chillies ground with salt. This is an excellent substitute for fresh chillies: one teaspoon of *sambal ulek* is equivalent to two or three freshly ground red chillies.

You may find it convenient to buy a large amount of fresh red chillies at a time and grind them in a blender or food processor with a small amount of salt until a coarse paste results. Put the ground chilli in tiny packs, each containing about 4-6 teaspoons (the equivalent of 8-12 whole chillies) and store in the deep freeze. Allow to thaw before using, draining off any liquid before frying the paste.

COCONUT

The coconut is probably the world's most versatile plant. Quite apart from its numerous commercial uses, it is indispensable in a Singapore kitchen. Coconuts were once the major source of oil for Malay cooks, but these days it is impossible to find a commercial product that equals the rich flavour of home-made coconut oil. To make your own, you must grate the flesh of ten mature coconuts, put them in a large *kuali* with water, and boil the contents for about four hours until the water evaporates and the oil comes out of the coconut. This provides just enough oil for one large bottle. No wonder Malay cooks now use other vegetable oils!

Coconut milk (*santan*) is the destiny of most of the thousands of coconuts sold daily in Singapore. Coconut milk is the liquid that is extracted from the grated white flesh of the coconut, *not* the water found in the middle of the nut. There are two types of *santan*: thick coconut milk (*pati santan*) which comes from the first squeezing of the grated flesh with just a small amount of water; and thin *santan*, which is made from the second squeezing of the coconut flesh with considerably more water. Occasionally, coconut 'cream' is prepared by squeezing the grated flesh without the addition of water.

In Singapore markets, you can buy fresh coconuts and have them grated on the spot, making extraction of *santan* an easy task. To obtain thick or *pati santan*, add ½ cup water to the grated flesh of one whole coconut (it will weigh around 500 g or 1 lb). Squeeze the flesh firmly, handful by handful, into a sieve set over a basin, keeping the squeezed flesh to one side. The resulting thick coconut milk is often added at the end of cooking to thicken and enrich a dish, or used in much the same way as dairy cream, poured over sweet dishes. To obtain thin *santan*, put the once-squeezed coconut back in a bowl with 2½ cups of water. Knead the grated coconut firmly for a minute or two, then repeat the handful-by-handful squeezing process to obtain a second lot of milk. Unless thick or thin coconut milk is specified in a recipe, the first and second extracts can now be combined to form the regular coconut milk required for recipes in this book.

Coconut flesh and milk deteriorate quickly in a hot climate, and if the milk is kept in the refrigerator for too long, the oily part becomes solid. The answer is to keep your grated coconut, bought the day you intend to use it, in the refrigerator until just before you need to make the *santan*. Most Singapore cooks add a pinch of salt to coconut milk if they are not using it immediately as this helps prevent it turning sour quickly.

Coconut milk can be stored satisfactorily in the deep freeze, provided it is going to be used for cooking, as the solid oily portion will integrate with the rest of the milk when heated.

Unless you are a very enthusiastic cook, I would not recommend buying fresh coconuts and grating them yourself to make coconut milk. Coconuts are generally expensive outside Asia, and Western kitchens lack the proper sort of utensil for grating the flesh sufficiently finely. However, if a small amount of grated coconut is required in certain vegetable dishes, chutneys and cakes, you can deal with fresh coconuts in the following manner. To open the nut, hold it in the palm of one hand and tap it in the centre with the back of a cleaver. Imagine it as a globe, and keep tapping the 'equator' as you turn the nut, and it will eventually split. To make the flesh shrink away from the sides of the shell to make extraction easier, put the two halves in a slow oven (120°C/250°F/Gas No. ½) for 15-20 minutes. Prise out the flesh, cut off the hard brown skin, then grate the flesh finely.

Substitutes: The following substitutes can be used for making coconut milk.

1 Creamed coconut, a solid preparation sold in plastic tubs, is easy to use and, in my experience, closest in flavour to genuine coconut milk. To make thick coconut milk, mix 100 g (3½ oz) creamed coconut with 1 cup boiling water. Stir until dissolved and, while still hot, strain through a fine sieve. For coconut milk of regular thickness, use 30 g (1 oz) creamed coconut to 1 cup water.

2 Frozen coconut cream, which is the thick coconut milk frozen solid, is marketed in some countries. To make coconut milk, allow the frozen cream to thaw and dilute with water to the required thickness.

3 Desiccated coconut makes the cheapest substitute for fresh coconut milk and, if you have an electric blender or food processor, it is easy to prepare. Put 2 cups of desiccated coconut in a blender with 2 cups hot water and blend at high speed for 30 seconds. Squeeze out the milk, handful by handful, to obtain thick coconut milk. Return the squeezed coconut to the blender with another 2½ cups of water and repeat the process to obtain thin coconut milk. Both extracts can be combined to form the regular coconut milk required in most recipes.

If you do not have an electric blender, the desiccated coconut should be left to soak in the required amount of hot water for 15 minutes and should be kneaded thoroughly before squeezing. The amounts of coconut and water required are the same as if you were using a blender.

When making desserts or cakes with coconut milk, use milk instead of water with the desiccated coconut for a richer flavour.

Cooking with coconut milk: Coconut milk will curdle if it is not stirred while coming to the boil. The milk should be lifted up with a ladle and poured down again, a process Malays call *timboh*. After thick coconut milk has been added to a dish towards the end of cooking, be sure to stir the mixture constantly until it thickens, then serve. Unless otherwise directed, do not cover the pan while cooking with coconut milk. The condensation will fall back into the pan and is likely to make the milk curdle.

When cooking curry dishes rich in coconut milk, you will find that after some time a little oil comes out of the coconut milk and floats on the top of the gravy. It usually takes on the colour of the chillies, and gives a lovely gloss and flavour, so don't be surprised if you see bright red oil floating on the top of your curry.

Grated coconut, either fresh or toasted, is often added to enrich certain dishes. To toast coconut (either fresh or desiccated), put it in a dry pan over low heat, stirring constantly and taking great care not to let it burn. It will take quite some time to start to change colour, but once it does, it must be watched closely as it quickly turns golden brown. Toasted coconut is usually lightly pounded with a mortar and pestle before being added to food.

If you are using desiccated coconut in place of fresh coconut for southern Indian vegetable dishes and chutneys, the flesh should be moistened with a little water. It will lack the rich flavour of fresh coconut and I always feel that for these dishes it is worth the bother of coping with fresh coconuts when they are available in Western countries.

Singapore cooks rarely use prepared commercial curry powders, preferring to blend their own at home or have them prepared by a spice merchant in the market.

COOKING OILS

Pure peanut oil, or a blend of peanut and other vegetable oils such as coconut, palm oil and safflower, is generally used in Singapore. Pure coconut oil, once the most popular oil with Malays, is seldom encountered these days. Chinese cooks prefer to use peanut oil, and I find it gives the most authentic flavour to Chinese food. Hokkien Chinese frequently use freshly rendered pork fat or lard in certain dishes; it gives a distinctive taste which cannot be reproduced by oil. Sesame oil is used only as a flavouring, not a frying, medium; a few drops are often added to a dish just before serving. Some Chinese cooks like to sprinkle just a little sesame oil into their frying oil (probably peanut) for extra flavour, a habit which did not escape the attention of one local manufacturer who now sells safflower oil with added sesame. Peanut, safflower and corn oil are all suitable for Malay and Indian cooking. Butter or *ghee* are used only occasionally by Singapore's Indian cooks, most of whom originate from the south where oil is the more common cooking medium. Olives are not produced in Southeast Asia, therefore olive oil should not be used in cooking food of the region, except for some Eurasian dishes of Portuguese origin.

Lovely to look at, even lovelier to taste: this selection of dried spices includes fenugreek, coriander powder, brown mustard seed and turmeric powder.

DRIED SPICES

Dried spices, including cloves and nutmeg which were once found only in Indonesia's Moluccan islands, are as important today as they were four hundred years ago when explorers and merchants braved incredible hardship to cross the world in search of this rich treasure. Many of these spices have been used for years in Western kitchens, while some are less familiar. With a few exceptions, ready-ground or powdered spices have no place in a Singapore kitchen. There is simply no comparison between the flavour of a dish made with freshly ground spices and one made with spices ground in a factory (and perhaps adulterated) goodness knows how long ago, and which may have sat on a supermarket shelf for months before reaching your kitchen.

Buy small quantities of whole spices and store them in screw-top jars. If you have a big freezer compartment in your refrigerator, or own a deep freeze, you can store whole spices in airtight jars almost indefinitely. The spices do not freeze up or deteriorate in any way, and keep their flavour remarkably well. To bring out the maximum flavour and to make spices very much easier to grind, shake them in a dry pan over low heat for several minutes. Most Singapore cooks use a mortar and pestle for grinding, but I find a small electric coffee grinder does an excellent job in a fraction of the time. For information on individual spices, please refer to the glossary (pages 53-63).

FLOUR

A number of different types of flour are used in Singapore, the most common being listed below.

Plain white wheat flour: This needs no introduction.

Wholemeal wheat flour: Known as *atta* by Indian cooks, who use this finely milled flour for *chapati* and other Indian breads. It can be bought still warm from the mill in Indian shops along Singapore's Serangoon Road. Health food shops in Western countries normally sell wholemeal flour (sometimes it is termed 'wheatmeal'). Be sure to buy the finely ground flour rather than the coarser varieties.

Rice flour: Fine white flour made from ground rice; known as *tepong beras* by Malay cooks.

Glutinous rice flour: This is made from white glutinous rice and is used for steamed savoury or sweet snacks. Known as *tepong pulot*.

Chickpea flour: Indian cooks use this flour, known as *besan*, to make batter for fish or vegetables, and in other savoury dishes. It is available in many health food shops overseas. Do not confuse it with green mung pea flour or green lentil flour.

Green mung pea flour: Made from the tiny green peas (*lok tau* or *kacang hijau*) which are sprouted to form beansprouts, this flour is frequently sold under the label 'tepong hoen kwe'. The best brands are Indonesian and are available in Chinese stores, often with the name 'green pea flour' stamped across the pack. Pack sizes range from 90 g (3 oz) to 150 g (5 oz), with 100 g (3½ oz) being the most common. The flour resembles arrowroot in appearance and cooking properties, and is used for cakes and desserts. It is sometimes sold coloured pink or green. Substitute arrowroot if green mung pea flour is not available.

NOODLES

There is an almost bewildering variety of noodles available in Singapore, made from different types of flour and cut in various sizes. They can be bought fresh or 'wet' from markets or noodle shops, or dried from provision stores and supermarkets. The main noodles are:

Fresh yellow or 'Hokkien' noodles: These heavy yellow noodles made from flour and egg are used mainly by Hokkien Chinese, although Malay and Indian cooks use them for *mee rebus* or *mee goreng*. They are not readily available in many Western countries, but dried wheat noodles or even spaghetti can be used as a substitute.

Fresh rice-flour noodles: Known as *kway teow* or *sa hor fun*, these wide flat rice-flour noodles have a creamy texture and mild flavour. They can often be obtained in flat sheets in Chinese delicatessens in Western countries. Cut the sheets into strips about 1 cm (½ in) wide, separate gently, and pour boiling water over to rinse. Dried rice-flour noodles can be used as a substitute. These must be soaked in boiling water for 30 minutes, drained, then soaked in a second lot of boiling water for a further 30 minutes.

Fresh laksa noodles: Also made from rice flour, these noodles are about as thick as spaghetti and about 4 cm (1½ in) long. Soak in boiling water for about 1 minute before using. Dried rice vermicelli can be used as a substitute.

Dried wheat-flour noodles: The most common of all, these noodles (called *mee*) are sold in packets or loose in rounds; eggs are often used in making these noodles, giving them a richer flavour, and this variety is sold as 'egg noodles'. Another variety of dried wheat noodles, known as *mee swa*, comes in very long thin strands and is traditionally served by the Chinese on birthdays. To cut the noodles on such an occasion would be to risk cutting short one's life. *Mee* (except *mee swa*) is generally cooked in plenty of boiling water with a dash of oil for about 3 minutes. It is then drained and either mixed with other ingredients or fried.

Dried Chinese rice vermicelli: Called *beehoon*, this is a fine white noodle made from rice flour. It is popular in soups, or fried with meat, seafood or vegetables. Soak in boiling water for 2 minutes before using. Sometimes known overseas as 'rice stick noodles'.

Dried green mung pea or 'cellophane' noodles: The name 'cellophane' is an apt description of these transparent noodles made from the flour of the dried green mung pea. They are known as *tunghoon* or *sohoon* in Singapore, but usually sold overseas under the name *fun see*. Soak in boiling water for 3 minutes before using.

'Indian' vermicelli: Used for desserts such as *payasam* (see page 202), this is a thin yellow vermicelli made from semolina, a wheat extract. The type sold in Singapore is manufactured in Australia.

Instant noodles: Popular in Singapore as a convenience food and readily obtained overseas, these packs contain dried cooked noodles, often with a sachet of seasoning. Many Singaporeans prefer to add their own seasoning, and consider the packaged variety to be somewhat synthetic in flavour. Instant noodles can be garnished with almost any kind of meat, poultry, egg, seafood and herb.

Popiah skins: Very thin fresh wrappers made from flour, eggs and water. Difficult to obtain, so make your own (see page 191) or use spring roll wrappers.

Wun tun skins: Similar to *popiah* skins, but cut into much smaller squares. Used for making dumplings which are either simmered in soup or deep fried. If you cannot obtain them packaged (either fresh or deep frozen) try your nearest Chinese restaurant, which will probably be prepared to sell you fresh ones.

Spring roll wrappers: Sold frozen in packages. Be sure not to allow them to dry out while using them or they will crack and be difficult to fold. Keep covered with a damp cloth except when handling.

THE ONION FAMILY

Four types of onions are used in Singapore: the tiny red shallot (*bawang merah*); the large red Bombay onion; the large white onion; and spring onions. The flavour and moisture content of various onions differs considerably, so if you want authentic results, try as far as possible to use the onion specified in the recipes.

Shallots, which are like tiny purplish-red onions, grow in clumps as does garlic. They are pounded or ground to form part of the seasoning paste (*rempah* or *masala*) in Malay, Indian and Nonya cooking. Shallots are also finely sliced and deep fried to form a crisp garnish for many local dishes.

If possible, use shallots where specified in the recipes. If they are not available, substitute 1 medium-sized red Bombay onion or brown-skinned Spanish onion for around 6-8 shallots. Shallots should be stored in a dry, airy cupboard. Incidentally, if you find they are starting to sprout, do not throw them away. Put them shoot upwards on the top of some soil in the garden or in a pot, and in a very short time you will have young green shoots that taste like chives.

Large red Bombay onions are used in some dishes. If necessary, substitute brown-skinned Spanish onions, not the white variety.

White-skinned onions are used in some Chinese dishes.

Spring onions, which are very important in Chinese cooking, are slender white stalks with green tops. In Australia they are widely (and confusingly) known as 'shallots', while in America spring onions are known as 'green onions' or 'scallions'.

Coarse chives, known as *kuchai* (also spelled *koo chye*), are used as a flavouring or garnish in several noodle dishes. They're very similar in flavour to garlic chives, but common chives or spring onions can also be used as a substitute.

Garlic is vital to all Singapore cooks (1,500 tonnes were imported to Singapore for a recent Chinese New Year season!). The Chinese often fry a crushed clove or two to flavour their cooking oil, discarding the cooked clove before adding other ingredients. Thinly sliced garlic is fried and used as a garnish for some soup or noodle dishes, and garlic is almost always part of the *rempah* or *masala* of curries. When frying garlic, take great care not to burn it or it will become very bitter. The easiest way to peel and chop garlic is to smash the unpeeled clove with the back of a knife or cleaver. Remove the loosened skin and then chop the smashed garlic finely.

ROOTS, LEAVES AND GRASSES

The wonderful aroma and flavour of many local dishes comes not only from dried spices but from a range of roots, herbs and grasses. Fresh ginger root and the related *lengkuas* (Bot: galangal) and fresh turmeric are commonly used. So too are lemon-scented grass (*serai*) and the southern Indian favourite, curry leaf (*karuvapillai*). Fragrant screwpine or pandanus leaf (*daun pandan*), the young leaves of a special aromatic lime (*daun limau perut*) and a pungent herb called *daun kesom* (Bot: polygonum) all contribute unique flavours.

Unfortunately, not all these plants will grow in a temperate climate, but dried or powdered substitutes are generally available in speciality stores. Conimex, a Dutch company, markets a number of items under their Indonesian names (which are still written in the old spelling). Please refer to the glossary (pages 53-63) for a full description of individual roots, leaves and grasses.

RICE

Many different types of rice are prepared in almost every way imaginable in Singapore — except for Mary Jane's detested rice pudding! When I was a child, rice meant just this: rice baked with milk, sugar and egg, and flavoured with nutmeg. As I grew older and encountered the soggy boiled rice that some Western cooks inflict on their guests at buffets, I decided that I definitely did not like rice.

I was totally unprepared for the quality and variety of rice dishes in Singapore: there was savoury Chinese rice porridge boiled with pork;

sweet black glutinous rice porridge with a heavenly fragrance; nutty Basmati rice prepared by Indian cooks with spices, fruit and nuts, extravagantly decorated with tissue-thin silver leaf; steamed white rice; yellow rice glistening with oil; rice fried in either Chinese or Malay style; Indian rice boiled with lentils; Malay rice simmered in coconut milk; glutinous rice steamed in lotus leaves; sweet cakes made from sticky rice — the list is never-ending.

All of Singapore's rice is imported. The long-grain Thai rice is generally acknowledged to be the best of the white varieties, and the price reflects this. For certain Indian dishes, Basmati rice (usually from Pakistan) is required. This rice has a long thin grain, is light beige in colour, and has a distinctively nutty flavour. It is considerably more expensive than other types of rice, but well worth it. It is sometimes marketed overseas as Patna rice, and is usually available in health food or gourmet shops. In Singapore, Basmati rice is obtainable from Indian provision stores along Serangoon Road.

Glutinous white rice (*pulot*) and glutinous black rice (*pulot hitam*) are used for cakes, savouries and sweet porridge. White glutinous rice is normally available from Chinese stores overseas, but unfortunately black rice is rarely found outside of Asia.

Natural unpolished or 'brown' rice, which has a higher nutritional value than polished rice, is unfortunately looked down upon by most Asians and is not used in Singapore cooking.

How to cook rice: My Malay *amah* used to look in amazement at my early attempts to cook rice. She couldn't understand how I could turn out complex Western dishes, bake bread, make cheese and chutneys, and yet invariably produce gluggy unpalatable rice. For cooks with a similar problem, I strongly recommend an automatic rice cooker which produces separate fluffy grains every time, and also keeps the rice warm for as long as you wish. Hundreds of thousands of Asian cooks, from Japan right down through Singapore to Indonesia, use rice cookers daily.

Plain white rice is cooked in two major ways in Singapore (by those without rice cookers, that is). Indian cooks boil rice in lots of water until the grains are just tender. The water is then thoroughly drained off and the rice set over very low heat to dry out. The evaporation method used by Malay and Chinese cooks (and most other cooks throughout Southeast Asia) involves boiling the rice rapidly with a certain amount of water until the water is totally absorbed. The grains are then dried out slowly over very low heat. (See page 85 for full instructions.)

Rice sold in Singapore (and most other Asian countries) is unwashed, so you must wash it thoroughly before cooking. Put the rice in a saucepan, half-fill it with water, and rub the rice grains with your hands for a few moments. Tip the water out and repeat the process at least four times until the water runs clear. This step is crucial to good rice cooking. Since most Western countries market packaged, prewashed rice, it is unnecessary to wash it again before cooking.

Glossary

A NOTE ON FOREIGN NAMES

When buying Asian ingredients overseas, the English name is usually adequate for identification. However, there are instances where a knowledge of the Chinese, Hindi or Malay helps; furthermore, some products used in Malay cooking are marketed only under their Indonesian names abroad, so where this occurs, I have provided the Indonesian name.

In Singapore, four major languages or dialects are spoken (Malay, Hokkien, Tamil and English), as well as a number of other dialects. Although the English names for many ingredients are fairly widely understood in Singapore, it is helpful to know the local names. Malay, the old language of the market place, has been the *lingua franca* of much of Southeast Asia for centuries, and you'll find it is still useful when shopping in Singapore. Although Cantonese is more widely spoken among Chinese living in Western countries, I have also provided the Hokkien names by which many products are commonly known in Singapore. Similarly, I have provided Tamil as well as Hindi, for the majority of Singapore's Indian population speaks Tamil or Malayalam — Hindi won't, as I quickly discovered, be of much help in the Indian provision shops along Singapore's Serangoon Road.

Foreign names are abbreviated thus: **M** Malay; **C** Cantonese; **H** Hokkien; **T** Tamil; **Hin** Hindi; **Indon** Indonesian.

The spelling of certain Malay and Indonesian words was altered in 1972; this new spelling is used throughout the book. Thus the 'ch' in words like *blachan* (dried shrimp paste) and *kachang* (beans) is now spelled 'c' (e.g. *blacan*).

Using the glossary: If you cannot find a particular item listed in the glossary, check the index for references to that item in other sections of the book. Alternatively, look through the preceding pages (43-51) if the item seems likely to belong in any of the following categories: chillies, coconut, cooking oils, dried spices, flour, noodles, onions, rice, roots, leaves and grasses. Individual items are also described in some detail in the introductions to the recipe sections on Vegetables (page 107) and Seafood (page 129).

1 *Giant white radish,* 2 *yam bean,* 3 *dried shrimp paste,* 4 *tamarind,* 5 *Chinese sausage,* 6 *dried salted radish,* 7 *salted soya beans,* 8 *salted duck eggs,* 9 *dried beancurd twists,* 10 *dried beancurd sheets,* 11 *soft beancurd,* 12 *hard beancurd,* 13 ikan bilis, 14 *dried black mushrooms,* 15 *dried prawns,* 16 *dried lily buds,* 17 *Szechuan pepper.*

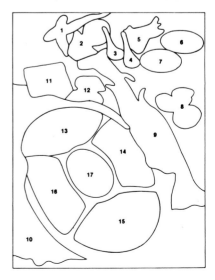

AGAR AGAR

Made from seaweed and used like gelatine. It sets hard without refrigeration, so is ideal in a tropical climate. Strips of agar agar can be bought, although the powdered variety is much easier to use. One teaspoon of powder will set 1-2 cups of liquid, depending on the firmness required. Agar agar is obtainable from Chinese stores or health food shops overseas.

ASAFOETIDA
T: *perunkayam*
Hin: *hing*

A gum derived from a Persian plant, used in some Indian dishes.

ASAM GELUGOR (M)

Slices of dried tamarind fruit used for their sourness in certain Malay and Nonya dishes. Dried tamarind pulp can be used as a substitute.

BAMBOO SHOOTS
M: *rebong*
C: *juk sum*

If you can obtain fresh bamboo shoots, peel off the tough skin and simmer shoots in water for 30 minutes. Canned bamboo shoots (especially the more tender winter bamboo shoots) make an acceptable substitute. They should be boiled in water for 10 minutes before use. Store bamboo shoots, covered with fresh water, in the refrigerator; if water is changed daily, they will keep for about 3 days.

BARBECUE SAUCE

see Sweet Red Sauce

BEANCURD

Several types of fresh and dried soya beancurd products are used in Singapore; although generally bland in flavour, beancurd products are delicious when imaginatively prepared, and are a good source of protein.

Hard beancurd (C: *taukwa*): Often stained yellow on the outside with a dye now banned as a possible health hazard in Singapore, this firm beancurd comes in pieces about 6-8 cm (2½-3 in) square. As it holds its shape well, it is used for stuffing, deep frying, etc. Available at Chinese delicatessens.

Soft beancurd (C: *taufu*): Used mainly in soups, steamed or scrambled. Tinned *taufu* can be bought overseas, and it is possible to make 'instant' *taufu* from a packaged Japanese mix. Fresh soft beancurd is usually available in Chinese stores, and can be stored covered with water in the refrigerator for 2-3 days, provided the water is changed daily.

Brown beancurd (C: *taufu pok*): Squares of fried beancurd usually hung on strings in markets. Used in some noodle soups.

Dried beancurd sheets (C: *taufu juk*): Used as a wrapper. Sold in large sheets that should be wiped with a damp cloth to clean and soften; cut to the required size with scissors. Sold packaged.

Dried beancurd twists (C: *taufu kee*): Sticks or twists of beancurd skin used in meat or vegetable dishes. They should either be fried in hot oil, which makes them puff up, or soaked in hot water for 15 minutes before use.

Fermented red beancurd (C: *nam yee*): Small cakes of reddish beancurd, sold in jars or tins; they have a salty, slightly fermented flavour and are used as a seasoning.

BEANSPROUTS
M & C: *taugeh*

Usually made from the small round green mung pea, although sprouts of the soya bean are also sold in Singapore markets. Fresh beansprouts are obtainable from many vegetable sellers overseas, and will always be found in Chinese stores. Will keep refrigerated for 2-3 days if wrapped in plastic, or kept in water in a bowl. Before using beansprouts, rinse in a bowl filled with cold water so that any loose skins will float to the top and can be removed. Some fussy cooks pull off the straggly root end of the beansprouts for the sake of appearance — fine if you have all day in the kitchen, but not necessary.

BIRD'S NEST

Sounds rather gruesome, but this is the highly prized gelatinous material that the tiny swift uses to line its nest. Dried bird's nests are usually available packaged. The nest should be soaked in warm water for 30 minutes and any feathers or other foreign matter picked out. Change the water, soak a further 10 minutes, then drain. Almost flavourless, bird's nests are used mainly for texture and medicinal properties in savoury or sweet soups.

BITTER GOURD
M: *peria*

A pale-green elongated vegetable (usually about 25 cm or 10 in long). The skin and central pithy portions are discarded before cooking.

BLACK CHINESE VINEGAR

Sometimes called Tientsin vinegar, this is similar to thick black soya sauce in consistency. Less acidic than other types of vinegar, it is used sparingly as a flavouring for some dishes such as shark's fin soup.

BLACK CUMMIN
Hin: *kala jeera*

Although translated into English as black cummin, this hard, irregular-shaped seed is not true cummin and has a completely different flavour. Used mostly in Punjabi dishes.

BLIMBING (M)

A tiny pale-green oblong fruit, rather like a cucumber in appearance, used for its acidity by Malay and Nonya cooks. Tamarind or lemon juice can be used as a substitute.

BROWN MUSTARD SEED

see Mustard Seed

CANDLENUTS
M: *buah keras*
Indon: *kemiri*

Cream-coloured waxy nuts that are almost identical to Queensland Bush Nuts or macadamias, which make a perfect substitute. They are always finely ground before being added to Malay and Nonya dishes for flavour and texture. Almonds are an acceptable substitute.

CAPSICUM

Large green or red bell-shaped peppers with a mild flavour. Eaten as a vegetable, and should not be confused with small red chillies.

CARDAMOM
M: *buah pelaga*
T: *elakai* or *elam*
Hin: *illaichi*

A tough, straw-coloured fibrous pod containing small black seeds with a superb lemony fragrance that earned them the name 'grains of Paradise' in fifteenth-century Europe. Slit the pods on one side and give a blow to bruise the seeds lightly before using whole. If you cannot buy whole cardamom pods, buy the whole seeds and use 6-8 seeds to replace 1 pod. Powdered cardamom should be avoided, with the exception of McCormick's brand which is excellent.

CELERY LEAVES
M: *daun sop*
H: *kin chye*

'Local' or 'Chinese' celery, as it is called in Singapore, is smaller and more pungent than the large white celery grown outside Asia. The leaves and top portion of the centre of large celery can be used as a substitute.

CHILLI OIL
C: *lat yau*

Bottles of Japanese-manufactured chilli oil are available overseas. Chilli oil can be made by frying 10 pounded dried red chillies (previously soaked) in 10 tablespoons of oil for several minutes. Strain and reserve oil. Keeps indefinitely.

CHILLI POWDER
M: *serbok chilli*
    or *serbok lombok*

Hot seasoning made from ground dried red chillies. Do not confuse it with American chilli powder, which contains a mixture of paprika, cummin, oregano and other spices, and is relatively mild.

CHILLI SAUCE

A hot sauce made from red chillies, ginger, garlic and seasonings, often sweetened with fruit. Try to buy either Singapore or Malaysian brands as other chilli sauce is either too hot (e.g. Tabasco), too bland (American products especially) or too bitter (Chinese chilli sauce).

CHILLIES

see Chillies, page 43, for a full description

CHINESE RICE WINE

see Rice Wine

CHINESE SAUSAGE
C: *lap cheong*

Mottled red sausages sold in pairs. They do not need refrigeration. Delicious steamed on top of rice or added to fried rice or noodles. Sold in Chinese stores overseas.

CHINESE TREACLE SAUCE

see Sweet Black Sauce

CHIVES, COARSE
H: *kuchai*

Fairly similar to the common chive in flavour, these are flat leaves about 3 mm (⅛ in) wide. Garlic chives are the best substitute, although common chives or even spring onions will do.

CHOKO
M: *labu Siam*

A pear-shaped pale-green marrow with a rough skin and large seed, originating in South America where it is known as *chayote*. Any green marrow can be used as a substitute.

CINNAMON
M: *kayu manis*
T: *karuvapaddai*
Hin: *darchini*

Thick chunks of bark from the cassia tree are more commonly used in Southeast Asia than true cinnamon, which comes from Sri Lanka (Ceylon) and is very thin (about 2 mm or 1/16 in). Recipes in this book use the thick bark sold in Singapore and overseas. If you are using true cinnamon, about 4 pieces of bark should be used in place of 1 thick piece of cassia.

CLOUD EAR FUNGUS
C: *mok yee*

A shrivelled black fungus that should be thoroughly washed to remove grit, then soaked in hot water for about 10 minutes until it softens and swells. Used in soups and some vegetable dishes for its slightly chewy texture.

CLOVES
M: *bunga cingkeh*
T: *karambu*
Hin: *laung*

One of the world's best-known spices, frequently used, like cinnamon, in savoury dishes. Always use whole cloves where specified.

COCONUT

see Coconut, pages 44-46, for a full description

CORIANDER
M: *ketumbar*
T: *kotamalee*
Hin: *dhania*

Probably the most frequently used spice in Singapore, this small round seed with a faintly orangey smell is an indispensable ingredient in most curries.

CORIANDER LEAVES
M: *daun ketumbar*
C: *wan swee*
T: *kotamalee elai*
Hin: *dhania sabz*

Used by almost all local cooks for flavouring and garnishing, this leaf has a delightful, faintly peppery taste. It is often called 'Chinese parsley' overseas, although in Europe it is known as *cilantro*. Coriander leaves can easily be grown in the garden or in a pot from the whole coriander seeds bought as a spice. Pick when the plant is about 20-25 cm (8-10 in) high. Coriander leaves can be stored in an airtight container in the refrigerator for about 1 week, provided the condensation is wiped off the inside of the lid every day or so.

CUMMIN
M: *jintan puteh*
T: *peeru jeeragam*
Hin: *zeera sufaid*

Another important curry spice, somewhat similar to carraway seeds in shape and flavour. It is often used in conjunction with fennel seeds.

CURRY LEAVES
M: *daun kari*
T: *karuvapillai*
Hin: *karipattar*

Small dark-green leaves used in just about everything by southern Indian cooks, and also popular among Malays for fish curries. Curry leaves have a unique flavour and are not, as is sometimes suggested, the same as the Indonesian *daun salam*, which is a type of bay leaf with a very different flavour. Dried curry leaves are sometimes available overseas. When a sprig is called for in a recipe, this means about 10-12 leaves.

DAUN KESOM (M)

Known only by its Malay name in Singapore, this dark pungent leaf (Bot: polygonum) is about the size of a mint leaf. It is used in some fish and noodle dishes by Malay and Nonya cooks, and is very popular in Thailand and Indo-China. I have not encountered it outside Southeast Asia, but know from personal experience that it will grow in Australia. Although some books suggest basil or mint as a substitute, the flavour is quite different.

DAUN LIMAU PERUT (M)

see Fragrant Lime Leaf

DAUN PANDAN (M)

see Pandan Leaf

DAUN SALAM (M)

A type of bay leaf used in dishes of Indonesian origin. The dried leaf often available overseas is an acceptable substitute. In Singapore, it is difficult to obtain this leaf, so when I come across it, I buy a large quantity and keep it in the deep freeze.

DRIED BLACK MUSHROOMS
C: *tung ku*

Available in two types, the light-coloured brown mushrooms and the more highly prized thick dark-black mushrooms. The former are adequate as a seasoning, but thick black mushrooms should be used if they are to star in a dish (braised mushrooms, for example). Dried mushrooms should be soaked in hot water for 30 minutes before use.

DRIED LILY BUDS
C: *khim chiam*
H: *gum kum*

The Chinese name, which translates as 'golden needles', is an apt description of this dried yellow flower which is about 8 cm (3 in) long. It is usually knotted before being added to soup or vegetable dishes, although this fiddly task is not essential.

DRIED PRAWNS
M: *udang kering*
H: *hay bee*
C: *har mai*

Sun-dried small prawns or shrimps used in Chinese, Malay and Nonya cooking. They give a distinctive flavour and are not interchangeable with fresh prawns. Soak in hot water for about 10 minutes and discard any shell or hard material before using.

DRIED SHRIMP PASTE
M: *blacan*
Indon: *trassi*

Various types of paste or sauce made from fermented shrimps, prawns or fish are found throughout Southeast Asia. Although dried shrimp paste smells distasteful — some might even say revolting—before being cooked, it develops a delicious pungency when fried and adds a remarkable flavour to food.

Two types of *blacan* are available in Singapore: a light pinkish-brown soft cake or roll; and a firm, thin, dark-brown square. I prefer to use the latter, as do most Malay and Nonya cooks. *Blacan* should be stored in a tightly covered jar after opening or the smell may permeate your entire house. It keeps indefinitely.

Blacan should always be cooked before being eaten. It is usually ground and fried together with onions and other 'wet' spices, but if other ingredients in a particular dish are not to be cooked, flatten the *blacan* to about 5 mm (¼ in) thick, put in a dry pan and cook for about 3 minutes on either side. The *blacan* can also be placed on a small square of aluminium foil and grilled.

Dried shrimp paste is normally available overseas; if it is necessary to use a substitute, try concentrated anchovy sauce.

FENNEL
M: *jintan manis*
T: *peeru jeeragam*
Hin: *soonf*

This spice seed, which is similar to cummin although slightly whiter and fatter, has a sweet fragrance and flavour. It is often wrongly described as aniseed; although the smell is similar, fennel is completely different in appearance to true aniseed.

FENUGREEK
M: *alba*
T: *ventayam*
Hin: *methi*

A hard, almost square yellow-brown seed with a bitter flavour, and highly regarded for its medicinal properties, it is most frequently used by Indian cooks in fish dishes. If the smell reminds you of old-fashioned ready-made curry powders, that's because it was often used with too heavy a hand in such products.

FERMENTED SOYA BEAN CAKE
M: *tempe*

A thin (2 cm or ¾ in) cake made from pressed fermented soya beans. It originated in Java where it is a major source of cheap protein. It is wrapped in large leaves and sold in most Singapore markets. Dried *tempe* can sometimes be bought overseas, but, being salted, must be soaked overnight before use.

FIVE-SPICE POWDER
C: *ng heong fun*

A seasoning made from ground star anise, fennel, cloves, cinnamon and Szechuan pepper. Sold in powdered form in packets. Buy in small quantities as it looses its flavour if stored too long.

FLOUR

see Flour, pages 47-48, for a full description of all types

FRAGRANT LIME LEAF
M: *daun limau perut*
Indon: *daun jeruk perut*

A large sweet-smelling leaf from a particular type of lime. Sometimes called a 'kaffir' lime, the fruit has very rough, knobbly skin. The young leaves of any citrus tree can be used as a substitute, although they lack the distinctive fragrance of this variety.

GARAM MASALA (Hin)

A mixture of ground spices used in cooking or sprinkled over food immediately before serving. The combination of spices differs regionally, but commercially packaged brands are readily available overseas. Do not store for more than 3 months (except in a deep freeze) for, like any ground spice, it looses its flavour. See also page 36.

GHEE (Hin)

Clarified butter used by Indian cooks. It is preferable to ordinary butter because there is no residue which may cause the food to stick or burn during cooking. *Ghee* can be bought in tins and stored unopened on the shelf, even in a hot climate.

GINGER
M: *halia*
C: *keong*
T: *injee*
Hin: *adrak*

Fresh root ginger is an essential item in many Singapore dishes. It is either used in slices, finely chopped or crushed, or the juice is extracted. Peel the fine skin off the root before using. Where a 'slice' of ginger is specified in the recipes, use a slice about 3 mm (⅛ in) thick.

To make ginger juice, use the very young light-coloured ginger or the tender shoots of the old root if possible. Pound with a mortar and pestle or in a blender and squeeze juice out of the pounded flesh with a piece of cheesecloth. Another method is to chop the ginger finely and press it in a garlic crusher. If you are forced to use old ginger, moisten it a little with cold water before squeezing.

Ginger can be stored in dry earth in a pot, or wrapped in kitchen paper and put in a plastic bag in the refrigerator. It can also be kept in a closed jar filled with dry sherry. This sherry can later be used as a substitute for Chinese rice wine.

Never use dried ginger powder as a substitute for fresh ginger.

GINGER BUD, PINK
M: *bunga siantan*

The fragrant bud of a variety of ginger plant, used as a garnish for several Singapore dishes. No substitute.

GREEN MUNG PEAS
M: *kacang hijau*
C: *lok tau*
Hin: *mung ki dhal*

This tiny round dried green pea is very versatile: it is ground to make flour; sprouted to make beansprouts; boiled to make soup and sweet porridge; and made into transparent noodles (*tunghoon* or *soohon*).

HOISIN SAUCE (C)

A sweet reddish-brown sauce sold in jars or tins. Covered, it will keep in the refrigerator for several months.

HOT BEAN PASTE

Mixture of soya beans, chilli and seasoning used in Szechuan cooking; often contains sesame oil. Available in jars or tins.

HUNDRED-YEAR EGGS
C: *peh dan*

Duck eggs that have been covered with a mixture of lime, rice husks and salt and left for several months. To use, remove coating and shell and cut egg into quarters. Serve as an *hors d'oeuvre* with slices of pickled ginger to counteract the faintly sulphurous taste of the egg.

IKAN BILIS (M)
Indon: *ikan teri*

A tiny whitebait that is salted and dried. It is highly nutritious and comparatively inexpensive. *Ikan bilis* are fried to make snacks and *sambals,* and are sometimes added to Malay vegetable dishes. Remove the head and black intestinal tract of each fish before using, unless you have bought the very tiny thin variety (not more than 2.5 cm or 1 in long) that is sometimes sold as 'silver fish'. If you live in a humid climate, you may find it necessary to dry the *ikan bilis* in the sun or in a low oven before frying. They are usually quite salty, so taste any dish using *ikan bilis* before adding extra salt. Most Chinese stores sell *ikan bilis.*

KRUPUK (M)

Dried wafers, usually made from shrimp (*krupuk udang*) or fish (*krupuk ikan*). *Krupuk emping* or *melinjo,* made in Indonesia from a bitter nut, are sold in Singapore and some shops overseas. They have a slightly bitter but wonderful flavour.

Make sure the *krupuk* are thoroughly dry before cooking. Drop a few at a time in deep hot oil and swirl around with a slotted spoon until they puff up. Remove immediately, drain, and store in an airtight container until needed. Add salt only when serving or they will become soggy.

LEMON GRASS
M: *serai*
T: *vasanelalang*
Hin: *sera*
Indon: *sereh*

This lemon-scented grass is one of the loveliest of all local seasonings and is very important in Malay and Nonya cooking. It looks rather like a miniature leek. Only the bottom 8 cm (3 in) of the plant should be used. Slice finely before pounding.

Lemon grass grows easily even outside Asia. If you can obtain a few stems of freshly cut lemon grass, keep them in a jar of water in a sunny spot until the roots start sprouting. Plant out in a large pot or in a sunny position. In a cold climate, the lemon grass should be kept indoors during winter.

Strips of dried lemon grass are sometimes available in Western countries. Use 12 strips as a substitute for 1 stalk of fresh lemon grass. A powdered form known as *sereh poeder* is also sold; use 1 teaspoon in place of 1 stalk of fresh lemon grass. Failing these substitutes, use a small strip of lemon peel.

LENGKUAS (M)
Indon: *laos*

Always called by its Malay name in Singapore, the botanical name for this ginger-like root is 'greater galangal'. It is used frequently by Malay and Nonya cooks, particularly in fish dishes. Powdered *lengkuas* is sometimes marketed under the Indonesian name, *laos.* Half a teaspoon of *laos* powder is roughly equivalent to 1 slice (3 mm or ⅛ in) of fresh *lengkuas.* Dried slices of *lengkuas* are sometimes available overseas; soak in boiling water for 30 minutes then use as you would the fresh root.

LENTILS
Hin: *dhal*

The name *dhal* is given to any sort of lentil, dried bean or pea. *Dhal* is particularly important to vegetarians, being a valuable and inexpensive source of protein. There are many different types of *dhal*, the major ones used in Singapore being:

Channa: A round brownish pea known in the West as chickpea, or by its Spanish name, *garbanzos*. The Malay name is *kacang kuda*. Some Indian cookbooks written for Westerners refer to *channa dhal* as Bengal gram. This *dhal* is ground to make a flour called *besan*; it is often boiled and salted for eating as a snack.

Masur: Salmon-pink lentils, similar in shape to the common brown lentil well known in Western and Middle Eastern countries.

Mung: The small round green pea used extensively in Chinese cuisine (see Green Mung Peas); Indians use this for sweet porridge and cakes.

Parupoo or tuvar: Also known as *tuar* and *arhar*, this is a pale-yellow split pea, sometimes known in English as pigeon pea. The taste is different from that of ordinary split green peas, although these can be used as a substitute.

Ulundoo or urad: Called 'blackgram' in English, this is frequently used as a seasoning for vegetable dishes by southern Indians, and should not be soaked before being fried. It is also ground to make *dosay* (see page 104) and other savoury snacks such as *vaday* (see page 193). It is usually possible to buy husked *ulundoo*, but if it still has a black skin, it must be soaked and the skins rubbed and floated off before use.

LIMES

Although the large lime resembling a lemon in size and shape (M: *limau nipis*) is sold in Singapore, a small round green lime called 'local' lime or Chinese lime (M: *limau kesturi*) is generally preferred. The flesh is yellow and the juice fragrant and sharp. A squeeze of *limau kesturi* gives piquancy to curries, noodle soups and chilli *sambals*. Half-ripe kumquats make an excellent substitute; failing these, use lemon juice. A third type of lime, *limau perut*, is occasionally used for its very fragrant leaves; the skin is also grated and used in some Nonya dishes.

MONOSODIUM GLUTAMATE
C: *mei chen*

Excessive use of this fine white crystalline powder, which intensifies the natural flavour of food, can lead to indigestion or heartburn. Some cooks prefer to omit it, but as long as you do not exceed the amount specified in the recipes, it should not have any side effects. It is sold under brand names such as Aji-no-moto, Vetsin, Vesop and Ac'cent.

MUSTARD SEED
M: *biji sawi*
T: *kardugoo*
Hin: *rai*

A small brownish-black mustard seed, used mostly in southern Indian cooking. The flavour is totally different from the larger yellow European mustard seed, so be sure not to confuse the two.

NOODLES

see Noodles, pages 48-49, for a full description of all types

NUTMEG
M: *buah pala*
T: *jathikka*
Hin: *jaiphal*

A firm oval nut usually sold inside its hard shell in Singapore, though shelled elsewhere. Grate or pound just before using. Never use powdered nutmeg as it looses its flavour more quickly than any other spice.

OIL

see Cooking Oils, page 47

OYSTER SAUCE
C: *ho yau*

Made from oysters, but very mild in flavour, this sauce has the surprising ability to heighten the flavour of the food it is cooked with.

Hongkong brands are generally acknowledged as the best, and are sold in Chinese stores overseas.

PALM SUGAR
M: *gula Melaka*
T: *jaggery*
Indon: *gula Jawa*

Sold in flat cakes or in rolls, and generally called by its Malay name, *gula Melaka* (previously spelled *gula Malacca*). It is brownish-black in colour, and usually made from the sap of the aren tree, although a milder, lighter-coloured variety is made from the coconut palm.

To dissolve palm sugar, break into small pieces and put in a pan with a little water and, if possible, a *pandan* leaf. Simmer gently until sugar is dissolved, then pour through a strainer to remove any grit or even pieces of insect that were attracted to the sugar sap while drying.

Brown sugar, or a mixture of brown sugar with maple syrup or golden syrup, can be used as a substitute.

PANDAN LEAF
M: *daun pandan*

An aromatic member of the .pandanus family, sometimes called fragrant screwpine in English. A couple of leaves, first scraped lightly with a fork then tied in a knot, are often added to rice, sweet dishes, or even curries, while the juice is extracted for cakes and desserts.

Dried *pandan* leaves are obtainable under the Sinhalese name, *rampé*, in some shops specialising in curry ingredients. If these are not available, omit *daun pandan*.

PEPPER
M: *lada hitam* (black)
    lada puteh (white)
T: *mooloogoo*
Hin: *kali mirch*

Black peppercorns are preferred in most spicy dishes, although some mild curries require white peppercorns. Chinese cooks often sprinkle food with a liberal amount of ground white pepper just before serving.

PICKLED GINGER
C: *shin keong*

Young root ginger finely sliced and preserved in vinegar. Sold in glass jars in Chinese or Japanese stores. An ideal accompaniment to most fish dishes, and to hundred-year eggs.

PICKLED RADISH
H: *tang chye*
C: *tung choy*

A chewy, salty accompaniment to rice porridge and many other Chinese dishes. Sold in plastic bags in Chinese or Japanese stores; keeps indefinitely on the shelf if stored in a screw-top jar.

POPIAH SKINS

see Noodles, pages 48-49

POPPADUM

Thin wafers made from lentil flour and spices. They should be completely dry before being fried in hot oil for a few seconds on either side so that they puff up. Fry only just before eating to ensure crispness, and be sure the oil is sufficiently hot or the *poppadum* will be leathery and heavy. Available in packets at specialty food stores overseas.

POPPYSEEDS
Hin: *kas kas*

This ancient spice, known to the Egyptians over three and a half thousand years ago, is used as a thickening in Indian and some Malay curries. Only the fine white poppyseeds, similar to grains of sand, are used; they are much milder than the black poppyseeds used in European cooking. Blanched almonds can be used as a substitute.

RICE

see Rice, pages 50-51, for a full description of all types

RICE WINE

Sold in bottles by Chinese stores. Substitute dry sherry.

ROSE ESSENCE
M: *ayer mawar*

A wonderfully evocative flavouring originating in the Middle East (and used to flavour Turkish Delight). It is usually obtainable from chemists overseas. A few drops are sufficient to flavour milk desserts, cakes and cordials. If you are buying rose water rather than the concentrated essence, you may need to use up to one tablespoonful as a substitute for a few drops of essence.

61

SALTED BLACK BEANS
C: *tau see*

Small black beans sold either moist in tins or jars, or dried (in packets). If using moist beans, rinse under running water for a few seconds. The dried beans should be soaked in hot water for 5 minutes and drained before use.

SALTED CABBAGE
C: *ham choy*
H: *kiam chye*

Available in tins, and also sold from large wooden tubs, this is usually very salty and must be soaked in cold water for up to 1 hour, changing the water several times.

SALTED DUCK EGG
M: *telur asin*

A traditional accompaniment to a lavish curry meal, these eggs are usually halved and served in the shell by local cooks, although most Westerners peel the egg and dice it finely. The eggs are usually sold with a coating of black soil which should be washed off. Put the eggs into cold water, bring to the boil and simmer 10 minutes. Salted duck eggs can sometimes be bought from Chinese stores overseas.

SALTED SOYA BEANS
C: *taucheong*
H: *taucheo*

A popular seasoning in Singapore, these beans are usually sold in semi-paste form, with soft beans in a light-brown sticky sauce. Some brands sold by Chinese stores overseas label *taucheo* in rather vague terms as 'bean sauce', even though it is a thick paste rather than a sauce of pouring consistency. *Taucheo* is usually lightly pounded or crushed with the back of a spoon before cooking.

SAMBAL ULEK (Indon)

A mixture of ground fresh red chillies and salt, sold bottled in many countries, it makes a convenient, easy-to-store substitute for freshly ground chillies (1 teaspoon *sambal ulek* = 2-3 fresh red chillies). Also spelled 'oelek'.

SESAME OIL
C: *ma yau*

Strongly flavoured oil made from sesame seeds, and used sparingly as a seasoning.

SESAME SEEDS
C: *tse mah*
M: *bijan*

These small oval seeds have a delightful nutty flavour and high nutritional value. They are often lightly toasted in a dry pan before being crushed. Black sesame seeds are used in some Chinese dishes, but unless otherwise specified, the white variety should be used in recipes. Obtainable from health food stores.

SHARK'S FIN

Delicious but expensive. Whole dried shark's fin can be bought at Chinese stores; it should be simmered for several hours then shredded. It is easier to buy prepared shredded dried shark's fins which need about 30 minutes' soaking in boiling water to soften them before cooking. Shark's fin has a rich taste and interesting gelatinous texture that makes it a true gourmet item.

SOYA SAUCE

Made from salted soya beans, this sauce is universally known. Three types of soya sauce are used in Singapore, and their flavours are markedly different, so be sure to use the type specified in the recipes.

Light soya sauce (C: *pak si yau*): Literally 'white' sauce in Chinese, this is the most commonly used sauce and is thinner and lighter in flavour than other types.

Black soya sauce (C: *hak si yau*): A black, thicker sauce with a stronger flavour, it is generally used in stewing.

Sweet soya sauce (M: *kicup manis*): A thick sweet sauce used in dishes of Javanese origin. Obtainable from most Chinese stores. The following makes an acceptable substitute: boil together 1 cup thick black soya sauce, ¼ cup molasses and 3 tablespoons brown sugar until well blended; store in an airtight jar.

SPRING ROLL WRAPPERS

see Noodles, pages 48-49

STAR ANISE
M: *bunga lawang*
C: *pak kok*

A dark-brown star-shaped spice made up of eight petals or 'points'. Used in Chinese, Nonya and Malay cooking, and an ingredient in Chinese five-spice powder.

SWEET BEAN PASTE
C: *tau sa*

Made from cooked and mashed red beans, and available tinned. An almost identical Japanese product, used as a filling for *toriyaki* cakes, is sold under the name *yokan*.

SWEET BLACK SAUCE
C: *tim cheong*

The name *tim cheong* (literally 'sweet sauce') is given to several types of sauce in Singapore. The most common are sweet red sauce, sometimes labelled 'barbecue sauce'; thin black sweet sauce sold in bottles; and very thick treacle-like black sweet sauce that is smeared inside *popiah*.

SWEET RED SAUCE
C: *tim cheong*

Sometimes labelled 'barbecue sauce', this is a very salty sweet red sauce available in jars or cans. Keeps indefinitely if refrigerated.

TAMARIND
M: *asam*
T: *pulee*
Hin: *imlee*

The fruit of the tamarind tree is prized for its acidity and slight fragrance, while Indian cooks also claim it has digestive properties. The dried pulp of the fruit, known in Malay as *asam Jawa*, is most commonly used, although some Malay and Nonya dishes require dried slices of the fruit (*asam gelugor*).
  To make tamarind water from dried tamarind pulp, soak 1 heaped tablespoon of pulp in ¼ cup warm water for 5 minutes. Squeeze with the fingers to extract the juice and strain out any fibrous matter, stones or skins. In Singapore, tamarind generally contains some seeds; if you are using dried tamarind pulp that has had all the stones removed, use 1 scant tablespoon per ¼ cup water.
  Instant tamarind exported from India in small plastic pots provides a quick easy substitute; use 1 teaspoon to replace ¼ cup tamarind water. Some form of tamarind is usually available overseas, but as a last resort, lemon juice or half-ripe tomato can be substituted for that touch of sourness.

TEMPE

see Fermented Soya Bean Cake

TEPONG HOEN KWE

see Flour, page 48

THICK SHRIMP PASTE
M: *petis*
H: *hay koh*

An almost black treacle-like paste used in making sauce for *rujak*. Do not confuse with dried shrimp paste (*blacan*), which is quite different in flavour and consistency.

TURMERIC
M: *kunyit*
T: *manjal*
Hin: *huldi*

Often misleadingly called Indian saffron, this is generally sold as a powder. It is made from the crushed dried root of the turmeric plant, and it bears no resemblance whatsoever to the flavour of true saffron. It is used mainly for its bright yellow colour. The flavour is slightly bitter, so be sure not to use more than the specified amount. Fresh or dried turmeric root is often preferred to powdered turmeric in Singapore, and the shredded leaf is sometimes added to the cooking pot or sprinkled over food. Ground turmeric or turmeric powder, although lacking the fragrance of the fresh root, is a satisfactory substitute.

WUN TUN SKINS

see Noodles, pages 48-49

YOGHURT
T: *tairu*
Hin: *dahi*

Plain yoghurt is used by Indians as a side-dish, a meat tenderiser, a salad dressing, and combined with iced salty water to make a refreshing drink (see *lassi*, page 203). Home-made yoghurt is superior to the commercial product.

Getting down to Cooking

UTENSILS AND METHODS

Many Western cooks are amazed at the simplicity of Asian kitchens and find it hard to believe that such superb meals are cooked with so few utensils — a clay pot, a *kuali* (*wok*), a charcoal brazier or kerosene cooker, and there you have it. I am not advocating a return to extreme simplicity; my experiences in a Javanese kitchen equipped only with one charcoal brazier and a hand-pumped well have made me an ardent supporter of modern kitchens. But the advantage of the uncomplicated approach to cooking means that you won't need to spend a lot of money buying suitable equipment for producing Singapore food in your own home.

Every Singapore kitchen is certain to have at least one *kuali*, the wide pan with a curving base that is better known overseas by its Chinese name, *wok*. You *can* manage without a *kuali*, but once you've used one, you'll wonder how you ever coped with an ordinary frying pan: the high sloping sides of the *kuali* heat up for even cooking throughout; stir-fried food falls back into the pan and not out over the edge as you toss it; less oil is required for deep frying; and the wide mouth permits the correct degree of evaporation so important when cooking dishes using coconut milk. I hope you are convinced and will go right out and buy a *kuali*. But do not buy an electric model, it cannot reach the high temperature required for a lot of Chinese cooking and is not really satisfactory; furthermore, those with a non-stick lining prevent the ground spices and other ingredients from frying correctly.

When buying your *kuali*, choose a heavy iron one as it is less likely to tip over when in use and there is less chance of the food sticking and burning during cooking. Some cooks keep an aluminium *kuali* for cooking dishes such as *opor ayam* which might discolour if cooked in an iron pan, although an enamelled saucepan or casserole will do. If you don't have a gas cooker, you may need a metal ring to hold the *kuali* steady over the radiant coil of your electric stove and to help direct the heat upwards. These are obtainable from most Chinese stores.

Singapore cooks like to season their *kuali* before its first use, and treat the *kuali* with the respect a French cook gives an omelette pan. One favourite method of seasoning is to rub the inside of the *kuali* with half an onion, then to fry the onion in oil for a few minutes. The *kuali* is then rinsed out in hot water and dried thoroughly before being stored.

Whether you want a plaster elephant moneybox or a jumbo-sized metal pan, a coconut-husk spoon, a plastic vegetable rack or just a plain ordinary earthenware cooking pot, if it's for the kitchen you'll find it in shops like this.

65

Abrasive powders and scouring pads should never be used on a *kuali*.

Terracotta pots with a curving bottom, sometimes called curry pots, were once used by Malays (who call them *belangah*) and Indians (who call them *chatty*). They are supposed to improve the flavour of curries, especially those made with fish, but few cooks bother to use them these days. A coarse clay pot with a sandy texture and colour, glazed inside, is a favourite among some Chinese cooks; they are available in many Chinese stores overseas and are very decorative.

One indispensable item is a large heavy cleaver, obtainable from Chinese stores. It is essential for chopping poultry; for mincing meat finely (unless you happen to have a food processor — an ordinary mincer makes the meat too dry); for slicing vegetables; for chopping crabs in half; and so on. You will also need a thick wooden chopping board to use with the cleaver. Laminated surfaces are not advised as the food tends to slither around.

Indian cooks use a circular iron disc, very slightly concave, as a griddle for frying various types of bread. This is called a *tawa*, and, if not obtainable overseas, can be replaced by a heavy iron frying pan.

Steaming is a favourite Chinese cooking method, also used by Malays on occasion. A bamboo steamer is a useful and very attractive addition to the kitchen, although it is not essential if you already have a metal steamer. The Chinese steamer, now fairly widely available overseas, is a simple affair made from hoops of bamboo with a split bamboo base and woven bamboo lid. It is designed to sit in a *kuali*, resting on the sides about 5 cm (2 in) above the boiling water in the bottom of the *kuali*. When steaming items that are not wrapped in banana leaf or foil, place them in a bowl or on a plate and set inside the steamer. A simple substitute for a steamer is to invert a low metal bowl or ring in the bottom of a deep pan (a preserving pan is ideal). Put in a little water and place the dish or bowl containing the ingredients to be steamed on top of the inverted bowl or ring, well above the level of the water. Cover the pan and simmer, adding to the boiling water when necessary.

For grinding ingredients such as dry spices, onions, chillies and ginger, there is a choice of utensils. Traditionally, a granite mortar and pestle (*batu lesong*) is used for dry spices and small amounts of wet spices, while a heavy granite slab with a roller (*batu giling*) is preferred when large amounts of wet spices such as onions, chillies, fresh turmeric and garlic are to be ground to a paste. Both the *batu lesong* and *batu giling* need a fair amount of practice to be used successfully, and they are almost impossible to obtain outside Asia.

This is where a food processor or an electric blender comes to the rescue. When recipes call for ground or pounded ingredients, grating or chopping simply won't produce the same result. An electric blender or food processor will smash up wet ingredients and produce the same result as traditional methods if used properly. I find whole dried spices such as coriander and cummin are most successfully ground in a small electric coffee grinder. To grind wet ingredients such as onion, chillies, lemon grass and so on, I cut the items into small pieces and put them in the food processor and grind for about 1 minute. I then scrape down the sides and add just enough liquid (about 1 tablespoon) to keep the ingredients moving. If the ingredients being ground are to be fried, I add oil; if they are to be simmered in coconut milk or water, I add coconut milk or water. You may need to add a little more liquid (say another tablespoon) and keep grinding for up to 5 minutes to get ingredients fine enough.

I cannot stress too strongly how important it is to use the right type of blender or food processor. I tried again and again with several blenders and had to admit defeat. The blender *must* have a small narrow jar, preferably of glass, or the blades won't even touch the contents. It must have a strong motor, and preferably four sharp blades.

As you grind the ingredients, you will need to stop the machine every so often to scrape down the sides of the jar. At the risk of sounding like a commercial, I must confess that my Magimix food processor has revolutionised my kitchen. Although it is an expensive machine, it has more than justified the initial cost. I find it indispensable for grinding wet spices (and it does it far more finely than my blender used to); great for chopping pork, liver, and other meat; perfect for smashing up fish for fish balls; ideal for quick and even slicing of vegetables; good for making paste out of soaked rice and lentils; and so on.

If you wish to use a granite mortar and pestle (*batu lesong*) for grinding both 'wet' and 'dry' spices, there are several points that should be noted. 'Dry' spices should always be heated gently in a dry pan for a few minutes, then put into the mortar and ground while still hot. Tap the spice seeds with the pestle for about 1 minute to break them up slightly, then use a firm circular motion with the pestle to grind the seeds finely.

'Wet' ingredients should always be cut into small pieces to make grinding easier. Because the texture of various items differs considerably, it is better to grind them in a certain order, making sure each item is well ground before adding the next. When using any or all of the following ingredients, grind them in this order: lemon grass, *lengkuas*, ginger, fresh turmeric, chillies, candlenuts, dried shrimp paste, garlic and finally shallots.

In Singapore, food is often wrapped in banana leaves before steaming or roasting over charcoal. To ensure the leaves are clean and pliable, cut them to size with an oiled knife (watch out for the juice, which will stain material) and cover them with boiling water for a few minutes. Aluminium foil can be substituted for banana leaves, although food cooked in foil lacks the subtle flavour imparted by the leaves.

Ovens have only recently become popular in Singapore homes. Baking or roasting are not methods traditionally used by Malay or Indian cooks, while the Chinese generally buy ready-cooked roasted meat as they have no facilities for preparing it at home. Frying, steaming and boiling are carried out over a kerosene or gas burner, or occasionally over a charcoal brazier. Grilling over charcoal (*panggang*) is another method adopted by Malay cooks; an electric or gas grill can be used instead of a barbecue.

Stir-frying is often called for in Chinese recipes: sliced food is continuously stirred around in a little very hot oil until well coated, then the temperature is lowered slightly and the stirring process continued until the food is cooked. Chinese cooks often add a few spoonfuls of stock or water after the food is coated with oil, and continue stir-frying until the liquid has evaporated. If the *kuali* is covered, and the liquid subsequently thickened, the food is considered braised rather than stir-fried.

HOW TO BUY THE INGREDIENTS

Most big Western cities have their 'Chinatown' area where Chinese and often Indian, Malay and Indonesian items can be found. Gourmet sections of many big supermarkets also stock these products, while Chinese delicatessens sell fresh beancurd, Chinese sausages, red barbecued Chinese pork (*char siew*), fresh chicken and duck, roasted poultry, and Chinese vegetables. Health food shops often stock spices, various flours and lentils, and many other items used in Singapore cooking. When buying spices, be sure you buy whole spices sold in airtight packages; some health food stores keep them in open drawers which make it impossible to retain their freshness.

In Singapore and neighbouring countries, buying ingredients presents no problems except for newcomers unfamiliar with local markets. Certain areas of Singapore specialise in foods that may be unobtainable elsewhere. For Malay and Indian items, shops in Serangoon Road and the Kandang Kerbau market area provide an unrivalled source of spices, lentils, flours, *krupuk*, *tempe*, noodles, vegetables, herbs, fresh fish, mutton and cooking utensils. You can even buy incense, peacock feathers, a garland of jasmine and a cassette tape of Indian music to put you in the mood while you cook! Geylang Market is also famous for its Malay ingredients.

Chinese items are sold in practically every Singapore market. What you won't find there will be in the nearby provision shop or Chinese Emporium. The excellently stocked shops along New Bridge Road are certain to have every Chinese ingredient you could ever want.

An array of utensils commonly used in Singapore kitchens: at the back, a kuali *or* wok *with a bamboo steamer set inside; in front, from left to right, a chopping block with cleaver, spoons and a frying shovel, a metal griddle or* tawa, *a clay pot, a* belangah *or* chatty *with a wire-mesh scoop, and a mortar and pestle (*batu lesong).

HOW TO PRESENT A MEAL

The normal practice when serving food in Singapore homes is to place all the dishes in the centre of the table at the beginning of the meal, and for everyone to help themselves as the meal progresses. This is different from Chinese restaurant procedure, where normally one course is presented at a time. In some of the more conservative Malay and Indian homes, the husband, sons and other menfolk eat first, with the women and girls following. In large households, the serving dishes are often left

in the centre of the table (with large conical rattan or plastic covers on top to keep out any insects) for members of the family who want to eat later. It is common for many Malay and Indian dishes to be eaten at room temperature, although all Singaporeans insist that their rice should be steaming hot.

It is considered polite to put only a small amount of food onto your plate at one time, replenishing it as the meal progresses. It is not essential to eat from every dish put on the table; Singaporeans are accustomed to large families (although these are fast becoming a thing of the past) and are not perturbed by individual preferences. If a dish of liver is served, for example, and you can't stand liver, concentrate on other dishes and no-one will mind.

The question of the appropriate drinks to serve with Singapore food· is fairly easily answered. Chinese food is often served with glasses of hot tea (without milk or sugar, of course); cold water is generally the rule with other types of food, although a glass of *lassi* (iced yoghurt drink) is sometimes taken with Indian food. Alcoholic drinks are seldom served, except at Chinese banquets when the men often consume vast quantities of neat cognac. I feel quite strongly that European wines do not blend well with any Asian food, although cold beer goes excellently with almost all Singaporean dishes.

There is no need to rush out and buy a complete one-hundred-piece set of Chinese tableware for presenting the food. For home-style Chinese meals, the ideal table setting per person is one small plate (the size of a bread-and-butter plate) to eat from and put bones on; one soup bowl plus a porcelain spoon; one rice bowl; a pair of chopsticks; and a

Round-table dining adds to the convivial atmosphere of a Chinese meal, where dishes are placed in the centre of the table for all to share.

tiny sauce bowl. You will also need several medium to large bowls and an oval plate or two for serving the food. Most Chinese stores sell moderately priced porcelain or china tableware; in Singapore many families prefer to use unbreakable plastic from Japan. Just a word on the use of chopsticks. It is well worth attempting to use them correctly (watch Chinese in your local Chinese restaurant), for when you pick up the morsels of food, they are covered by just the amount of sauce intended by the Chinese who created the recipes; a spoon tends to scoop up too much sauce.

Malay and Indian food is much easier to eat from a shallow bowl than a flat plate; a set of bowls about 4-5 cm (1½-2 in) deep and 20-24 cm (8-9½) in diameter is ideal. These also do service for all kinds of Singapore noodle soups. Malay and Indian food is traditionally eaten with the right hand (the left is considered unclean by Muslims), although some households use a spoon and fork. It's up to you to use which you prefer. A surprisingly large number of Westerners feel quite uncomfortable using their hands, although my son, born and raised in Singapore, has always eaten Malay and Indian food with his hand and has great trouble remembering not to dive into Western food, picking up peas or lamb chops with his fingers!

If you are entertaining, you might like to dress up your table with a cheap cotton *sari* (for Indian food), a plain white or coloured cloth (for Chinese food) and a piece of *batik* cloth for Malay or Nonya food. A few bright flowers scattered around add to the atmosphere. Squares of banana leaf are ideal for casual outdoor entertaining, provided you have a table to put them on, for they're even more limp than the proverbial paper plate.

All these suggestions are merely to help make your Singapore meals more enjoyable. You could, of course, eat the food from the normal tableware you already have in your home, but because Singapore food is such an adventure, why not extend the fun?

HOW TO PLAN A MENU

The prospect of preparing a full-scale Asian meal is rather intimidating for many Western cooks — and, I've discovered, for many inexperienced Singapore cooks as well. It is best to take things slowly. If you try to prepare an eight-course Chinese dinner or a vast rice and curry spread to impress your friends, your chances of success are slight. Even if the meal is fantastic, you'll probably be far too exhausted by mental and physical strain to enjoy it. So, *pelan, pelan* (slowly, slowly)! Begin with one or two simple dishes until you feel confident enough to add another. If you've decided upon one fairly complex dish, make sure the others are simple and that at least one can be prepared in advance.

When planning a meal — whether dinner for two, a family barbecue, a large sit-down dinner or a cocktail party — the first thing to consider in which *type* of Singapore food you wish to prepare. Generally speaking, food from the different ethnic communities should not be mixed at the one meal. If you plan on a couple of Chinese dishes, then don't include an Indian mutton curry or a Malay vegetable dish. There are, of course, dishes that go well together; when you are thoroughly familiar with the taste of different foods, you may find that certain Malay and Indian dishes can be served at the same meal, and that a number of Nonya and Malay dishes complement each other.

Rice is the basis of all main meals in Singapore. At a normal family meal, it will generally be accompanied by three to five other dishes, plus condiments. A Chinese meal will probably include a soup, a fish dish, something made with pork, and vegetables. Nonya meals include a dish with coconut-milk gravy, a hot spicy dish, several other dishes (meat, fish, poultry or vegetable) with little or no gravy, a chilli *sambal* and vegetable pickle (*acar*). Malay families serve fish, chicken or meat, a vegetable dish, and a chilli *sambal*. Indian meals follow a fairly similar pattern, except for vegetarian meals which include a range of vegetable and lentil dishes, plus a thin soup (*rasam*), yoghurt, and several small savoury items.

Desserts are seldom served at the end of meals in Singapore, although fresh fruit is very popular. There are, of course, exceptions, but sweet cakes, porridges and other 'desserts' are usually served as between-meal snacks. You may like to serve a dessert after a lunch of noodle soup, or a salad such as *gado gado*, to make the meal somewhat more substantial, but if you serve a full dinner of rice and several other dishes, you will probably find, like Singaporeans, that you have little room for desserts.

My family were guinea pigs during my early days of experimenting with Singapore food. I began with rice, a vegetable dish, and one other dish of either fish, poultry or meat. Sometimes I bought from the market a little cooked red barbecued pork (*char siew*) or steamed chicken to flesh out the meal, or even cheated by buying a clay pot or casserole to 'take-away' from a well-known Cantonese restaurant. If I was serving Malay food, I fried some *krupuk* and prepared a chilli *sambal* to add variety. Indian meals were an excuse for *poppadums*, which we all love, and before I learned to make chutneys, I used the commercial variety. When entertaining, I planned (and still do) at least one dish that could be prepared in advance, such as Chinese braised aniseed beef or almost any of the Malay, Nonya or Indian curry-style dishes with gravy.

A number of Chinese stewed dishes, as well as Malay, Nonya and Indian curries, can be deep frozen and re-heated successfully. I sometimes prepare double quantities of a dish that will freeze, making sure I remove the portion to be stored just before the end of cooking time so that it won't be too soft when re-heated. It will keep, packed in a plastic tub, for two to three months.

One point to remember when planning meals is that there should be a certain amount of contrast. Don't serve more than one dish with a lot of gravy; if you're serving a dish with plenty of coconut-milk sauce, look for a dry one to complement it. Don't serve more than one deep-fried dish at the same time; if you plan on fried fish, then cook your meat or poultry in some sort of gravy. Don't have all your dishes spicy hot; a fiery *rendang daging* is balanced by a soothing mild cabbage in coconut milk.

To help ensure that your meal will be a success, sit down with a pen and paper and jot down the dishes you'd like to have. Think carefully whether they complement each other, then go ahead. Even after a decade of preparing Singapore food, I still find it helpful to make a list.

To illustrate how you can plan meals, I have suggested some menus, all of which contain recipes from this book. There are sample menus for a sit-down dinner for six to eight people for each of the four cuisines covered. Because many people like to entertain out-of-doors in a relaxed fashion, I have listed a number of local dishes that are ideal for barbecues; most of them can be prepared well in advance, which makes your task as hostess a lot easier. If you are entertaining a fair number of people (say about twelve) you might like to serve a buffet; Chinese food does not generally lend itself well to a buffet, for many dishes need to be served piping hot, but I have suggested other dishes that I have found successful at buffets. And finally, if you're looking for interesting snacks for serving with drinks (what we call *makan kecil*, literally 'small eats', in Singapore), you will find them listed under 'cocktail suggestions'.

SAMPLE MENUS

DINNER FOR 6-8

Chinese

Soup with stuffed cucumbers
Long beans with prawns
Fish in taucheo sauce
Stewed pork leg
White rice

Abalone soup
Fried beancurd with spring onions
Har loke (prawns in shell)
Claypot beef
White rice

Szechuan sour hot soup
Quick-cooked broccoli
Diced chicken with dried chillies
Steamed whole fish
White rice

Duck and salted cabbage soup
Peking duck with pancakes
Fried beansprouts
Toffeed apples

Malay

Kangkong tumis ayer (simmered water
  convolvulus)
Gulai ayam (chicken curry)
Sambal udang (chilli-fried prawns)
Cucumber and pineapple sambal
Fried krupuk or tempe
White rice

Kobis masak lemak (cabbage in coconut
  milk)
Sambal goreng hati (liver in coconut
  chilli sauce)
Ayam goreng (fried chicken)
Acar (vegetable pickle)
Fried krupuk
White rice or roti jala

Pumpkin and long bean curry
Ikan goreng (fried fish)
Ayam korma (mild chicken curry)
Nasi kunyit (turmeric rice)
Ikan bilis goreng (fried dried whitebait)
Sambal blacan (chilli and shrimp paste
  sambal)

Urap (vegetable and coconut salad)
Rendang daging (beef in spicy coconut
  gravy)
Ikan moolie (fish in coconut milk)
Sambal telur (eggs in chilli sauce)
Nasi lemak (rice cooked in coconut
  milk)

Indian

Mutton Mysore
Goan prawn curry
Pilau
Okra bhaji
Onion and tomato salad
Mango chutney

Spiced mutton chops
Cauliflower masala
Kabuli channa (chickpeas)
Tomato and cucumber salad
Poppadum
Rice

Dhansak (Parsi meat, lentil and
  vegetable stew)
Puri (fried wholemeal bread)
Onion sambal

(Vegetarian)
Carrot pachadi
Southern Indian cabbage
Simple dhal stew
White rice or dosay
Rasam (hot sour soup)
Poppadum
Plain yoghurt
Lime pickle

Nonya

Bakwan kepiting (pork, prawn and crab
  ball soup)
Ayam lemak (chicken in rich coconut
  gravy)
Sambal timun (spicy cucumber dish)
White rice

Gulai ikan Penang (sour hot fish stew)
Babi lemak (pork in coconut milk)
Kiam chye goreng (fried salted cabbage)
Sambal brinjal (eggplant with dried
  prawn topping)
Nasi lemak (rice cooked in coconut
  milk)

Ayam tempra (chicken cooked with
  soya sauce and lime juice)
Hati babi (pig's liver balls)
Gulai udang nanas (sour prawn and
  pineapple)
White rice

DISHES SUITABLE FOR BARBECUES

Spiced chicken wings
Ayam panggang (barbecued chicken)
Tandoori chicken
Ikan panggang (barbecued fish)
Otak otak (spicy fish in banana-leaf packets)

Satay with gravy, cucumber chunks and compressed rice cakes
Gado gado (Indonesian salad)
Urap (vegetable and coconut salad)

Most of the above dishes can be prepared well in advance, and just cooked over the barbecue for the required time. For dessert, serve fresh fruits such as bananas, pieces of pineapple or papaya (pawpaw), slices of melon, orange wedges. *Kueh naga sari*, a chilled banana blancmange cake wrapped in banana leaf, is always a popular end to any meal and can be prepared in advance.

COCKTAIL SUGGESTIONS

Koftas (deep-fried meatballs)
Fried wun tun with apricot sauce
Ikan bilis goreng (fried dried whitebait)
Curry puffs
Samosa
Spring rolls

Prawn toast
Sandwiches with filling of sambal udang kering (dried prawn sambal)
Savoury stuffed sweet potato balls
Lobah (deep-fried pork and prawn rolls)
Fried prawn balls

BUFFET FOR 12

Ayam goreng Jawa (Javanese fried chicken)
Sambal goreng udang (chilli-fried prawns in coconut milk)
Gulai kambing (mutton curry)
Cucumber and pineapple salad (double amount)
Ikan bilis goreng (fried dried whitebait)
Salted duck eggs
Krupuk
Nasi goreng or white rice
Kueh naga sari

Lamb biryani
Koftas
Cucumber with yoghurt (double amount)
Onion sambal (double amount)
Tomato and cucumber salad
Poppadum
Carrot halwa

Recipes

There are four broad categories of food in Singapore: home-style food, stall food, restaurant food and banquet food. Although there tends to be a certain amount of overlapping, each category is different. Restaurant and banquet food (especially Chinese) tends to be more expensive than the home variety; it involves more complex techniques and sometimes requires equipment not available in the average kitchen. Stall food covers a wide range of dishes, some easy, some complex; most eating stalls concentrate on only one type of food, such as *satay*, *murtabak* (Indian savoury pancakes), fried noodles and substantial noodle soups. Home cooking, while no less delicious than restaurant food, uses less expensive ingredients and simpler techniques.

Most of the recipes in this book fall into the category of home cooking and stall food; some relatively easy restaurant dishes, now so popular in Singapore that they are prepared at home, are also included. I have tested every one of the recipes, and although authenticity has been my main criterion, I have on occasion modified the amount of certain ingredients to suit general tastes.

Many cookbooks specify the number of people each recipe will serve. This is almost impossible with Singapore food, since it depends on the number of other dishes being served at the same meal. Obviously, a fish curry that is adequate for eight people when five other dishes are being served won't be adequate if presented to the same number of people with only two other dishes. Generally speaking, however, the amounts given in these recipes will serve four to six persons at a meal where rice and three other dishes are presented. Please refer to page 70 for further advice on menu planning.

If, when you are using the recipes in this book, any technique or ingredient is not clear, refer to the index or glossary.

Nangka lemak (recipe page 117) and pachadi buah nanas (recipe page 120).

Soups

A meal without soup 'to help wash down the rice' would be unthinkable to most Chinese, especially the Cantonese. Soups range from stock made with a few chicken or pork bones cooked with leafy green vegetables, such as watercress, to elaborate gourmet soups using shark's fin and crabmeat.

During family meals, the Chinese put a bowl of soup in the centre of the table and everyone helps themselves throughout the meal. At more formal dinners or banquets, rich thick soups or those containing highly prized ingredients are served before fish, poultry and meat dishes, with thin 'cleansing' soups appearing towards the end of the meal to help cleanse the palate.

Light soups are rarely eaten by Malays, who prefer substantial noodle soups that are a meal in themselves (see Rice, Noodles and Breads). Indians do not prepare a wide range of soups, although *rasam*, a type of pepperwater, is drunk as an aid to digestion by many southern Indians, and a substantial mutton soup is a popular hawkers' dish.

CHINESE

SZECHUAN SOUR HOT SOUP (picture page 79)

30 g (1 oz) pork, shredded
30 g (1 oz) chicken breast, shredded
2 teaspoons peanut oil
2 heaped tablespoons cloud ear
    fungus (*mok yee*), soaked
4 large dried black mushrooms,
    soaked and shredded
100 g (3½ oz) soft beancurd (*tauhu*),
    diced
3 cups chicken stock (see page 77)
1 teaspoon light soya sauce
1 teaspoon Chinese rice wine or dry
    sherry
1 teaspoon sesame oil
2-3 teaspoons malt vinegar
¼-½ teaspoon chilli oil (optional)
salt to taste
1 tablespoon cornflour, mixed with
    ¼ cup water
1 egg, lightly beaten
white pepper
spring onion, finely chopped

This soup is rarely found in Singapore homes, but it is so delicious, and so popular in local Szechuan restaurants, that I have included it here.

Fry the pork and chicken gently in peanut oil until they change colour. Add the soaked and drained fungus and mushrooms and stir. Put in beancurd and stock and simmer 10 minutes. Add all the seasonings except pepper and simmer 3 minutes. Thicken with cornflour mixture.

Just before serving, stir in beaten egg, sprinkle very liberally with white pepper and garnish with spring onion.

CHINESE
BASIC STOCK (picture page 79)

1 teaspoon oil
1 clove garlic, lightly crushed
about 500 g (1 lb) pork bones; or
    chicken bones, head, feet and gizzard;
    or fish head and bones
2 slices fresh ginger
1 medium onion, sliced
2 stalks 'local' celery with leaves, or 1
    stalk large celery
8 black peppercorns
¼ teaspoon monosodium glutamate
salt to taste
4-6 cups water

Many Chinese recipes call for pork, chicken or fish stock. Although stock made with cubes is often an acceptable substitute, it is a good idea to make up stock whenever you have leftover bones or trimmings. It will keep for some time in the refrigerator if boiled up every two or three days, or can be deep-frozen.

Heat oil and gently fry garlic until golden. Discard garlic and add all other ingredients to the oil. Simmer for 1 hour, then strain.

To serve a simple soup as part of a Chinese meal, add a few vegetable leaves such as lettuce, spinach, silver beet, watercress, mustard greens, Chinese celery cabbage, or diced marrow or sliced lotus root. Sprinkle with chopped spring onion or coriander leaf and serve piping hot.

CHINESE
WUN TUN SOUP

Dumplings:
125 g (4 oz) *wun tun* wrappers (fresh or
    frozen)
125 g (4 oz) lean pork
60 g (2 oz) raw prawns
1 spring onion, including green top
½ teaspoon salt
½ teaspoon light soya sauce
pinch monosodium glutamate (optional)
dash of white pepper
1 dried black mushroom, soaked and
    finely shredded

Soup:
6 cups chicken stock (see page 77)
few drops of sesame oil
1 spring onion, finely sliced

Prepare dumplings first. If using frozen *wun tun* wrappers, allow to thaw. Chop pork, prawns and spring onion together very finely, or put in food processor until a very fine mince results. Add seasonings and mushroom, mixing to blend thoroughly. Make dumplings one at a time. Take one wrapper and moisten each corner with a wet finger. Put about ½ teaspoon of filling into the centre of each wrapper. Gather up the corners and press the edges firmly together to seal. This should make around 40 dumplings.

Bring a large saucepan full of lightly salted water to the boil. Add dumplings and simmer, uncovered, for 7 minutes. Drain dumplings and put into a serving bowl.

Heat chicken stock. Add a few drops of sesame oil and pour soup over the dumplings. Sprinkle with spring onion and serve immediately with a side-dish of pickled green chillies (recipe page 187).

CHINESE
RICH SWEETCORN SOUP

1 chicken drumstick
1 chicken stock cube
4 cups water
1 × 440 g (1 lb) tin creamed sweetcorn
2 dried black mushrooms, soaked and
    shredded
1 teaspoon light soya sauce
2 spring onions, finely sliced
salt and white pepper to taste
2 tablespoons cornflour
¼ cup cold water
30 g (1 oz) cooked crabmeat (optional)
1 egg, lightly beaten

Boil the chicken drumstick in water until tender. Reserve water. Remove chicken and finely shred the meat. Add stock cube to the water and simmer until thoroughly dissolved. Add the sweetcorn, mushrooms, soya sauce and half the spring onion. Simmer 2-3 minutes then add salt and plenty of white pepper to taste. Thicken with cornflour mixed with water and simmer for 2 minutes.

Add chicken and crabmeat and heat through. Just before serving, add the beaten egg, stirring constantly. Serve sprinkled with the remaining spring onion.

CHINESE

SOUP WITH STUFFED CUCUMBERS (picture opposite)

2 cucumbers, each about 18-20 cm (7-8 in) long
150 g (5 oz) minced pork
1 egg
¼ teaspoon salt
white pepper
pinch monosodium glutamate
1 teaspoon Chinese rice wine or dry sherry
1 tablespoon cornflour
12 large dried black mushrooms, soaked for 2 hours, with stems removed
5 cups good chicken stock (see page 77)

Peel cucumbers and cut each into 6 slices. Hollow each slice out to within 1 cm (½ in) of the base, making little cups.

Mix pork, egg, salt, pepper, monosodium glutamate, wine and cornflour. Press a little of this mixture into each of the cucumber cups. Top each cup with a mushroom, underside face down.

Put the mushroom-capped cucumber pieces in one layer in a wide saucepan and carefully add just enough stock to cover. Simmer very gently for 30 minutes. Bring rest of the stock to the boil in a separate pan, then add carefully to the cucumbers. Reheat and serve.

CHINESE

DUCK AND SALTED CABBAGE SOUP

500 g (1 lb) salted cabbage (kiam chye or ham choy)
4 cups stock made with giblets and carcass of duck
1-2 chicken stock cubes (optional)
1 large tomato, cut in wedges
white pepper

Salted cabbage (kiam chye or ham choy) is sold from wooden tubs in Singapore, but the tinned product available overseas is a very good substitute. Although duck stock is used in this recipe, a soup made from either chicken or pork stock is also popular and cheaper.

Soak salted cabbage in cold water for 1 hour, changing water 2 or 3 times. Squeeze out moisture, rinse under running water, and squeeze again. Chop roughly.

Add chicken cubes to duck stock if the flavour is not rich enough, then add cabbage and simmer for 30 minutes. Add tomato and cook a further 5 minutes. Sprinkle liberally with white pepper and serve.

CHINESE

BAT KOOT TEH
PORK BONE SOUP

500 g (1 lb) meaty pork ribs
2 whole cloves garlic, skins left on
2 teaspoons salt
1½ tablespoons thick black soya sauce
½ teaspoon monosodium glutamate
5 cups water

This soup is believed to be very nourishing and is normally eaten as a late-night snack or for breakfast.

Buy the pork ribs cut into pieces about 8 cm (3 in) long. Bruise the garlic lightly, but do not smash completely. Put pork ribs, garlic, and all other ingredients into a covered bowl and steam for 2-3 hours until the meat is tender. Serve in large soup bowls with a side-dish of sliced fresh red chilli in light soya sauce.

For a Nonya version of this soup, tie the following spices, lightly crushed, in a muslin bag and cook with the other ingredients: 5 cm (2 in) stick cinammon; 6 cloves; 2 points star anise; ½ teaspoon white peppercorns; ½ teaspoon coriander; ½ teaspoon cummin; ½ teaspoon fennel. Remove spices before serving.

Soup with stuffed cucumbers (recipe this page), Szechuan sour hot soup (recipe page 76) and basic stock (recipe page 77).

SHARK'S FIN AND CRABMEAT SOUP

125 g (4 oz) packaged dried shark's fin
1 large fresh crab, with roe if possible,
    or 100 g (3½ oz) tinned crabmeat
4 cups chicken stock, made with 2
    drumsticks and chicken cubes
salt to taste
½ teaspoon monosodium glutamate
½ teaspoon white pepper
2 teaspoons light soya sauce
2 teaspoons sugar
2 teaspoons sesame oil
4 tablespoons cornflour mixed with
    ½ cup cold water
1 or 2 eggs, lightly beaten
black Chinese (Tientsin) vinegar

Soak the shark's fin in hot water for 30 minutes. If it is still tough, simmer gently until soft and gelatinous. Drain.

If using fresh crab, chop in half and reserve the roe. Steam crab for 10 minutes, then pick out all the flesh.

Bring chicken stock, salt, monosodium glutamate, pepper, soya sauce, sugar and sesame oil to the boil. Add the shark's fin and crabmeat. Simmer for a couple of minutes then thicken with cornflour. Just before serving, beat in the roe with 1 egg (or, if not using roe, use 2 eggs) and stir briskly into the hot soup.

Serve immediately, passing a small jug of black vinegar for each person to add to taste (about ½ teaspoon per bowl).

FISH BALL SOUP

500 g (1 lb) fish balls (see page 136)
1 tablespoon oil
2 cloves garlic, finely sliced
4 cups fish or light chicken stock
    (see page 77)
salt and pepper to taste
4 lettuce leaves, torn in half
60 g (2 oz) cellophane noodles
    (*tunghoon* or *sohoon*), soaked in hot
    water for 5 minutes, then cut into
    small pieces

Garnish:
fried onion flakes (see page 188)
young celery leaves
fresh red chilli, sliced
fresh coriander leaves

If making your own fish balls, save the fish bones and head to make stock. Otherwise purchase fish balls from a Chinese shop or market and make chicken stock.

Heat oil and gently fry the garlic until golden. Add stock, salt and pepper and bring to the boil. Add the fish balls and simmer for about 10 minutes, until cooked, then add lettuce leaves and noodles. Cook just another 30 seconds and serve, garnished to taste.

ABALONE SOUP

1 tablespoon oil
1 clove garlic, very finely chopped
2 slices fresh ginger, very finely chopped
2½ cups mild pork or chicken stock
    (see page 77)
3 dried black mushrooms, soaked and
    shredded
50 g (1½ oz) lean pork, shredded
½ teaspoon Chinese rice wine or dry
    sherry
salt and white pepper to taste
pinch monosodium glutamate
250 g (8 oz) tinned abalone, sliced
2 lettuce leaves, torn into small pieces
1 spring onion, finely sliced

Heat oil in a saucepan and gently fry garlic and ginger until golden. Add stock, mushrooms, pork, wine and seasonings and simmer gently for 30 minutes.

Just before serving, put in the abalone and lettuce. Bring back to the boil and serve immediately, sprinkled with spring onion. (Prolonged cooking will make the abalone shoe-leather tough!)

Bakwan kepiting (recipe page 82).

BAKWAN KEPITING (picture page 81)
PORK, PRAWN AND CRAB BALL SOUP

Meatballs:
250 g (8 oz) lean pork
125 g (4 oz) raw prawns, shelled, or
    white fish
125 g (4 oz) crabmeat, finely shredded
2 dried black mushrooms, soaked and
    finely shredded
1 tablespoon grated carrot, boiled for
    1 minute
1 spring onion, finely sliced
1 egg
1 teaspoon cornflour
½ teaspoon salt
white pepper to taste
pinch monosodium glutamate

Soup:
2 cloves garlic, finely sliced
1 tablespoon oil
5 cups chicken stock
1 cup finely shredded bamboo shoot
salt to taste

Garnish:
fried onion flakes (see page 188)
fried sliced garlic
fresh coriander leaves

Chop the pork and prawns together until finely minced. Combine with crabmeat and other meatball ingredients. Mix well and set aside while preparing soup.

Fry the garlic gently in oil until golden. Remove and keep aside for garnish. Pour out oil if stock already oily. Add chicken stock and bamboo shoot to the oil in which the garlic was fried and simmer 15 minutes.

Shape the pork mixture into balls about 2.5 cm (1 in) in diameter and drop into the simmering stock. Cook 10-15 minutes. Serve in a large bowl decorated with garnish ingredients.

KAMBING SOUP
INDIAN MUTTON SOUP

6 shallots (bawang merah), or 1 small
    red or brown onion, finely sliced
2 tablespoons oil
2 tablespoons ghee or butter
1 medium red or brown onion, sliced
2 slices fresh ginger, very finely chopped
4 cloves garlic, very finely chopped
1 sprig curry leaves (karuvapillai)
2.5 cm (1 in) stick cinnamon
2 cardamom pods, bruised
3 cloves
375 g (12 oz) mutton or lamb, cubed
1 teaspoon finely ground black pepper
½ teaspoon chilli powder
3 teaspoons coriander powder
½ teaspoon cummin powder
4 cups water
1 teaspoon salt
1½ cups coconut milk (see page 44)
lime or lemon juice to taste

This is a substantial version of the mutton soup sold by Indian hawkers in Singapore, and usually known by its Malay name, sop kambing. *It is served with chunks of white bread, and is similar to mulligatawny, an Anglo-Indian soup based on pepperwater or* mooloogoo thani.

Fry shallots in hot oil until crisp and golden brown. Drain and set aside in a screw-top jar for garnish.

Heat *ghee* and gently fry onion, ginger, garlic, curry leaves, cinnamon, cardamom and cloves for 3-4 minutes, stirring frequently. Add meat, pepper, chilli powder, coriander and cummin and fry gently for a few minutes until meat is well coated with spices. Add water and salt, cover pan and simmer until meat is tender. Add coconut milk and cook for another 10 minutes.

Sprinkle with lime or lemon juice to taste, and garnish with fried shallot. Serve with chunks of French bread.

INDIAN

RASAM (picture page 118)
HOT SOUR SOUP

½ cup yellow lentils (*parupoo dhal*)
3 cups water
¼ teaspoon cummin
½ teaspoon black peppercorns
pinch turmeric powder
½ teaspoon salt, or more to taste
2-3 cloves garlic, unpeeled and lightly
  crushed
1 ripe tomato, skinned and crushed
pea-sized chunk of asafoetida
2 teaspoons tamarind, soaked in ¼ cup
  water and strained

Final addition:
3 teaspoons oil
½ teaspoon brown mustard seed
2 shallots (*bawang merah*), or ¼ red or
  brown onion, finely sliced
1 sprig curry leaves (*karuvapillai*)
1 dried red chilli, broken into 1 cm
  (½ in) pieces

A southern Indian favourite, this soup is believed to aid diges-
tion. Try to obtain asafoetida (see glossary), as it makes all
the difference to the flavour.

Wash lentils thoroughly and soak in cold water to cover for 1
hour. Drain lentils and put in saucepan with 3 cups water.
Simmer for 30 minutes. Drain off water and keep. Discard
lentils.

Grind cummin and black pepper together and put in a saucepan with lentil water and all other ingredients (except 'final addition'). Bring to the boil and simmer gently for 10 minutes,
stirring from time to time to make sure asafoetida has dissolved.

To prepare 'final addition', heat oil in a small pan and fry
mustard seed for 30 seconds. Add all other ingredients and fry
gently, stirring frequently, until the dried chilli turns brown.
Add fried ingredients to the saucepan, taking care as the oil will
sizzle when it meets the hot soup. Bring back to the boil and
serve immediately.

SRI LANKAN

SOTHI
COCONUT-MILK SOUP

1 tablespoon oil
½ teaspoon brown mustard seed
½ teaspoon fennel
2 sprigs curry leaves (*karuvapillai*)
1-2 fresh red chillies, sliced
1-2 fresh green chillies, sliced
8 shallots (*bawang merah*), or 1 medium
  red or brown onion, finely sliced
2 cups thin coconut milk (see page 44)
½ teaspoon turmeric powder
1 medium potato, diced
125 g (4 oz) white fish, diced, or small
  raw prawns, peeled
½ cup thick coconut milk (see page 44)
½ teaspoon salt
lime or lemon juice to taste

Strictly speaking, this dish from Sri Lanka (Ceylon) is not
drunk on its own as a soup but it is served with rice and
spooned over it. However, it can be served separately as a
soup at lunch or as part of a meal with rice.

Heat oil in a heavy-bottomed saucepan and gently fry the
mustard seed, fennel, curry leaves, chillies and shallots until
golden. Add thin coconut milk and turmeric. Bring gently to the
boil, stirring constantly. Simmer uncovered for 5 minutes, then
add potato and cook a further 5 minutes. Put in the fish or
prawns and continue to simmer for another few minutes until
cooked.

Add the thick coconut milk and salt, and stir over low heat
until the soup thickens. Just before serving, squeeze in lime or
lemon juice.

Rice, Noodles & Breads

Rice is such an essential item that the words for 'meal' and 'rice' are the same in most Asian languages. To many Western cooks, rice presents a problem. Here are recipes to help you prepare not only simple rice dishes but some of the more unusual treats encountered in Singapore.

Australians have their meat pies, the English their fish and chips, and Americans their hot dogs and hamburgers, but to Singaporeans there's nothing like a bowl of noodles for a snack. You see noodle lovers everywhere — coolies squatting on their heels downing a bowl of noodle soup for breakfast, smart young office workers seeking out the best *char kway teow* in a tiny coffee shop, Malay families rounding off a night at the movies with a bowl of *soto ayam* or *mee rebus*, and Indian men talking far into the night over their Singapore-style *mee goreng*. (For detailed descriptions of the various types of noodle used, please refer to page 48.)

The bread recipes in this section include several popular Indian breads as well as Chinese steamed buns — all surprisingly good for people thought to specialise in rice.

WHITE RICE

1 cup raw long-grain white rice for every 2 people

One of the hardest things for many Western cooks is to learn to prepare fluffy white boiled rice. After trying many different ways, I have found that the absorption method used by almost all Southeast Asian cooks is the most effective. This involves covering the rice with a certain amount of water, boiling until every drop has evaporated, then drying the rice out over low heat.

Wash the rice thoroughly in at least 3 changes of water, unless you are using packaged rice that has been pre-washed.

Choose a saucepan with a heavy bottom and tight-fitting lid. Put in the washed rice and cover with sufficient cold water to rise above the surface of the rice to the first joint of your forefinger (about 2.5 cm or 1 in). Cover pan and bring rapidly to the boil, stirring a couple of times to prevent the rice from sticking.

As soon as the water boils, put the lid to the side of the pan so that it is half-covered. Lower the heat slightly and boil at a reasonably fast pace until every drop of water has evaporated and holes appear on the surface of the rice like little volcanic craters. This will probably take about 10 minutes from the time the pan was first put on the stove. Do not stir the rice at this stage. Cover pan tightly and put over the lowest heat possible,

Rice porridge with pork and peanuts (recipe page 86).

85

using an asbestos mat if necessary. Leave for 20 minutes until the rice has swelled and dried. Fluff it up with a fork or chopstick and leave to stand over very low heat for another 10 minutes. The rice can be kept warm for at least another 30 minutes by standing it on the back of the stove.

CHINESE

CHOW FAN
FRIED RICE

2 tablespoons oil
1 stalk celery, finely chopped
1 medium red or brown onion, sliced
250 g of any or several of the following items: red barbecued pork (char siew); sliced Chinese sausage (lap cheong); lean ham, diced; prawns, raw or cooked; cooked chicken
2 dried black mushrooms, soaked and shredded
2 eggs
¼ teaspoon salt
2 teaspoons light soya sauce
4-5 cups cold boiled rice
2 tablespoons cooked green peas
2 spring onions, finely chopped
sliced fresh red chilli and celery leaves to garnish

An easy way of using leftover boiled rice. The meats can be varied according to taste and availability.

Heat oil and gently fry celery and onion until soft. Add prawns if using raw and cook until they turn pink. Add remaining meats and dried mushrooms and cook gently for 3 minutes.

Beat eggs with salt and soya sauce and add to pan. Stir over high heat until set. Add rice and green peas and cook, stirring constantly, for 2 minutes. Mix in half the spring onion and serve garnished with remaining onion, chilli and celery leaves.

CHINESE

FAH SANG CHOK (picture page 84)
RICE PORRIDGE WITH PORK AND PEANUTS

2 cups short-grain rice
¾ cup skinned raw peanuts
2 chicken stock cubes
water to cover rice by 10 cm (4 in)
250 g (8 oz) lean pork, sliced and shredded
2 teaspoons cornflour
liberal sprinkling of white pepper
2 teaspoons light soya sauce
½ teaspoon sesame oil
few very thin slices pig's liver (optional)

Garnishes:
½ cup oil
6-8 cloves garlic, thinly sliced
8 shallots (bawang merah), or 1 medium red or brown onion, thinly sliced
1-2 fresh red chillies, sliced
pickled radish (tang chye or tung choy)
fresh coriander leaves
light soya sauce
eggs (optional)

Like any Westerner who has grown up to regard porridge as synonymous with oatmeal, I was initially horrified when a friend suggested we have pork porridge for breakfast. Rice porridge is an easily digested, mild dish consisting of rice boiled with lots of water plus optional extras. It is an introduction to solid food for most Chinese babies, and is enjoyed as a breakfast or late-night supper dish by adults. I like to serve it at lunch, enlivened with as many garnishes as possible.

Wash rice thoroughly, then put into a deep saucepan with peanuts, stock cubes and water. Bring to the boil, cover and simmer gently for about 45 minutes until a mushy porridge results. Add more water during cooking if necessary to ensure a fairly liquid consistency.

While rice is cooking, sprinkle pork with cornflour, pepper, soya sauce and sesame oil and leave aside while preparing the garnishes.

Heat oil and gently fry garlic until golden. Remove from oil and drain. Fry shallots in same oil until golden brown then set aside. Put all garnish ingredients in separate small dishes.

Using oil in which garlic and shallots were fried, stir-fry pork over high heat until it changes colour. Reduce heat and fry for about 2 minutes, then add to the cooked rice porridge. Simmer pork in porridge for 10 minutes, then add pig's liver and cook for 2-3 minutes. Taste and add salt if necessary.

Serve porridge in bowls, sprinkled with a liberal amount of white pepper. Each person adds garnishes to taste, breaking a whole egg into the porridge and stirring it around to cook it if desired.

MALAY

NASI GORENG
FRIED RICE

6 cups cold cooked long-grain rice
8 shallots (*bawang merah*) or 1 medium
   red or brown onion
4 tablespoons oil
1 heaped tablespoon raisins
1 egg, lightly beaten
2 fresh red chillies
2 cloves garlic
250 g (8 oz) raw prawns, peeled
1-2 spring onions, finely sliced

A great way of using leftover rice, nasi goreng *used to be a popular breakfast dish in Singapore. It can be served on its own as a light meal (add a little steak if you wish to make it more substantial), or can accompany other dishes at dinner.*

Stir rice with a fork to make sure grains are separate.

Slice half the shallots or onions and fry gently in oil until crisp and golden brown. Set aside for garnish. Fry raisins gently in same oil for 1 minute and set aside. Pour egg into pan and make a thin omelette. When cool, shred finely for garnish.

Pound remaining shallots or onions, chillies and garlic together and fry gently for 3-4 minutes, then add prawns and stir-fry until they turn pink. Increase heat, and add a little more oil if necessary. Put in rice and stir-fry for 2 minutes. Serve on a large platter, garnished with fried shallots, raisins, egg and spring onions.

MALAY

NASI LEMAK
RICE COOKED IN COCONUT MILK

2 cups long-grain rice
2½ cups coconut milk (see page 44)
1 teaspoon salt
1 *pandan* leaf (optional)

Although the name 'nasi lemak' means rice cooked in coconut milk, it also includes the dishes that usually accompany such rice. It is particularly popular for breakfast in coffee shops and roadside stalls, where the rice is normally served with fried ikan bilis *(dried salted whitebait), boiled egg, cucumber, and chilli sambal. Some cooks steam the rice before mixing it with coconut milk, but I find the following method the easiest.*

Wash rice thoroughly, drain and set aside. Bring coconut milk slowly to the boil, stirring constantly. Add rice, salt and *pandan* leaf, stir, and simmer with the saucepan lid slightly ajar until all the liquid has evaporated. Cover saucepan tightly and turn off the heat. Put an asbestos mat under the saucepan and allow to stand for 5 minutes. Turn on heat as low as possible and cook for about 20 minutes. Fluff up the rice with a fork, cover saucepan, and leave to stand at the back of the stove until needed. Take great care during cooking or the bottom of the rice will burn.

MALAY

NASI KUNYIT (picture page 174)
TURMERIC RICE

2 cups glutinous rice
2.5 cm (1 in) fresh turmeric (*kunyit*) or
   1 teaspoon turmeric powder
boiling water
banana leaf or *pandan* leaves
½ teaspoon salt
½ cup thick coconut milk (see page 44)

Nasi kunyit, gleaming golden glutinous rice, has a strong ritual significance for Malays, and also for Nonyas who adopted the custom of preparing this rice for important religious ceremonies. Nasi kunyit has a special meaning for me too: my amah, knowing my longing for a son, promised an offering of bananas and nasi kunyit at a keramat (sacred place) should our prayers be answered. The son duly arrived, the offerings were made, and all was well.

Wash rice thoroughly and put in a glass or china bowl. Pound fresh turmeric and extract juice. Add juice or turmeric powder to the rice and pour over boiling water to cover. Allow rice to stand for at least 10 hours, preferably overnight.

   Drain soaking liquid from rice, and rinse rice well. Line a bamboo or metal steamer with banana leaf or *pandan* leaves and spread the rice on top. Put over boiling water and steam for 5 minutes. Uncover rice, make several holes in it using a chopstick (this is to allow the steam to circulate more easily), then cover and steam again for at least 45 minutes. Check to see if rice is tender. Put into a bowl, stir in salt and coconut milk, and return rice to steamer for another 5 minutes.

   If preferred, instead of steaming the rice, cook it in the normal manner as directed on page 85. After adding coconut milk, put back over very low heat for about 10 minutes.

MALAY

KETUPAT
COMPRESSED RICE CAKES

2 cups short-grain rice
2½ cups water
banana leaf or aluminium foil
oil for greasing

Ketupat, served with satay and lontong, are traditionally made by pouring uncooked rice into intricately woven little baskets of young coconut-palm leaves, and boiling them. I once passed an hour-long boat trip in the South China Sea trying to learn the art of weaving these baskets from a ten-year-old Malay girl who giggled helplessly at my efforts. I still can't make ketupat baskets, but have found the following method produces much the same result.

Boil the rice in the normal manner (see page 85). While the rice is cooking, choose a rectangular dish that will hold the rice to a depth of about 2.5 cm (1 in) when spread. A dish roughly equivalent to 25 cm by 35 cm (10 in by 14 in) should be adequate. Cut two pieces of banana leaf to fit into the bottom of this dish. Lightly oil the dish and both pieces of banana leaf, then place one piece of leaf on the bottom of the dish.

   As soon as the rice is cooked, spoon it into the lined dish, pressing it in firmly and smoothing the top with the back of an oiled spoon. Place the second piece of banana leaf on top of the rice and press firmly with your hands to compress the rice as much as possible. Place weights on top of the banana leaf and leave at room temperature for several hours until firmly set. Cut with a wet knife into 5 cm (2 in) squares.

Kon loh mee (recipe page 91).

LAMB BIRYANI

Garnish:
8 shallots (*bawang merah*), or 1 medium
    red or brown onion, finely sliced
3 tablespoons *ghee* or butter
½ cup raw cashew nuts, split in half
½ cup raisins
fresh coriander leaves

Lamb curry:
1 medium red or brown onion, chopped
2.5 cm (1 in) fresh ginger, finely
    chopped
4 cloves garlic, finely chopped
4 cm (1½ in) stick cinnamon
6 cloves
6 cardamom pods, slit and bruised
½ teaspoon freshly ground black pepper
½ teaspoon black cummin seeds
    (optional)
3 tablespoons meat curry powder
    (see page 189)
750 g (1½ lb) boneless leg lamb, cut in
    2.5 cm (1 in) cubes
3-4 tomatoes, roughly chopped
½ cup plain yoghurt
½ cup water
1 teaspoon salt
2 tablespoons chopped mint

Rice:
4 cups Basmati rice
1 tablespoon salt

Additional items:
2 tablespoons *ghee* or butter
½ cup evaporated milk
yellow food colouring (optional)
few drops rose essence

This festive Muslim dish has come to Singapore from the Middle East via India. It is a three-stage dish involving cooking lamb in a curry sauce, parboiling rice, then combining both and finishing the dish in the oven. As most of the preparation can be done well in advance, biryani *is an ideal dish when entertaining. This recipe serves 8.*

Prepare the garnish first. Pat the sliced shallots dry. Heat *ghee* and fry shallots gently until golden brown. Drain and set aside. Fry cashews very gently in the same *ghee*, stirring constantly, until golden brown. Drain and set aside. Fry raisins in *ghee* for just 1 minute, drain and set aside leaving *ghee* in the pan. When fried garnishes are cold, store in an airtight container.

To prepare lamb curry, gently fry onion, ginger and garlic in leftover *ghee* for 2 minutes. Add cinnamon, cloves, cardamom, pepper and black cummin and continue frying for another 2 minutes. Combine curry powder with enough cold water to form a stiff paste. Add paste to the pan and fry for 2 minutes, then put in the lamb and fry until it changes colour. Add tomatoes and cook until they begin to soften, then put in yoghurt and stir for a moment or two before adding water, salt and mint. Cover pan and cook meat gently until it is soft and the gravy has almost dried up. If there is more than about ¼ cup of gravy left, cook with the lid off the pan to reduce.

While lamb curry is cooking, prepare the rice. Wash thoroughly in several changes of water, then drain in a sieve or colander for at least 15 minutes. Heat a large saucepanful of water with 1 tablespoon salt added, and when it is boiling vigorously, pour in the rice in a thin stream, stirring all the time. Stir until the water comes back to the boil, then continue boiling with the lid off the pan for 5 minutes. Drain rice thoroughly.

To assemble *biryani* for the final stage, melt 1 tablespoon *ghee* in a very large casserole. Swirl around so that the sides of the casserole are greased. Mix half the reserved garnish ingredients with the rice, and spread half the rice on the bottom of the casserole. Arrange the meat over this, then top with the remaining rice. The *biryani* can be left aside for several hours at this stage.

Roughly 30 minutes before the *biryani* is required, melt 1 tablespoon *ghee* and combine with evaporated milk, yellow food colouring and rose essence. Spoon this mixture over the top of the assembled casserole, cover tightly, and put in a low oven (150°C/300°F/Gas No.2) for 30 minutes. Serve piled onto a large platter with the remaining garnish ingredients and fresh coriander leaves scattered on top. *Biryani* goes well with onion *sambal* and cucumber with yoghurt.

PILAU

3 tablespoons *ghee* or butter
1 heaped tablespoon slivered almonds
8 shallots (*bawang merah*), or 1 medium
    brown or red onion, finely sliced
2 slices fresh ginger, finely chopped

Fry almonds gently in *ghee* until golden. Drain and set aside.

In same *ghee* gently fry shallots, ginger, garlic and spices until golden. Add rice and raisins and cook for 3 minutes, stirring constantly, to coat rice with *ghee*. Add water and salt and bring quickly to the boil. Partly cover the pan and boil until every

1 clove garlic, finely chopped
3 cardamom pods, slit and bruised
4 cloves
4 cm (1½ in) stick cinnamon
2 cups Basmati rice, washed and drained
1 heaped tablespoon seedless raisins or
   sultanas
2¼ cups water
1 teaspoon salt
fried onion flakes (see page 188)
fresh coriander leaves

drop of water has evaporated and holes appear in the surface of the rice. Turn down heat as low as possible, or put pan on an asbestos mat, cover tightly and leave rice to dry out for 20 minutes. Fluff up rice with a fork and let pan stand over very low heat for another 10 minutes.

Serve garnished with fried almond slivers, fried onion flakes and coriander leaves. Excellent with lamb or mutton curries.

CHINESE

KON LOH MEE (picture page 89)
SIMPLE NOODLE DISH

2 packets individual serve 'instant
   noodles'
4 cups water
4-6 stalks Chinese mustard greens (chye
   sim or choy sam), or any other leafy
   green vegetable
1 teaspoon peanut oil
2 teaspoons sesame oil
2 teaspoons black soya sauce
2 teaspoons chilli sauce
any of the following: slices of red
   barbecued pork (char siew); shredded
   cooked chicken; braised black
   mushrooms; cooked prawns

This is a quick and easy version of one of the most popular noodle snacks served by Singapore hawkers. Sufficient for 2.

Unpack the noodles and discard the packaged seasoning. Heat water and simmer the green vegetable until just tender. Drain and reserve water. Cook noodles in the vegetable water for the time specified on the noodle package, then drain.

Combine peanut and sesame oils, soya sauce and chilli sauce and toss in a large bowl with the noodles. Serve garnished with the vegetable and other ingredients. These noodles would normally be accompanied by a small bowl of light chicken soup and a side-dish of pickled green chillies (see page 187).

CHINESE

MEE SWA SOUP

4 small bundles *mee swa* noodles, or
   250 g (8 oz) Chinese rice vermicelli
   (beehoon)
6 shallots (bawang merah), or 1 small
   red or brown onion, finely sliced
3 tablespoons oil
250 g (8 oz) lean minced pork
1 teaspoon pickled radish (tang chye or
   tung choy), finely chopped (optional)
¼ teaspoon salt
¼ teaspoon white pepper
pinch monosodium glutamate
   (optional)
1 teaspoon cornflour
4 cups light pork or chicken stock (see
   page 77)
150 g (5 oz) sliced pig's liver (optional)
6 lettuce leaves

A traditional Chinese birthday dish; the long mee swa *noodles symbolise longevity and should never be cut. If you cannot obtain* mee swa, *Chinese rice vermicelli (beehoon) can be substituted.*

If using Chinese rice vermicelli, soak in hot water for 2 minutes, drain and set aside. Do not soak *mee swa*.

Fry shallots gently in oil until they turn crisp and golden brown. Drain and set aside.

Mix together pork, pickled radish, salt (add ¼ teaspoon more if pickled radish is not used), pepper, monosodium glutamate and cornflour. Form into balls 2.5 cm (1 in) in diameter. Bring stock to the boil and add pork balls. Simmer for 10 minutes, then add liver and cook another 2 minutes. Put in *mee swa* or Chinese rice vermicelli and lettuce leaves, torn into 3 or 4 pieces. Stir and serve immediately in 4-6 soup bowls. Sprinkle on extra white pepper and garnish with fried shallots.

CHINESE

BEEHOON SOUP

500 g (1 lb) Chinese rice vermicelli
    (*beehoon*)
200 g (6½ oz) beansprouts
250 g (8 oz) pork, in one piece
6 cups basic pork stock (see page 77)
1 chicken stock cube
salt to taste
¼ teaspoon monosodium glutamate
1 tablespoon oil
250 g (8 oz) raw prawns
24 fish balls, bought or home-made (see
    page 136)
2 flat fried fish cakes, sliced (optional)
small bunch leafy green vegetable, such
    as Chinese mustard greens (*chye sim*
    or *choy sam*), spinach or Chinese
    celery cabbage
2 spring onions, finely chopped
fried onion flakes (see page 188)
white pepper

Soak *beehoon* in boiling water for 3 minutes. Drain and divide between 6 large soup bowls. Blanch beansprouts in boiling water for 30 seconds, refresh in cold water, drain, and put on top of *beehoon*.

Put pork into pork stock. Add stock cube, salt to taste, and monosodium glutamate, and simmer until cooked. Remove, cool, then slice pork finely. Divide between soup bowls.

Put oil into a small saucepan. Peel prawns, keeping heads and shells. Heat oil and fry prawn heads and shells for 3 minutes. Add 2 cups of the prepared stock, cover, and simmer for 10 minutes. Sieve, pressing firmly on prawn shells to extract all their juices, then discard shells. Simmer peeled prawns for just 3 minutes, then drain. Combine prawn stock with rest of the pork stock, and divide cooked prawns between the soup bowls.

Cook leafy vegetable in boiling water, with 1 teaspoon of oil added, for just 1 minute. Drain and divide between soup bowls. Heat stock, add fish balls and simmer for about 10 minutes. Add fish cake and simmer for 1 minute.

To serve, pour hot stock, fish balls and fish cake into the soup bowls. Garnish with spring onion, fried onion flakes, and sprinkle with white pepper.

CHINESE

FRIED HOKKIEN NOODLES

500 g (1 lb) fresh yellow noodles
    ('Hokkien' *mee*)
250 g (8 oz) raw prawns
3 tablespoons oil
1 cup water
250 g (8 oz) boiled belly pork
250 g (8 oz) beansprouts
8-10 cloves garlic, pounded
2 eggs, lightly beaten
salt and pepper to taste

Garnish:
1-2 fresh red chillies, finely sliced
    lengthwise
2 spring onions, cut in 2.5 cm (1 in)
    lengths
few stalks 'local' celery, or sprigs young
    celery, finely chopped

Many cooks use lard rather than vegetable oil to fry the noodles. I prefer oil as it helps to lighten a very heavy, substantial dish.

Put the noodles in a bowl and pour over boiling water to cover. Stand for 1 minute, then drain and set aside.

Peel the prawns, keeping shells and heads. Heat 1 tablespoon of oil in a saucepan and fry the shells and heads, stirring constantly, for 1 minute. Add water and bring to the boil. Cover pan and simmer for 5 minutes, then pour through a sieve and discard shells. Simmer prawns in this stock until cooked. Strain and reserve stock.

Slice the pork finely. Rinse the beansprouts and discard any black husks. Heat remaining 2 tablespoons of oil in a large *kuali* and fry garlic gently until golden, to flavour the oil. Discard garlic. Raise heat, and when oil is really hot pour in beaten eggs. Stir constantly for 1 minute, then add noodles, beansprouts and ½ cup of the prawn stock. Cook over high heat for 1 minute,

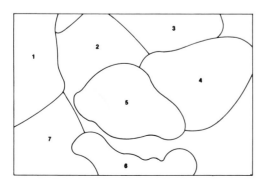

1 *Dried wheat-flour noodles* (mee), 2 *fresh rice-flour noodles* (kway teow), 3 *fresh yellow or 'Hokkien' noodles,* 4 *fresh laksa noodles,* 5 *mee swa noodles;* 6 *dried mung pea or 'cellophane' noodles,* 7 *dried Chinese rice vermicelli* (beehoon).

stirring constantly, then add pork, prawns and salt and pepper to taste. Stir-fry for another 2-3 minutes, adding more prawn stock if the noodles appear to be sticking.

Serve on a large platter decorated with garnish ingredients.

CHINESE

CHAR MEE
FRIED WHEAT NOODLES

250 g (8 oz) dried wheat noodles (mee)
3 tablespoons oil
1 slice fresh ginger, very finely chopped
1-2 cloves garlic, very finely chopped
6-8 shallots (bawang merah), or
   1 medium red or brown onion, sliced
100 g (3½ oz) raw prawns
2-3 dried black mushrooms, soaked and
   shredded
small bunch Chinese mustard greens
   (chye sim or choy sam) or 4 leaves
   silver beet
100 g (3½ oz) red barbecued pork (char
   siew), sliced
1 tablespoon light soya sauce

Cook noodles in plenty of rapidly boiling water for 2-3 minutes, separating strands with chopstick or fork. Drain and toss with 1 tablespoon of the oil to prevent noodles sticking together. Spread out and leave aside.

Heat remaining oil in kuali and gently fry ginger, garlic and shallots until soft and golden. Add prawns and mushrooms and cook, stirring, until prawns turn pink. Tear vegetable leaves into small pieces and add to kuali. Cook for 2-3 minutes, then add meat and heat through for 30 seconds.

Raise heat and add noodles. Cook for 1 minute, stirring constantly. Pour over soya sauce and serve immediately. The mee can be garnished with sliced red chilli and spring onion, and served with a chilli sambal.

CHINESE

CHAR KWAY TEOW
FRIED FRESH RICE-FLOUR NOODLES

100 g (3½ oz) hard pork fat
4 cloves garlic, very finely chopped
2 fresh red chillies, pounded
200 g (6½ oz) lean pork, shredded
375 g (12 oz) raw prawns, peeled
200 g (6½ oz) squid (optional)
1 tablespoon light soya sauce
1 tablespoon dark soya sauce
2 teaspoons oyster sauce
½ teaspoon salt
pepper to taste
250 g (8 oz) beansprouts
1 kg (2 lb) fresh rice-flour noodles
   (kway teow), cut in strips 1 cm
   (½ in) wide
fresh red chilli, sliced
fresh coriander leaves

Cut pork fat into pieces roughly 1 cm (½ in) square and put into a dry kuali over medium heat until the lard runs out and the pieces of fat turn golden and crisp. Remove crisp pieces of fat and leave 3 tablespoons of lard in kuali.

Fry garlic and chilli gently in the lard until garlic starts to turn golden. Raise the heat, add pork, and stir-fry for 2 minutes. Put in the prawns and squid and stir-fry for another 2 minutes. Add the sauces, salt, pepper and beansprouts. Mix well and stir-fry for just 2 minutes.

Add the noodles, previously scalded with boiling water and drained, to the kuali and stir-fry to heat through for 2-3 minutes. Stir in the fried fat crisps and serve kway teow on a large platter, garnished with chilli and coriander. The kway teow can be fried in oil rather than lard, and the fat crisps omitted, but the dish will lack its characteristic flavour.

CHINESE

FRIED BEEHOON

500 g (1 lb) Chinese rice vermicelli
   (beehoon)
4 tablespoons oil
2 cloves garlic, lightly crushed
500 g (1 lb) white fish or cooked chicken
   and chicken liver

Scald beehoon in boiling water for 1 minute. Drain and set aside.

Heat 1 tablespoon of the oil in a kuali and gently fry garlic until golden. Discard. In garlic-flavoured oil fry fish together with mushrooms, stirring frequently, until cooked. If using cooked chicken and chicken liver, fry mushrooms alone for 2

4 dried black mushrooms, soaked and
   shredded
10 shallots (*bawang merah*), or
   1½ medium red or brown onions,
   sliced
2 teaspoons crushed red chillies or
   sambal ulek
1 teaspoon salt
250 g (8 oz) beansprouts
2 eggs, lightly beaten
1 spring onion, finely chopped
fresh coriander leaves

minutes, add chicken and liver, and cook another minute. Remove contents of *kuali* and set aside.

Put remaining oil in *kuali* and gently fry shallots and chilli for 1 minute. Add *beehoon*, stir well for 1 minute, then sprinkle in salt. Make a space in the centre of the *kuali*, put in the beansprouts and cover them completely with *beehoon* so that they can cook, covered, for about 3 minutes. Stir *beehoon* and beansprouts thoroughly together then push to the sides of the *kuali*. Pour beaten egg into centre of *kuali*, a little at a time. As each portion of egg sets, flick it up onto the *beehoon* before adding the next. Add cooked fish or chicken mixture and spring onion. Stir thoroughly to mix and heat through for a couple of minutes. Serve on a large platter garnished with coriander leaves.

NONYA

MEE SIAM
SIAMESE-STYLE NOODLES IN SPICY GRAVY

500 g (1 lb) Chinese rice vermicelli
   (*beehoon*)
oil for deep frying
2 cakes hard beancurd (*taukwa*)
500 g (1 lb) beansprouts
375 g (12 oz) cooked prawns, peeled
1 cup coarse chives (*kuchai*), garlic
   chives or spring onions, chopped in
   2.5 cm (1 in) lengths
3 hardboiled eggs, peeled and quartered
6-8 Chinese limes (*limau kesturi*),
   halved, or 2 limes or lemons,
   quartered

Spice paste:
10 dried red chillies, soaked
12 shallots (*bawang merah*) or 2 small
   red or brown onions
1 stalk lemon grass (*serai*) or substitute
1 teaspoon dried shrimp paste (*blacan*)
3 tablespoons oil
2 heaped tablespoons salted soya beans
   (*taucheo*), lightly crushed
1 teaspoon salt
1 tablespoon sugar

Gravy:
5 cups thin coconut milk (see page 44)
1 heaped tablespoon dried tamarind
½ cup warm water

*This makes a fabulous luncheon dish, especially if decorated with sliced pink ginger buds (*bunga siantan*). A basically Malay-style gravy is given an intriguing flavour by the addition of salted soya beans (*taucheo*), and the finished dish is liberally sprinkled with lime or lemon juice for further titillation of the tastebuds and nose!*

Prepare the spice paste first. Grind the chillies, shallots, lemon grass and dried shrimp paste together to make a paste. Heat oil in a *kuali* and gently fry the spice paste for 3-4 minutes. Add the salted soya beans and cook for 1 minute, stirring all the time. Sprinkle in the salt and sugar and continue frying for another minute. Remove half this mixture to use in making the gravy. Set aside the *kuali* with the remaining mixture.

To make the gravy, put half the fried spice paste into a large saucepan and add the coconut milk. Bring to the boil, stirring all the time, then add the dried tamarind which has been soaked in warm water and strained. Simmer for 2-3 minutes, stirring all the time, then set aside.

Soak the rice vermicelli in boiling water for 1 minute, then drain and set aside. Heat oil in a pan and deep fry the beancurd for 3-4 minutes, turning so that it cooks golden brown on both sides. Drain and slice coarsely. Have all other ingredients prepared and set on a plate for easy assembly of the dish.

Just before you wish to serve the *mee Siam*, heat the spice mixture left in the *kuali*, then add the beansprouts and cook over high heat, stirring constantly, for just 1 minute. Add half the cooked prawns and half the chopped chives. Cook for about 30 seconds, stirring constantly, then add the rice vermicelli a little at a time, stirring vigorously to mix well with other ingredients. When all the vermicelli has been added and thoroughly heated, put into a large serving dish. Scatter the remaining prawns and coarse chives on top. Arrange the eggs, fried beancurd and limes around the edge of the plate. Serve the gravy separately in deep bowl. The noodles should be put into individual bowls by each diner, and plenty of gravy added; the lime juice should be squeeze over the top. If you like really hot food, serve a fresh chilli *sambal* as well.

MALAY

SOTO AYAM
SPICY CHICKEN SOUP WITH NOODLES

½ small chicken or 500 g (1 lb) chicken
  pieces
4 cups water
1 teaspoon salt

Spices:
1 teaspoon black peppercorns
1 teaspoon coriander
4 candlenuts (*buah keras*) or
  macadamias
1-2 cloves garlic
4-6 shallots (*bawang merah*) or 1 small
  red or brown onion
1 slice fresh ginger
¼ teaspoon turmeric powder
2 tablespoons oil

Additional items:
1 cup coconut milk (see page 44)
1 fragrant lime leaf (*daun limau perut*)
  or young citrus leaf
1-2 waxy potatoes, boiled and sliced
100 g (3½ oz) beansprouts, scalded
few spinach or silver beet leaves, scalded
1-2 hardboiled eggs, sliced
100 g (3½ oz) cellophane noodles
  (*tunghoon* or *sohoon*) or Chinese rice
  vermicelli (*beehoon*)

Garnish:
fried onion flakes (see page 188)
fresh coriander leaves

This popular dish of Indonesian origin makes a good luncheon or supper.

Simmer chicken in water and salt until tender. Allow to cool in the liquid, then remove chicken and dice, reserving stock.

Grind the peppercorns and coriander. Then grind candlenuts, garlic, shallots and ginger until fine. Mix together both ground combinations with turmeric.

Heat oil in a heavy saucepan and gently fry the spice mixture for 3-5 minutes. Add chicken stock, cover pan, and simmer for 5 minutes. Put in coconut milk and lime leaf. Simmer gently, uncovered, stirring frequently, for another 5 minutes.

To serve the *soto*, put some noodles, potato, beansprouts, leafy vegetable, egg and chicken into the bottom of each bowl. Pour over the gravy, and garnish. Serve with chilli *sambal*.

MALAY

LAKSA LEMAK (picture page 103)
RICH NOODLE SOUP WITH SEAFOOD

250 g (8 oz) fine-fleshed fish such as
  ikan parang (wolf herring) or *ikan
  tenggiri* (Spanish mackerel), or 250 g
  (8 oz) fish balls (see page 136)
375 g (12 oz) raw prawns, in shells if
  possible
2 cups water
750 g (1½ lb) fresh *laksa* noodles or
  400 g (13 oz) Chinese rice vermicelli
  (*beehoon*)
200 g (6½ oz) beansprouts, scalded
several sprigs of *daun kesom* or mint,
  finely chopped
½ small cucumber, peeled and cut in
  matchsticks

Gravy:
4-6 dried red chillies, soaked

Two types of laksa *are made in Singapore: Penang* laksa, *a Nonya creation with a thin sour gravy, and* laksa lemak, *which has a rich coconut-milk gravy. If you cannot obtain fresh laksa noodles, dried Chinese rice vermicelli (*beehoon*) makes a perfectly acceptable substitute.*

If making your own fish balls (and this is strongly recommended), follow directions on page 136, adding only 2 tablespoons water and other ingredients exactly as specified in the recipe. Keep fish balls in refrigerator until needed.

Put prawns and water in saucepan, bring to the boil, simmer 2 minutes and strain. Keep stock aside. Peel prawns. Keep aside. Scald *laksa* noodles or *beehoon* in boiling water for 3 minutes and set aside.

Prepare gravy. Pound or grind first seven ingredients finely, adding about 1½ tablespoons of oil during grinding if using a blender or electric food processor. Mix in coriander. Heat remaining oil in a clay pot (*belangah*) or large saucepan and

1 stalk lemon grass (*serai*) or substitute
8 shallots (*bawang merah*) or 1 medium
    red or brown onion
4 slices *lengkuas* or substitute
1 cm (½ in) fresh turmeric (*kunyit*) or
    1 teaspoon turmeric powder
4 candlenuts (*buah keras*) or
    macadamias
½ teaspoon dried shrimp paste (*blacan*)
2 teaspoons coriander, freshly ground
2 heaped tablespoons dried prawns,
    soaked and pounded
4 tablespoons oil
3 cups thin coconut milk (see page 44)
½ cup thick coconut milk (see page 44)
1 teaspoon salt
pinch monosodium glutamate

gently fry the ground ingredients, stirring frequently, for 4-5 minutes. Add pounded dried prawns and fry a further 2 minutes. Pour in thin coconut milk and reserved prawn stock and bring to the boil, stirring constantly. When simmering, add fish balls and simmer for 5 minutes. Add thick coconut milk, salt and monosodium glutamate and simmer until the gravy thickens.

To serve the *laksa*, put a little noodles into 6 deep bowls. Put some beansprouts on top then pour over the gravy. Garnish with the prawns, chopped herbs and cucumber. Serve with extra pounded fresh red chillies, if liked.

MALAY

MEE REBUS
NOODLES WITH MEAT AND RICH SAUCE

500 g (1 lb) beef in one piece (topside or
    round)
1 celery stalk with leaves
1 teaspoon salt
plenty of freshly ground black pepper
cold water to just cover meat

Gravy:
8-12 dried red chillies, soaked
3 candlenuts (*buah keras*) or
    macadamias
8-10 shallots (*bawang merah*) or 1½
    medium red or brown onions
3 slices *lengkuas* or substitute
2 tablespoons oil
2 teaspoons coriander, freshly ground
2 teaspoons salted soya beans (*taucheo*),
    mashed
½ cup mashed boiled sweet potato

Additional items:
500 g (1 lb) fresh yellow noodles
    ('Hokkien' *mee*) or 250 g (8 oz) dried
    wheat noodles
250 g (8 oz) beansprouts, scalded

Garnish:
2 spring onions, finely chopped
fried onion flakes (see page 188)
few stalks 'local' celery, or young leaves
    of large celery
1 fresh green and 1 fresh red chilli,
    sliced
3 pieces hard beancurd (*taukwa*), deep
    fried and sliced
3-4 Chinese limes (*limau kesturi*),
    halved, or 1 lemon cut in wedges

Put beef into a saucepan with celery, salt, pepper, and just enough water to cover, and simmer gently until cooked. Dice meat and reserve 2 cups beef stock.

To prepare gravy, grind chillies, candlenuts, shallots and *lengkuas* together and fry in oil in a deep pan for 3-5 minutes. Add coriander and cook another minute before putting in salted soya beans. Fry gently for another couple of minutes then add diced beef. Mix thoroughly and add sweet potato. Slowly add stock, stirring well to incorporate the sweet potato which acts as a thickening agent. Heat gravy through thoroughly.

If using fresh noodles, scald in boiling water for 1 minute, then drain thoroughly. If using dried noodles, boil as directed on the packet until just cooked, then drain.

To serve *mee rebus*, put some of the noodles and beansprouts into the bottom of large individual bowls and pour over gravy. Garnish with listed items. Alternatively, if you have a very large deep bowl, the *mee rebus* can be served in this, with each diner helping himself.

INDIAN

INDIAN MEE GORENG (picture opposite)
INDIAN FRIED NOODLES

500 g (1 lb) fresh yellow noodles
  ('Hokkien' *mee*)
½ cup oil
1 square hard beancurd (*taukwa*), cut
  into small dice
1 medium red or brown onion, chopped
1 medium tomato, finely chopped
2 tablespoons roughly chopped coarse
  chives (*kuchai*) or spring onion
1 sprig curry leaves (*karuvapillai*), finely
  chopped
2 tablespoons tomato sauce
1 tablespoon chilli sauce
2 teaspoons light soya sauce
2 eggs, lightly beaten
1 boiled potato, skinned and cut into
  small dice
1 fresh green chilli, sliced

*A most unusual dish, sold by Indian hawkers, that you
certainly won't find in India. It is a combination of Chinese,
Indian and Western ingredients; makes a tasty luncheon or
snack.*

Rinse noodles in warm water, drain and set aside. Heat oil in a
kuali and fry the beancurd until golden brown. Drain and set
aside. Cook the onion in the same oil for 2-3 minutes, until soft,
then add the drained noodles, tomato, chives, curry leaves and
three types of sauce. Cook over gentle heat, stirring frequently,
for 3-4 minutes.

Pour over beaten egg and leave to set for about 45 seconds
before stirring to mix it in well with the noodles. Add the potato
and beancurd, stir, cook for another 30 seconds and put on a
large serving dish. Garnish with green chilli and serve with additional tomato and chilli sauce to be added according to each
person's taste.

CHINESE

CHAR SIEW POW
STEAMED BUNS WITH BARBECUED PORK FILLING

Filling:
1 tablespoon oil
2 shallots (*bawang merah*), or ¼
  medium red or brown onion, finely
  sliced
1 clove garlic, finely chopped
125 g (4 oz) red barbecued pork (*char
  siew*)
2 leaves Chinese celery cabbage (*wong
  ah pak*) or 2 spring onions, chopped
½ teaspoon light soya sauce
pinch monosodium glutamate
white pepper
¼ teaspoon salt
½ teaspoon sugar
few drops sesame oil

Dough:
2½ cups plain flour
2½ teaspoons baking powder
1 tablespoon sugar
½ teaspoon salt
1 tablespoon peanut oil
few drops sesame oil
½ cup warm water

To make filling, heat oil and gently fry shallots and garlic until
golden. Add all other ingredients and cook gently, uncovered,
for 5 minutes. Leave to cool.

Sift flour and baking powder into a bowl and add sugar and
salt. Stir in both oils and water and knead to a soft dough.
Cover and leave for 1 hour.

Knead dough for 5 minutes then divide into 8 portions. Roll
each piece into a ball and flatten out with the hands, making the
disc a little thinner around the edge. Put some of the cooled
filling into the centre and pinch the outside edge into the centre
to seal in the filling. Place each bun, joined side down, on a piece
of oiled greaseproof paper about 10 cm (4 in) in diameter. Put
into a steamer and cook for ½ hour. Serve hot.

Sweet *pow* can be made using the same dough filled with
sweet bean paste (*tau sa*), obtainable in tins.

Indian mee goreng (recipe this page).

INDIAN

ROTI PARATHA

2 cups plain white flour
1 scant teaspoon salt
⅓-½ cup warm water
100 g (3½ oz) melted *ghee* or butter

This light flaky bread, rich with ghee, *is served with 'wet' curries to help mop up the gravy. It is so delicious that some Malay cooks prepare it as a snack, serving it with nothing more than a sprinkle of sugar.*

Sift flour and salt and add sufficient water to make a soft dough. Knead thoroughly for 5 minutes. Add 2 teaspoons of melted *ghee* and continue kneading for a further 5 minutes. Roll dough into a ball and put in a greased plastic bag or cover with a damp cloth. Leave in a warm place for 30 minutes.

Divide dough into 12 pieces and roll into balls. Flatten each ball into a circle with your hands, then roll out as thinly as possible with a rolling pin. Spread each circle with 1 teaspoon *ghee* and fold in three crosswise. Spread the surface with a little more *ghee* and fold in three lengthwise. Cover with greased plastic and leave for 10 minutes. If you wish, the dough can be left for several hours provided it is well covered.

Press each piece of dough into a circle with your hands, then roll out to about 20 cm (8 in) in diameter. Heat a metal griddle (*tawa*) or heavy iron frying pan and put in 1 teaspoon of *ghee*. Put in a *paratha* and pour a little more melted *ghee* around the edges as it cooks to help make it puff up. When the underside is evenly golden, turn it over and cook another ½ minute until golden. Serve hot.

INDIAN

CHAPATI
UNLEAVENED BREAD

2 cups fine wholemeal flour (*atta*)
about ½ cup warm water
2 teaspoons softened *ghee* or butter
  (optional)

Like all Indian bread, the dough for chapati *must be properly kneaded for a light-textured result. I know 10 minutes sounds like a long time to stand kneading, but it can be a very relaxing pastime, especially if you take the chance to chat to your children or even read a propped-up magazine as you work.*

Mix flour and water together to make a reasonably stiff dough. The amount of water required varies slightly with the quality of the flour and the humidity of the climate. Be careful to keep the dough soft but not sticky, adding a little more flour if necessary to achieve this. Add butter or *ghee*, if using, and knead the dough on a lightly floured board for 10 minutes.

Roll dough into a ball and put in a greased plastic bag or cover with a damp towel and leave for at least 1 hour. The dough can even be left in the refrigerator overnight, provided it is properly wrapped.

Knead dough for another 3-5 minutes, then break off pieces the size of a golf ball. Flatten each ball with the hands then, using a rolling pin, roll out into thin circles about 20 cm (8 in) in diameter.

Heat a griddle (*tawa*) or heavy iron frying pan until very hot. Put on a *chapati* and leave to cook for about 1 minute until brown spots appear on the underside. Turn over and cook on the other side, pressing the top of the *chapati* with a clean towel to help make air bubbles form and keep the *chapati* light. As each *chapati* is cooked, wrap in a clean cloth to keep warm while the rest are cooking. Serve hot with curries, *dhal* or vegetables.

INDIAN

NAAN (picture page 159)
LEAVENED BREAD

2 cups flour
1 teaspoon baking powder
½ teaspoon salt
4 tablespoons plain yoghurt
1 tablespoon oil
1 egg, lightly beaten
1 tablespoon *ghee* or butter, melted
sprinkle of black cummin seeds
  (optional)
few slivered almonds (optional)

A simplified version of the bread cooked in a tandoor *oven.*

Sift flour, baking powder and salt into a bowl and stir in yoghurt, oil and egg. Add a little warm water if necessary to make a pliable, reasonably soft dough. Knead on a board for 5 minutes, then cover with a floured cloth and leave in a warm place for 3 hours.

Knead bread for a minute or two, then divide into six pieces. Using your hands, pull each piece of dough into a teardrop shape about 20 cm (8 in) long. Heat a metal griddle or heavy frying pan and put a *naan* on to cook. Leave for about 2 minutes, then turn and cook for another two minutes until golden brown and puffed slightly. Brush each *naan* on one side with a little melted *ghee* or butter and sprinkle with a few black cummin seeds and almond flakes, if using. Put under a pre-heated griller for about 2 minutes. Serve warm with *tandoori* chicken or any dishes with gravy.

INDIAN

PURI
FRIED WHOLEMEAL BREAD

2 cups fine wholemeal flour (*atta*)
about ½ cup warm water
2 teaspoons softened *ghee* or butter

Puri *are almost identical to* chapati, *except that they are deep fried in hot oil so they puff up. The secret in cooking* puri *is to keep spooning or flicking the oil over the top of it while it is frying on the underside. A kuali is the perfect utensil for frying* puri.

Make as for *chapati* (page 100). When the dough has been rolled out into 20 cm (8 in) circles, heat a generous amount of oil in a *kuali* (filling it about ⅓ full).

When oil is very hot, put in one *puri* and immediately start spooning or flicking oil over the top side of the *puri* as it cooks. As soon as it swells up and is golden underneath, flip the *puri* over and cook on the other side until golden. Drain and serve hot with curries, *dhal* or vegetables.

INDIAN

POTATO PURI
FRIED POTATO BREAD

250 g (8 oz) potatoes
2 cups plain white flour
2 teaspoons salt
6-7 tablespoons warm water
oil for deep frying

These puri *are deliciously light and can be guaranteed to puff up in a spectacular fashion.*

Peel potatoes and boil until tender. Drain well, then put back in dry saucepan over very low heat for a couple of minutes to allow them to dry out thoroughly. Mash well and leave to cool.

Sift flour and salt into a bowl, then add mashed potatoes. Mix with a wooden spoon and add the water, a little at a time, until a firm dough is formed. Flour your hands and a board or table and knead the dough thoroughly for at least 5 minutes, preferably 10. Roll dough into a ball, cover, and leave to stand for at least 30 minutes. (The dough can be stored in the refrigerator for several hours, if wrapped well in plastic.)

Divide dough into 16, roll each piece into a small ball, then flatten with the hands into a circle. Roll each piece out carefully until it is about 15 cm (6 in) in diameter.

Heat oil until very hot. Put in one *puri* and immediately start spooning or flicking oil over the top side so that it puffs up. As soon as the *puri* is golden on the underside, flip it over and cook for another moment or two until the second side is golden. Drain and serve hot with curries, *dhal* or vegetables.

MALAY

ROTI JALA (picture page 155)
LACY PANCAKES

1½ cups plain flour
½ teaspoon salt
3 eggs, well beaten
2¼ cups thin coconut milk (see page 44)
    or ½ cup evaporated milk mixed with
    1¾ cups water
oil for greasing pan

These make a pleasant change from rice as an accompaniment to curry-style dishes. Batter is poured through a special cup with four narrow spouts to get the lacy effect; a kitchen funnel, the opening slightly closed off with the forefinger, can be used as a substitute. I have been told that some Malay women in the villages merely dip their hands in the batter and allow it to trail off their fingers to get the right effect.

Sift flour and salt into a bowl. Add eggs and milk gradually, stirring to blend well and avoid lumps. Allow the batter to stand for 5 minutes. Heat a frying pan (non-stick is preferable) and grease lightly with oil. Hold a *roti jala* cup (see page 155) over the pan in your right hand and with your left, pour in about ¼ cup of batter. Swirl the cup in circles so that it forms a lacy pancake. Allow pancake to set on top, then turn over and cook for another 30 seconds. Pile cooked pancakes on a plate and continue cooking until all the batter has been used. Serve hot.

INDIAN

MURTABAK
STUFFED INDIAN PANCAKES

Dough:
1½ cups plain flour
½ teaspoon salt
½ cup warm water
2 teaspoons oil
½-1 cup oil to cover dough

Filling:
1 tablespoon oil
½ medium onion, finely chopped
1 clove garlic, very finely chopped
1 slice fresh ginger, very finely chopped
½ teaspoon turmeric powder
¼-½ teaspoon chilli powder
250 g (8 oz) finely minced lamb or beef
½ teaspoon *garam masala* (see glossary)
½ teaspoon salt

Additional items:
1 egg, lightly beaten
1 medium onion, finely sliced

The Indian murtabak *man who flings a small lump of dough around and around in a circle until it becames an almost transparent sheet is one of the most spectacular sights in Singapore — even though you won't find it listed in any guide book. The* murtabak *is quickly fried on a griddle, usually with a filling of egg and raw onion. Cooked minced meat or, for vegetarians, green peas, are often added. This recipe will yield 6* murtabak; *double the amounts if you like.*

Prepare the dough first. Sift flour and salt into a mixing bowl. Mix water and oil together and pour into the flour, then mix well to make a soft dough. Flour your hands, then knead the dough for 10 minutes — the longer the dough is kneaded, the lighter it will be. Divide dough into 6 balls and put into a bowl just big enough to hold them. Cover with oil and allow to stand for about 1 hour.

Heat 1 tablespoon oil and gently fry the onion until it softens, then add the garlic and ginger and cook until they start to turn golden. Add the turmeric and chilli powder and fry for a few seconds, then put in the meat and stir-fry until it changes colour. Cover the pan and cook the meat gently for 15 minutes. If it seems to be drying out during cooking, add a tablespoon or two of water. Put in *garam masala* and salt, and cook for another 5 minutes. If meat is rather wet, remove lid to dry it during the last

Laksa lemak (recipe page 96).

stage of cooking, as the filling should not have any gravy or juice. Allow to cool.

It takes years of practice to fling the dough into shape in true Indian fashion, but a very good result can be obtained in the following way. Carefully remove each ball of dough from the oil (it can be kept for cooking, as it will still be clean) and put on a smooth flat surface. Do not flour the surface or your hands. Carefully flatten the dough into a circle, then using the fingers in a spreading motion, gradually push the dough from the centre out to the edges, stretching it as you work. Use the same spreading motion around the edges, until you have spread the dough into a circle about 30 cm (12 in) in diameter.

Heat a large frying pan until very hot, then grease with a little oil. Put in the circle of dough, taking care not to tear it with your hands, and quickly smear the top of the dough with a spoonful of the beaten egg. Add a few pieces of raw onion and ⅙ of the meat filling. Fold up the pancake, envelope fashion, then check to see that the underneath is golden. If it is, turn the *murtabak* over carefully, add a teaspoon of oil to the pan, and allow to cook on this side.

Keep each *murtabak* warm as you cook the next one. They can be served without any accompaniments, but if you want a more substantial meal, try *murtabak* with *brinjal pachadi* (recipe page 125) and tomato and cucumber salad.

INDIAN

DOSAY (picture page 118)
SAVOURY SOUTHERN INDIAN PANCAKES

1 cup blackgram *dhal* (*ulundoo* or *urad dhal*)
2 cups rice flour
about 3 cups water
1 teaspoon salt

Soak *dhal* overnight in plenty of cold water. Discard skins by filling a bowl with water, rubbing *dhal* with your hands, and scooping or pouring off the skins as they float to the top. Repeat until all the skins are removed. If you can buy husked *dhal* you save a lot of time. Grind soaked *dhal* to a fine paste in an electric blender or with a mortar and pestle, adding a little cold water.

Mix 1 tablespoon of the rice flour with ½ cup water and heat gently in a pan, stirring constantly, until thickened. Put ground *dhal*, the rest of the rice flour and salt in a large bowl and gradually add water until the mixture reaches the consistency of a thin cream, like normal pancake batter. Add thickened rice flour, stir, and cover bowl. Leave to stand at room temperature for about 6 hours. In hot climates, the batter must be kept cool after this or it will ferment.

When the *dosay* are required, stir batter and add a little more water if necessary to achieve right consistency. Rub a griddle (*tawa*) or heavy iron frying pan with a cloth or tissue moistened in oil. Heat griddle until very hot, then pour in about ¼ cup of batter, swirling it out from the centre with the back of a ladle or spoon to spread. Leave for about 45 seconds until the underside is golden and the top of the *dosay* is dry. Turn and cook for another 30 seconds. Serve *dosay* warm with fresh coconut chutney (recipe page 184) or filled with savoury potatoes (recipe page 124).

SRI LANKAN

APPAM
RICE-FLOUR PANCAKES

1½ cups broken rice or short-grain rice,
    or ¾ cup rice flour and ¾ cup
    ground rice
2 cups coconut milk (see page 44)
2 teaspoons fresh compressed yeast or
    ½ teaspoon dried yeast
1 teaspoon sugar
½ cup warm water
¾ teaspoon salt
oil for greasing pan
6-8 eggs (optional)

I first came across hoppers (as appam *are usually called in English) during my travels in Sri Lanka, and have been pestering Sri Lankan friends in Singapore for the recipe ever since. Local cooks prefer to grind their own rice flour, which gives the* appam *a better consistency than commercial rice flour; however a mixture of rice flour and commercial ground rice is acceptable. The dough is mixed with a fermenting agent (traditionally water from inside a coconut or freshly grated coconut and leftover cold rice) but yeast provides a quicker and equally delicious alternative. If you are grinding your own rice dough, you will need to start preparations at least 9 hours in advance. The following recipe makes about 8 hoppers or* appam.

If you have a heavy-duty blender or food processor and can make your own rice dough, soak the broken or short-grain rice in plenty of cold water for at least 8 hours. Drain, then process until a smooth dough results, adding up to 1 cup of coconut milk, a little at a time. If using rice flour and ground rice (the latter is of a coarser consistency, and is available at health food stores), combine and add 1 cup of coconut milk.

Dissolve yeast and sugar in warm water and leave for about 10 minutes until frothy. Add this mixture to the rice and coconut-milk dough and leave in a warm place for about 1 hour until doubled in size. Stir in salt and enough of the remaining coconut milk to make a batter the consistency of a thick cream. The batter is now ready for use, or can be refrigerated for several hours if desired.

To cook the *appam*, heat a *kuali* or a very small omelette pan until quite hot. Grease the bottom and sides of the pan with oil, then put in a large ladleful of batter. Hold both sides of the *kuali* and swirl it around so that some of the batter sticks to the sides. Cover with a lid and cook over low heat for 1 minute. Break a whole egg into the centre of the *appam* if liked, sprinkle with salt, and cover the pan. Continue cooking over low heat for 3-4 minutes. By this time, the lacy edges of the *appam* should be crisp and golden brown, and the centre and egg perfectly cooked. Slide onto a plate and serve with chilli and onion *sambal* (recipe page 183).

Appam with egg makes an excellent substantial breakfast or luncheon dish. Plain *appam* can be served with a meal to replace rice, or as a snack with brown sugar and freshly grated coconut.

Vegetables

Many of the vegetables eaten in Singapore are the same as those enjoyed in the West; others, widely used in Singapore but less well known in Western countries, can often be found overseas in vegetable markets or Chinese stores; and there are others still (such as the drumstick, a seedpod used by southern Indians, and *pete*, a bitter bean liked by the Malays and people of Indonesian origin) which are rather unusual and are popular only among small sections of the community.

In addition to the common round cabbage, familiar in the West, several varieties of Chinese cabbage are used in Singapore. These include Chinese celery cabbage or *wong ah pak* (also known as *wong bok* or *peh tsai*), a tall white vegetable with crinkled leaves; dark-green cabbage with white stalks and ribs (*pak choy*); bitter Chinese cabbage, with very broad pale-green stalks which are often stuffed (*kai choy*); and Chinese mustard greens (*chye sim* or *choy sam*), a leafy vegetable with bright yellow flowers.

Chinese broccoli or *kai lan*, sometimes referred to overseas as kale, is a highly regarded vegetable. Water convolvulus, called *kangkong* by Malays and *ong choy* by the Chinese, is a well-flavoured leafy vegetable with a high iron content; it is often available in Chinese stores overseas, and in some recipes spinach can be substituted. Several types of true spinach (*not* silver beet) are eaten, the most common being the variety known as Indian spinach. The common round lettuce is used, and can be substituted for the Singapore 'local' lettuce, which has long leaves and is similar to Romaine lettuce.

Snow peas, often called *mange-toute* or sugar peas abroad, are popular among the Chinese; the entire pod, containing rather undeveloped peas, is eaten after the removal of the stalk and the strings on both sides of the pod. Long beans, also called snake or yard beans, are inexpensive and are more popular than French or green beans.

Okra or ladies' fingers, a favourite among the Indians (who call them *bendi*), should be used while young and preferably not more than 15 cm (6 in) long; they are usually available at Greek stores overseas. Giant white radish, called *lobak* or 'white carrot' in Singapore, is an important vegetable generally milder in flavour than small round red radishes.

Many varieties of eggplant or aubergine, known in Singapore as *brinjal* or *terong*, are available. They range from tiny, marble-sized orange fruits (used raw) to slender white, pale-green and purple fruits as much as 20 cm (8 in) in length. The large oval eggplant more commonly available in Western countries is three to four times the size of the average Singapore variety.

Several types of tuber are eaten, the main ones being taro yam, a purplish-stemmed plant grown in water; sweet potato, both white and yellow fleshed; and tapioca root, which is sometimes grated and used to make cakes. Water chestnuts are highly prized for their crisp texture; *bangkwang* or yam bean is a larger, round tuber (averaging a diameter of 10 cm or 4 in) with a crisp texture and clean flavour (tinned water chestnuts can be substituted for both these vegetables); and bamboo shoots and beansprouts (see glossary) are also widely used.

Rujak (recipe page 116).

LONG BEANS WITH PRAWNS

375 g (12 oz) long beans
1 tablespoon oil
1 clove garlic, finely chopped
6-8 very small raw prawns, peeled
1 tablespoon water
¼ teaspoon salt

Remove stalk end from long beans then cut into 4 cm (1 ½ in) lengths.

Heat oil and fry garlic gently until it starts to turn golden. Add prawns and fry until they change colour. Put in the beans and stir-fry for 3 minutes. Sprinkle over the water and salt, cover *kuali* and simmer until beans are just cooked. If there is any liquid left, evaporate it by raising raise heat and cooking quickly with the lid off. Serve hot.

SNOW PEAS, MUSHROOMS AND BAMBOO SHOOT

6 dried black mushrooms
1 tablespoon oil
1 clove garlic, lightly crushed
large chunk bamboo shoot weighing
    about 125 g (4 oz), sliced
250 g (8 oz) snow peas, strings removed
½ teaspoon salt
½ teaspoon sugar
pinch monosodium glutamate

Fresh or canned bamboo shoot can be used for this dish. If using the canned vegetable, try to buy winter bamboo shoots as they are more tender and have a better flavour. Canned bamboo shoots should be boiled in fresh water for 10 minutes before use.

Rinse mushrooms and soak in hot water for 30 minutes. Drain, reserving soaking liquid; discard mushroom stems and cut caps in half. Heat oil in a *kuali* and fry garlic until golden. Discard garlic and raise heat. Stir-fry mushrooms for a few seconds, then add sliced bamboo shoot and stir-fry for another few seconds. Add snow peas and continue to stir-fry over high heat for 1-2 minutes. Put in 4 tablespoons of the mushroom soaking liquid, salt, sugar and monosodium glutamate, and continue to cook, stirring constantly, for about 2 minutes when all the liquid should have evaporated and the vegetables are cooked but still firm. Serve immediately.

BRAISED MIXED VEGETABLES

2 tablespoons oil
2 cloves garlic, finely chopped
1 sliced fresh ginger, very finely
    chopped
¼ small cauliflower, broken into
    flowerets
1 carrot, sliced
1 green capsicum, cut into chunks
6 water chestnuts, sliced
1 piece bamboo shoot, sliced (about
    100 g or 3 ½ oz)
12 green beans, cut into 2.5 cm (1 in)
    lengths, or 12 snow peas, strings
    removed
4 dried black mushrooms, soaked and
    halved
½ teaspoon salt
¾ cup chicken stock (see page 77) or
    mushroom soaking liquid
1 teaspoon cornflour mixed with 1
    tablespoon water

Heat oil and gently fry garlic and ginger for 30 seconds. Add the vegetables and cook for 2-3 minutes, stirring constantly, until well coated with oil. Put in salt and stock and cover pan. Simmer vegetables until just cooked. Thicken with cornflour and serve immediately.

VEGETABLES

CHINESE

FRIED BEANSPROUTS

250 g (8 oz) beansprouts
2 tablespoons oil
1 clove garlic, lightly crushed
4 slices fresh ginger
1 teaspoon light soya sauce
¼ teaspoon salt
2 spring onions, cut in 2.5 cm (1 in)
  lengths

Wash beansprouts. Drain thoroughly and pinch off any brown straggly tails.

Heat oil in a *kuali* and fry garlic until golden, then discard. Fry beansprouts and ginger in garlic-flavoured oil over high heat, tossing constantly, for 1 minute. Add soya sauce, salt and spring onion and continue to stir-fry for another minute. The beansprouts should still be slightly crisp.

CHINESE

FRIED BEANCURD AND SPRING ONION

3 squares hard beancurd (*taukwa*)
20 spring onions
3 tablespoons oil
½ teaspoon salt
2 tablespoons light soya sauce

A very simple, quickly cooked dish that tastes better than you'd expect and is also highly nutritious.

Pat the beancurd dry and cut into cubes 1 cm (½ in) square. Cut spring onions, including green tops, into 2.5 cm (1 in) lengths.

Heat oil in a *kuali* until very hot and fry beancurd, stirring it around from time to time, for a couple of minutes until crisp and golden. Add spring onions and continue to cook for another couple of minutes, stirring occasionally. Put in salt and soya sauce and cook another minute. Serve immediately.

CHINESE

CHAP CHYE
MIXED VEGETABLE DISH

2 tablespoons cloud ear fungus
  (*mok yee*)
2-3 sticks dried beancurd twist (*taufu kee*), cut in 2.5 cm (1 in) pieces
15-20 dried lily buds (*khim chiam* or *gum kum*)
4-6 dried black mushrooms
30 g (1 oz) cellophane noodles
  (*tunghoon* or *sohoon*)
1 tablespoon oil
3 cloves garlic, very finely chopped
2 slices fresh ginger, very finely chopped
1 teaspoon salted soya beans (*taucheo*), mashed
100 g (3½ oz) lean pork, shredded
1 cup soaking liquid (see method)
2 teaspoons light soya sauce
½ teaspoon salt
white pepper
½ small cabbage, sliced
60 g (2 oz) raw prawns (optional)
1 piece bamboo shoot (about 100 g or 3½ oz), sliced
2 teaspoons cornflour mixed with ¼ cup water
2 spring onions, finely sliced
1 piece hard beancurd (*taukwa*), deep fried and cut in strips

Rinse the cloud ear fungus thoroughly then put in a bowl with dried bean curd twists, lily buds and mushrooms. Cover with warm water and leave to soak for 15 minutes. Soak noodles in hot water for 10 minutes then cut with scissors into small pieces. When dried ingredients have finished soaking, reserve 1 cup of the liquid. Drain thoroughly, then remove stems from dried mushrooms and cut caps in half.

Heat oil and gently fry the garlic and ginger for ½ minute, then put in salted soya beans and fry another ½ minute. Add pork and cook, stirring frequently, for a couple of minutes until the meat changes colour. Add the soaking liquid, soya sauce, salt, pepper and all dried ingredients except the noodles. Cover pan and simmer for 15 minutes.

Add cabbage, bamboo shoot and prawns (if using) to the pan. Stir well and continue cooking until the cabbage is tender (about 10 minutes). Thicken with cornflour mixture. Stir in noodles, chopped spring onions and fried beancurd and serve, sprinkled with more white pepper.

STUFFED DRIED MUSHROOMS WITH BROCCOLI (picture opposite)

12 large dried black mushrooms
2 cups warm water
1 tablespoon oil
2 cloves garlic, smashed and chopped
½ chicken stock cube
2 teaspoons cornflour
1 tablespoon cold water
250 g (8 oz) fresh or frozen broccoli

Filling:
250 g (8 oz) raw prawns
100 g (3½ oz) fresh or tinned crabmeat
3 water chestnuts
1 tablespoon finely diced hard pork fat
½ teaspoon salt
sprinkle white pepper

Rinse mushrooms in cold water then leave to soak in 2 cups warm water for about 2 hours. Drain, reserving soaking liquid. Discard mushroom stems and squeeze mushrooms dry. Heat oil in a saucepan and gently fry garlic for about 15 seconds. Raise heat and add mushrooms. Stir-fry for 1 minute, then add mushroom soaking liquid and stock cube. Simmer very gently for about 1 hour or until mushrooms are tender. Remove mushrooms from cooking liquid and drain. Thicken cooking liquid with 1 teaspoon cornflour mixed with cold water and set this sauce aside.

While mushrooms are simmering, prepare the filling. Peel prawns, flake crabmeat, and peel the water chestnuts. If you have a food processor, put the water chestnuts and pork fat in and blend for about 30 seconds until a rough paste results. Add prawns, crabmeat, salt and pepper and process for another few seconds. If you do not have a processor, chop all filling ingredients together with a cleaver to get a fine paste.

When the cooked, drained mushrooms have cooled sufficiently to handle, sprinkle the inside of each cap with a little cornflour. Press on some of the filling, mounding it slightly. If desired, the mushrooms can now be stored in the refrigerator for several hours and the dish finalised just before the meal.

Put the stuffed mushrooms into an enamel plate or low-sided bowl and steam for 20 minutes. Cook the broccoli until it is just tender. Arrange mushrooms in the centre of a serving platter. Pour any liquid that has accumulated in the steaming plate into the prepared sauce. Re-heat and pour over the mushrooms. Arrange broccoli around the edge of the serving platter, sprinkle the mushrooms with a little white pepper, and serve immediately.

BRAISED BLACK MUSHROOMS

16 large thick dried black mushrooms
2 tablespoons oil
4 cloves garlic, very finely chopped
3 slices fresh ginger, very finely chopped
1½ tablespoons light soya sauce
1 tablespoon dark soya sauce
½ teaspoon sesame oil

A 'must' at festive gatherings, because the shape of the mushroom cap symbolises an umbrella covering the family and holding it together. It is important to use the very thick dark-black dried mushrooms, not the cheaper, lighter-coloured variety.

Rinse mushrooms thoroughly then soak in plenty of hot water for 10-15 minutes. Strain, reserving the soaking liquid. Remove stems.

Heat oil in an earthenware casserole if possible, and gently fry garlic and ginger until golden. Add drained mushrooms and fry, stirring frequently, for a couple of minutes. Cover with soaking liquid and put in light and dark soya sauce. Cover tightly and simmer over very low heat for 2 hours, checking occasionally to make sure liquid does not dry out, adding a little water if necessary.

Sprinkle with sesame oil just before serving.

Stuffed dried mushrooms with broccoli (recipe this page).

STRAW MUSHROOMS IN CRAB SAUCE

1 large tin (425 g or 1 lb) straw
    mushrooms
75 g (2½ oz) fresh or tinned crabmeat
250 g (8 oz) 'local' or Romaine lettuce
2 teaspoons oil
¾ cup chicken stock
½ teaspoon light soya sauce
sprinkle monosodium glutamate
pinch sugar
¼ teaspoon sesame oil
white pepper to taste
3 teaspoons cornflour.mixed with ¼ cup
    water

Drain the straw mushrooms and cut each one in half lengthwise. Flake the crabmeat and set aside. Drop the lettuce leaves in a pan full of boiling salted water with a little oil added and cook for 2 minutes only. Drain and put on a serving dish

Heat the oil and gently cook the mushrooms, stirring constantly for 1 minute. Add all the remaining ingredients except cornflour mixture and crabmeat, and simmer for 3 minutes. Mix in the crabmeat and then thicken with cornflour. Pour over the arranged lettuce leaves and serve.

CHINESE CABBAGE WITH PORK OR PRAWNS

½ Chinese celery cabbage (wong ah
    pak)
2 tablespoons oil or lard
1 clove garlic, finely chopped
4 shallots (bawang merah), or ½
    medium red or brown onion, finely
    sliced
60 g (2 oz) pork, shredded, or raw
    prawns, peeled
2 tablespoons water or chicken stock
    (see page 77)
¼ teaspoon salt
1 teaspoon light soya sauce

Wash cabbage and cut into 4 cm (1½ in) pieces, keeping stalks separate from leafy part.

Heat oil or lard in a *kuali* and gently fry garlic and shallots until soft. Add pork or prawns and fry quickly for a couple of minutes until they change colour. Put in cabbage stalks and stir-fry for 2 minutes then add leafy part and stir-fry a further 2 minutes. Sprinkle over water or stock, salt and soya sauce. Cover *kuali* and simmer cabbage for another 2-3 minutes until cooked.

QUICK-COOKED BROCCOLI

500 g (1 lb) broccoli or *kai lan*
1 tablespoon oil
1 teaspoon light soya sauce
1 tablespoon oyster sauce
¼ teaspoon salt
sugar to taste
pinch monosodium glutamate
2 tablespoons water

Regular broccoli or the similar Chinese vegetable known as kai lan *can be used.*

Wash the vegetable. Cut off the flowerets and separate the leaves. Discard tough outer leaves and tear large leaves in half. Cut stems in 4 cm (1½ in) lengths. If using *kai lan*, peel thick stems and cut in half lengthwise. Keep stems separate from leaves and flowerets.

Heat oil in *kuali* and stir-fry stems over high heat for 30 seconds. Reduce heat, cover *kuali* with a lid and cook stems for another 2 minutes. Add flowerets and leaves and stir-fry for 30 seconds. Add seasonings and water, cover *kuali* and simmer vegetable until just cooked. *Kai lan* is more bitter than broccoli, so you may need to add a little more sugar — about ½ teaspoon.

CHINESE

MARROW, CARROT AND EGG

375 g (12 oz) marrow or choko
1 large carrot, about 60 g (2 oz)
1 tablespoon oil
1 medium onion, thinly sliced
1-2 cloves garlic, very finely chopped
½ teaspoon salt
white pepper
pinch monosodium glutamate
1 egg, lightly beaten
1 teaspoon light soya sauce

Cut marrow and carrot in matchsticks. Heat oil in a *kuali* and gently fry onion and garlic until soft. Add marrow, carrot, salt, pepper and monosodium glutamate and stir-fry for a couple of minutes until vegetables are thoroughly coated with oil.

Cover the *kuali* and cook vegetables gently, stirring from time to time, until cooked but slightly crisp. Raise heat and add beaten egg mixed with soya sauce. Stir vegetables until egg is just set. Serve immediately.

NONYA

TAUKWA GORENG
SPICY BEANCURD SALAD

4-5 large pieces hard beancurd (*taukwa*)
oil for deep frying
1 small cucumber
150 g (5 oz) beansprouts

Sauce:
2-3 fresh red chillies
4 shallots (*bawang merah*) or ½ medium red or brown onion
2 tablespoons palm sugar (*gula Melaka*) or brown sugar
4 heaped tablespoons crunchy peanut butter
1 tablespoon thick black soya sauce
¼ cup tamarind water (see page 63)
salt to taste
4 tablespoons water

Wipe beancurd dry with paper towel and deep fry in hot oil for 4-5 minutes until golden brown. Drain, then cut into thick slices. Leave to cool.

Prepare sauce by grinding together chillies and shallots. Add palm sugar and pound to mix, then combine with all other ingredients. If using an electric blender or food processor, grind chillies and shallots with just a little of the water until fine. Add all other ingredients and blend for a few seconds. Put sauce into a bowl.

Scrape skin of cucumber with a fork, rub with a little salt, rinse, then slice finely. Blanch beansprouts in boiling water for 30 seconds, drain, run cold water over to refresh, then drain thoroughly. To serve the salad, arrange cucumber slices on a large platter. Put sliced beancurd on top and scatter beansprouts over the beancurd. Pour over the sauce and serve immediately. Makes a nice luncheon dish, followed with *bubor pulot hitam* (recipe page 196) or *bubor kacang hijau* (recipe page 196).

NONYA

SAMBAL TAUKWA
BEANCURD IN SPICY COCONUT-MILK GRAVY

6 pieces hard beancurd (*taukwa*)
3 tablespoons oil
250 g (8 oz) raw prawns, peeled
1 teaspoon salt
1 cup thin coconut milk (see page 44)
2 fragrant lime leaves (*daun limau perut*) or young citrus leaves (optional)
½ cup thick coconut milk (see page 44)

Spice paste:
1 stalk lemon grass (*serai*) or substitute
1 thick slice *lengkuas* or substitute
6-8 fresh red chillies
10-12 shallots (*bawang merah*) or 2 small red or brown onions
1 teaspoon dried shrimp paste (*blacan*)

Prepare the spice paste first. Cut all ingredients except dried shrimp paste into small pieces then grind everthing to a fine paste with a mortar and pestle or blender. If using a blender or food processor, add a little of the oil to keep the blades turning.

Wipe beancurd dry and cut each piece into three or four thick slices. Set aside. Heat oil in a pan and fry the spice paste gently for about 5 minutes. Put in the prawns, stir for a moment or two, then add salt and thin coconut milk, a little at a time. Bring coconut milk to the boil, stirring all the time, then simmer for 1 minute before adding beancurd and lime leaves (if used). Simmer for 10 minutes then add thick coconut milk and cook for a couple of minutes to allow the gravy to thicken. Serve with rice and other dishes.

NONYA

SAMBAL TIMUN (picture opposite)
SPICY CUCUMBER DISH

2 medium cucumbers
150 g (5 oz) belly pork, boiled in one
   piece and sliced, or 1 chicken liver
   and 1 chicken gizzard, boiled and
   sliced

Sambal:
3 tablespoons dried prawns
1 teaspoon dried shrimp paste (blacan),
   grilled
2 fresh red chillies
2 tablespoons Chinese lime juice (limau
   kesturi) or juice from half-ripe
   kumquat or lemon
1-2 teaspoons sugar
½ teaspoon salt

The young Nonya friend who gave me this recipe (in very general terms — 'a handful of this', 'just enough of that') described it as 'a sort of sour side-dish to help the food down.' It goes well with nasi lemak *(recipe page 87) and a pork or chicken dish.*

Prepare the *sambal* mixture first. Soak dried prawns in hot water for 10 minutes, then pound coarsely and set aside. Make sure dried shrimp paste is thoroughly grilled on both sides then pound with chillies. Add prawns, pound a little, then mix in all other *sambal* ingredients. Taste, adding more sugar and lime juice if desired. Keep aside in a covered container.

To remove any bitterness from the cucumber, cut 1 cm (½ in) off the top. Take the cut top portion of the cucumber and rub it in a circular motion for 30 seconds over the cut surface of the rest of the cucumber. A white 'scum' will accumulate on both cut surfaces. Discard the cut top portion. Cut another 1 cm (½ in) off the top of the rest of the cucumber and discard this also. Repeat the procedure with the other cucumber. Do not peel cucumbers, but cut in half lengthwise then cut across diagonally in pieces about 2.5 cm (1 in) wide.

Just before serving, combine cucumber, pork or chicken liver and gizzard, and *sambal* ingredients. Serve immediately to prevent softening.

NONYA

SAMBAL BRINJAL
EGGPLANT WITH DRIED PRAWN TOPPING

6 medium eggplants, long green variety
   if possible
½ cup oil
4 tablespoons dried prawns, soaked
4-6 shallots (bawang merah) or 1 small
   red or brown onion
2 cloves garlic
1 teaspoon chilli powder
2 teaspoons vinegar
2 teaspoons sugar
¼ teaspoon salt

Wipe eggplants but do not peel. Cut in half lengthwise and fry in hot oil, a few minutes on either side, until soft. Drain and set aside. Pound the soaked dried prawns until fine and set aside. Pound shallots and garlic together.

Add enough oil to the pan in which eggplant was fried to make 4 tablespoons. Heat oil and gently fry shallots, garlic and chilli powder for 1 minute. Add dried prawns, vinegar, sugar and salt. Cook for a few minutes until golden brown, then spread a little of this mixture over each of the fried eggplant halves. Serve warm.

NONYA

PICKLED WHITE RADISH

½ giant white radish (lobak)
1 medium carrot
1 teaspoon salt
½ cup cold water
1-2 teaspoons sugar
1 tablespoon white vinegar
1 fresh red chilli, seeded and sliced
   (optional)

A sharply flavoured side-dish often served with rich or fatty pork dishes. Adjust the amounts of vinegar and sugar to suit your taste.

Wash the radish and carrot and cut into very thin strips about 8 cm (3 in) long using a vegetable peeler. Rub in salt with the fingers, then add cold water and leave the vegetables to stand for 30 minutes.

Rinse vegetables thoroughly under running water and squeeze out excess moisture. Sprinkle with sugar then rub in with the fingers. Add vinegar and stir thoroughly. Serve garnished with fresh red chilli if liked.

Sambal timun (recipe this page).

NONYA

RUJAK (picture page 106)
SALAD WITH SPICY GRAVY

125 g (4 oz) beansprouts
½ yam bean (bangkwang) or 1 cup
  sliced water chestnuts or hard green
  pear
large handful water convolvulus
  (kangkong) or spinach leaves
2-3 squares hard beancurd (taukwa)
1 small cucumber
salt
1-2 pieces long fried Chinese doughnut
  (yau char kway)(optional)
1 pink ginger bud (bunga
  siantan)(optional)
2-3 lengthwise slices of slightly under-
  ripe pineapple

Sauce:
½ cup raw peanuts
3-4 fresh red chillies
1 teaspoon dried shrimp paste (blacan),
  well toasted
1 tablespoon thick shrimp paste (petis or
  hay koh)
1 tablespoon palm sugar (gula Melaka)
  or brown sugar
¼ cup tamarind water (see page 63)
1 tablespoon Chinese lime juice (limau
  kesturi) or lemon juice
½ teaspoon salt
1 tablespoon cold boiled water

This is the Nonya version of the much more simple Javanese rujak. Although the Nonyas developed this recipe, it is prepared by Chinese hawkers all over Singapore and is a very popular snack or luncheon dish. The pink ginger bud adds a unique flavour, although rujak *is still a delicious dish without it.*

Prepare sauce first. Gently fry the peanuts in a dry pan, stirring frequently, until light brown and cooked. Allow to cool slightly, then rub with the hands to loosen the skins. Shake and blow (in the garden) to discard skins. Pound the peanuts coarsely, using a mortar and pestle or electric blender. Set aside.

Pound the chillies and dried shrimp paste together, then blend in the thick shrimp paste. Add palm or brown sugar, tamarind juice, lime juice, salt and boiled water and mix thoroughly, then stir in peanuts. If using a blender or food processor, put in the chillies, both types of shrimp paste and sugar. Blend, adding a little of the tamarind water as necessary to keep the blades turning. When the mixture is fine, add rest of ingredients except peanuts, blend for a few seconds, then stir in peanuts.

Blanch the beansprouts in boiling water for just 30 seconds, then rinse under running water to refresh. Peel yam bean and cut into coarse slices. Steam vegetables leaves until just cooked, then chop coarsely and set aside. Deep fry beancurd in hot oil for about 4-5 minutes, turning to cook golden brown on both sides. Drain and cut into thick slices. Scrape skin of cucumber with a fork, rub salt into the skin, then rinse and slice cucumber.

Cut Chinese doughnut, if using, into 4 cm (1½ in) lengths. Slice pink ginger bud very finely, and cut pineapple into chunks. Arrange all vegetables and other items except pink ginger bud attractively in piles on a large platter. Sprinkle with pink ginger bud, pour over the sauce, and serve immediately.

NONYA

KIAM CHYE GORENG
FRIED SALTED CABBAGE

300 g (10 oz) salted cabbage
2 pieces hard beancurd (taukwa)
  (optional)
½ cup oil
2 cloves garlic, very finely chopped
100 g (3½ oz) belly pork, very finely
  sliced
2 teaspoons sugar
1 teaspoon thick black soya sauce
1-2 fresh red chillies, cut in lengthwise
  strips
white pepper

The salted cabbage used in this dish, known as kiam chye *in Hokkien and* ham choy *in Cantonese, can be bought loose from Singapore markets or in some Chinese stores overseas. It is also available canned. Must be well soaked to remove excessive saltiness.*

Soak the salted cabbage in cold water, changing the water two or three times, for about 1 hour. Rinse and squeeze thoroughly to remove all moisture, then chop finely.

Cut beancurd into small cubes. Heat oil in a *kuali* and fry beancurd, stirring occasionally, until crisp and golden brown. Remove from pan and drain.

Pour out all but 1 tablespoon of oil from the *kuali*. Heat, then add garlic. Fry for just 15 seconds then add the pork and stir-fry for 2 minutes. Add the vegetable and continue to stir-fry for another 5 minutes. Sprinkle over the sugar and soya sauce, and add chilli and fried beancurd. Cook for another 2 minutes. Sprinkle with white pepper and serve.

MALAY

KOBIS MASAK LEMAK
CABBAGE IN COCONUT MILK

1 tablespoon oil
4 shallots (*bawang merah*), or ½
    medium red or brown onion, finely
    sliced
1 clove garlic, finely sliced
1-2 fresh red chillies, sliced
2 cups thin coconut milk (see page 44)
½ medium cabbage, coarsely shredded
1 heaped tablespoon dried prawns,
    soaked
½ cup thick coconut milk (see page 44)
½ teaspoon salt

Cooking in coconut milk (masak lemak) is a common way of preparing vegetables, and can be used for green beans, spinach, water convolvulus (kangkong or ong choy), pumpkin, marrow, or any combinations of these.

Heat oil in a saucepan and gently fry shallots, garlic and chillies for 2-3 minutes until they soften. Do not allow to brown. Add the thin coconut milk, and bring to the boil, stirring all the time. Put in the cabbage and dried prawns and simmer gently with the pan uncovered until the cabbage is cooked. Add thick coconut milk and salt and cook for another couple of minutes.

MALAY

NANGKA LEMAK (picture page 74)
JACKFRUIT IN COCONUT MILK

750 g-1 kg (1½-2 lb) unripe jackfruit
    (*nangka*)
1 tablespoon grated fresh or desiccated
    coconut
1 teaspoon coriander
5-6 shallots (*bawang merah*) or 1 small
    red or brown onion
3 fresh red chillies
5 mm (¼ in) fresh turmeric (*kunyit*) or
    ½ teaspoon turmeric powder
2 tablespoons oil
1 fragrant lime leaf (*daun limau perut*)
    or young citrus leaf (optional)
1 stalk lemon grass (*serai*), bruised, or
    substitute
3 cups coconut milk (see page 44)
150 g (5 oz) small raw prawns, peeled
    (optional)
salt to taste

Jackfruit, which grows to an enormous size (up to 30 kilos in weight), is not only a delicious fruit when ripe but makes a lovely vegetable dish when cooked unripe. The large seeds should not be discarded, for when cooked they have a beautiful chestnut-like flavour. Most Singaporeans, in fact, save the seeds from the ripe fruit as well, and boil them in salty water to eat as a snack.

Cut the coarse skin away from the jackfruit with an oiled knife, then cut the flesh into chunks about 4 cm (1½ in) square. Cook in plenty of boiling salted water until the jackfruit is just tender. Drain and set aside.
    If using desiccated coconut, moisten with a little water. Pound fresh or desiccated coconut and set aside. Pound the coriander, then add shallots, chillies and fresh turmeric and pound until fine. Add pounded coconut and powdered turmeric (if using). Heat oil in a saucepan and gently fry the pounded ingredients for 3-5 minutes, stirring occasionally.
    Add the lime leaf, lemon grass and coconut milk and bring to the boil, stirring constantly. Add the prawns, salt and boiled jackfruit and simmer gently, uncovered, for 10 minutes.

MALAY

POTATO CUTLETS

500 g (1 lb) potatoes
½ teaspoon salt
white pepper
pinch monosodium glutamate
1 spring onion, finely sliced
6 shallots (*bawang merah*), finely sliced
    and fried till golden, or 2 tablespoons
    fried onion flakes (see page 188)
1 egg, beaten
oil for deep frying

Indonesian in origin, this is an easy dish that can be served as part of a main meal.

Boil potatoes whole. Cool slightly, peel, then mash roughly. Add salt, pepper, monosodium glutamate, spring onion, fried shallots or onion flakes, and stir to mix well. Leave until cold then form into 8 round balls. Flatten balls to a thickness of 2.5 cm (1 in), dip into beaten egg, and deep fry in very hot oil for about 2-3 minutes. Drain and serve.

MALAY

PUMPKIN AND LONG BEAN CURRY

10 shallots (*bawang merah*) or 1 large
  red or brown onion
2 fresh red chillies
½ teaspoon dried shrimp paste (*blacan*)
1½ tablespoons oil
1 heaped tablespoon dried prawns,
  soaked
1¾ cups coconut milk (see page 44)
½ teaspoon salt
375 g (12 oz) pumpkin,
  peeled and cut in chunks
150 g (5 oz) long beans, cut in 4 cm
  (1½ in) pieces

A simple and very tasty vegetable dish. Sweet potato and spinach can be used instead of pumpkin and long beans.

Grind shallots, chillies and shrimp paste together until fine. Heat oil in a saucepan and gently fry ground ingredients for 3-4 minutes, stirring frequently. Add dried prawns and fry for 2 minutes. Put in coconut milk and salt and bring to the boil, stirring constantly. Add pumpkin and beans and simmer uncovered until cooked.

MALAY

BEANSPROUT OMELETTE

250 g (8 oz) beansprouts
1½ tablespoons oil
2 cloves garlic, finely chopped
2 spring onions (including green tops),
  coarsely chopped
1 fresh red chilli, seeded and sliced
3 eggs, beaten
½ teaspoon salt
¼ teaspoon white pepper

Wash beansprouts and discard any pieces of skin clinging to them. Drain thoroughly in a colander or sieve. Heat oil in a 25 cm (10 in) diameter frying pan and fry garlic gently until golden, then add beansprouts, spring onions and chilli. Fry over medium heat for 2-3 minutes. Make sure any moisture that may have come into the pan from the beansprouts has evaporated, then raise heat. Season eggs with salt and pepper and pour into the pan. Cook until the bottom has set and turned golden. Cut omelette into four and turn over each piece with a fish slice or spatula to cook on the other side. Serve on a plate as part of a meal including rice and other dishes.

MALAY

KANGKONG TUMIS AYER
SIMMERED WATER CONVOLVULUS

375 g (12 oz) water convolvulus
  (*kangkong* or *ong choy*)
½ teaspoon dried shrimp paste (*blacan*)
½ cup water
1 medium red or brown onion, sliced
1 clove garlic, finely chopped
1 fresh red chilli, sliced
1 tablespoon oil

Wash water convolvulus thoroughly and cut stalks into 4 cm (1½ in) lengths, discarding the bottom thick part. Grill the dried shrimp paste on both sides, then pound in a mortar. Add water to the mortar and mix thoroughly.

Heat oil in a *kuali* and fry the onion, garlic and chilli for 2-3 minutes, stirring frequently. Pour in the shrimp paste water and add convolvulus. Stir, then cover *kuali* with a lid and cook quickly for 3-5 minutes.

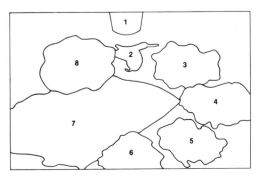

1 *Rasam (recipe page 83)*, 2 *chilli tairu (recipe page 193)*, 3 *savoury potatoes (recipe page 124)*, 4 *fresh coconut chutney (recipe page 184)*, 5 *southern Indian cabbage (recipe page 125)*, 6 *carrot pachadi (recipe page 124)*, 7 *dosay (recipe page 104)*, 8 *poppadum.*

PACHADI BUAH NANAS (picture page 74)
SPICY PINEAPPLE DISH

1 medium half-ripe pineapple, peeled
   and 'eyes' removed
water
1 heaped teaspoon turmeric powder
4 tablespoons oil
2 medium red or brown onions, finely
   sliced
1 whole star anise
5 cm (2 in) stick cinnamon
6 cardamom pods, slit and bruised
8 cloves
4 cloves garlic, very finely chopped
5 cm (2 in) fresh ginger, very finely
   chopped
1 cup water
1 teaspoon salt
1½ tablespoons sugar, or more to taste
2-3 fresh red chillies, sliced in half
   lengthwise

Cut pineapple in four lengthwise and remove core. Cut each piece in half crosswise. Put pineapple, enough water to cover it, and turmeric powder in a saucepan and simmer uncovered for 10 minutes. Drain pineapply and discard liquid.

Heat oil and fry onions and whole spices for 2 minutes. Add garlic and ginger and fry for another 2 minutes. Put in water, salt and sugar and boil rapidly for 2 minutes. Add chilli and pineapple and simmer for 2 minutes. Taste and adjust seasoning if necessary. The flavour should be hot and sour with a touch of sweetness.

SAMBAL BUNCIS
GREEN BEAN SAMBAL

8 shallots (*bawang merah*) or 1 medium
   red or brown onion
3 fresh red chillies
½ teaspoon dried shrimp paste (*blacan*)
4 candlenuts (*buah keras*) or
   macadamias
1 tablespoon oil
250 g (8 oz) green beans, cut in 2.5 cm
   (1 in) lengths
1½ cups coconut milk (see page 44)
½ teaspoon salt
8 small raw prawns, peeled, or 1
   tablespoon dried prawns, soaked

Grind shallots, chillies, dried shrimp paste and candlenuts until fine. Heat oil and fry the ground ingredients for 3-4 minutes. Add beans and fry for a minute. Put in coconut milk, salt and dried prawns. If using raw prawns, do not add yet.

Simmer with pan uncovered until beans are almost cooked. If using raw prawns, add and simmer another 3 minutes.

URAP (picture page 174)
VEGETABLE AND COCONUT SALAD

300 g (10 oz) green beans
200 g (6½ oz) beansprouts
1 fresh red chilli
1 small clove garlic
½ teaspoon toasted dried shrimp paste
   (*blacan*)
½ fresh coconut, grated after brown
   skin has been removed
½ teaspoon salt

Cut beans into 4 cm (1 ½ in) lengths and steam until just cooked but still crisp. Blanch beansprouts in boiling water for 30 seconds, then stand under running water to refresh. Drain. Allow vegetables to cool to room temperature. Pound chilli, garlic and dried shrimp paste together, then add salt and grated coconut, little by little, pounding to mix well. Combine pounded mixture with vegetables immediately before serving. Do not keep overnight, and do not store the coconut mixture outside the refrigerator or it will turn sour.

GADO GADO
INDONESIAN SALAD

waxy potatoes, boiled and sliced
cabbage, shredded and steamed
long beans or green beans, cut into 4 cm
  (1½ in) lengths, steamed
water convolvulus (*kangkong* or *ong
  choy*), steamed
beansprouts, scalded
hard beancurd (*taukwa*), deep fried and
  sliced
cucumber, skin left on, sliced diagonally
hardboiled eggs, sliced
gado gado sauce (see page 184)
fried *krupuk* to garnish

The amounts of the various vegetables that make up this just-cooked Javanese salad can be adjusted depending on the number of people being served. It is important that the vegetables should not be overcooked but remain crisp.

Prepare the vegetables and arrange on a large platter. Just before serving, pour over the *gado gado* sauce (which should be at room temperature) and garnish with *krupuk*.

SAMBAR
LENTIL AND VEGETABLE CURRY

1¼ cups yellow or red lentils (*parupoo*
  or *masur dhal*)
2 slices fresh ginger
3-4 cloves garlic, halved lengthwise
2 shallots (*bawang merah*) or ¼ medium
  red or brown onion
1 fresh green chilli, quartered
½ teaspoon salt
1 teaspoon oil or butter
½ teaspoon turmeric powder

Vegetables:
2 small potatoes, quartered
1 carrot, sliced thickly
4 small okra (ladies' fingers)
1 small eggplant, quartered lengthwise
4 green beans, cut into 4 cm (1½ in)
  lengths
2 tomatoes, quartered

Additional items:
¼ cup tamarind water (see page 63)
1 tablespoon oil
½ teaspoon brown mustard seed
2 dried red chillies, broken into 2.5 cm
  (1 in) lengths
1 sprig curry leaves (*karuvapillai*)
3-4 shallots (*bawang merah*), or ½
  medium red or brown onion, very
  finely sliced
¼ cup thick coconut milk (see page 44),
  optional

Rinse lentils and soak for 15 minutes. Put into a saucepan with ginger, garlic, shallots, chilli, salt, oil and turmeric with enough water to cover by 1 cm (½ in). Simmer gently until lentils are soft. Add vegetables and cook until soft, adding a little more water if necessary.

Add tamarind water to saucepan. Heat oil and gently fry mustard seed, chillies, curry leaves and shallots for 2-3 minutes then add to lentils and vegetables. Stir in coconut milk and cook a further minute. Serve hot.

INDIAN

SIMPLE DHAL STEW (picture opposite)

1 cup yellow or red lentils (*parupoo* or
 masur dhal)
1½ tablespoons *ghee* or oil
1 teaspoon brown mustard seed
1 medium red or brown onion, sliced
2 cloves garlic, finely chopped
2 slices fresh ginger, finely chopped
2 sprigs curry leaves(*karuvapillai*)
 (optional)
½ teaspoon turmeric powder
1 teaspoon *garam masala* (**see glossary**)
2-2½ cups water
1 teaspoon salt

Wash the lentils thoroughly and leave them to soak while
preparing other ingredients. Heat *ghee* and gently fry the
mustard seed until it pops. Add onion, garlic, ginger and curry
leaves and fry until the onion is soft and golden. Sprinkle in the
turmeric and *garam masala*. Stir thoroughly, then add the
lentils, well drained, and stir over low heat for a couple of
minutes until all the *ghee* is absorbed.

Add the water and salt and simmer until the lentils are soft.
Serve as part of a dinner, or for lunch, accompanied by *puris*
and a chutney.

INDIAN

KABULI CHANNA (picture opposite)
SPICY CHICKPEAS

1¼ cups dried chickpeas (*channa dhal*)
1 teaspoon salt
1 fresh green chilli, halved lengthwise
2 tablespoons *ghee* or oil
1 medium onion, grated
½ teaspoon cummin
2 cardamom pods
2 teaspoons coriander
4 cloves
2.5 cm (1 in) stick cinnamon
2.5 cm (1 in) fresh ginger
6 cloves garlic
½-1 teaspoon chilli powder
2 medium tomatoes, skinned and
 chopped
fresh coriander leaves to garnish

Wash the chickpeas thoroughly and discard any grit. Cover with
water and allow to soak overnight. Add salt and green chilli and
simmer until chickpeas are tender. Drain, and reserve the
cooking liquid.

Heat *ghee* and gently fry onion until soft. Grind the whole
spices. Chop the ginger and garlic very finely, and add to the
onion. Fry for 2-3 minutes, then add ground spices and chilli
powder and fry for another minute. Add the tomatoes and continue cooking, stirring frequently, until they soften and blend
with the onion and spices. Put in the drained chickpeas and cook
gently for 10 minutes, adding a little of the cooking liquid every
few minutes until ¾ cup has been used. Serve sprinkled with
coriander leaves.

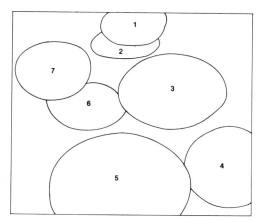

1 *Ulundoo* or *urad dhal*, 2 *parupoo* or *tuvar dhal*, 3 *simple dhal stew*
(*recipe this page*), 4 *channa dhal*, 5 *kabuli channa* (*recipe this page*),
6 *masur dhal*, 7 *mung dhal*.

INDIAN

SAVOURY POTATOES (picture page 118)

500 g (1 lb) potatoes
2 tablespoons *ghee* or oil
½ teaspoon brown mustard seed
1 large red or brown onion, chopped
½ teaspoon turmeric powder
½-1 teaspoon chilli powder
¾ teaspoon salt
few grindings black pepper

Used as a filling for dosay *(see page 104), these potatoes also make a good accompaniment to meat and other vegetable dishes.*

Boil potatoes until cooked but not too soft. Peel and cut into cubes of about 1 cm (½ inch). Heat *ghee* or oil and fry mustard seed until it starts popping. Add onion and fry gently, stirring from time to time, for 5 minutes. Add spices, salt and pepper and stir for few seconds, then put into diced potato and continue to fry, stirring from time to time, for another 5 minutes.

INDIAN

AVIAL
VEGETABLES WITH YOGHURT

750 g (1½ lb) mixed vegetables
4 fresh green chillies, halved lengthwise
1 teaspoon salt
¼ teaspoon turmeric powder
¼ teaspoon cummin powder
1 cup freshly grated coconut or ⅔ cup desiccated coconut
4-6 shallots (*bawang merah*) or 1 small red or brown onion
½ cup plain yoghurt

Avial, *popular with the Malayalee people from the southwestern state of Kerala, is very similar to the* pachadis *of Madras (Tamil Nadu). Use any of the following vegetables, either on their own or in combination: marrow, choko, cabbage, okra (ladies' fingers), green beans, potatoes.*

Cut vegetables into cubes or shreds. Combine with chillies, salt, turmeric and cummin. Add just enough water to prevent vegetables from drying out and cook in a covered pan until just-cooked. Remove lid and evaporate any liquid that may be left in the pan.

Pound freshly grated coconut and shallots together, then add together with yoghurt to the cooked vegetables. Stir to mix and serve.

If using desicated coconut, mix with the yoghurt before preparing and cooking vegetables to allow coconut to soften.

INDIAN

CARROT PACHADI (picture page 118)

3 medium carrots, grated
4-6 shallots (*bawang merah*), or 1 small red or brown onion, very finely sliced
½ fresh red chilli, seeded and sliced
½ teaspoon salt
½ cup freshly grated coconut or ⅓ cup desiccated coconut
2 teaspoons brown mustard seed
1 tablespoon oil
1 dried red chilli, broken in 2.5 cm (1 in) lengths
½ cup plain yoghurt

Another superb southern Indian creation that can be made in advance and served at room temperature with dosay *(see page 104) and two or three other vegetable dishes.*

Combine carrots, shallots, fresh red chilli and salt and set aside. Pound freshly grated coconut with 1 teaspoon of mustard seed.

Heat oil and fry the other teaspoon of mustard seed together with the dried chilli until chilli turns brown. Add the pounded coconut mixture and cook, stirring constantly, for 1 minute. Put in the carrot mixture and fry, tossing all the time, for just 1 minute. Put into a bowl and, when cool, add yoghurt.

(If you are using desiccated coconut, add it to the oil together with the carrot mixture. Add a little more yoghurt to compensate for the amount the desiccated coconut absorbs.)

INDIAN

BRINJAL PACHADI
EGGPLANT PURÉE

250 g (8 oz) eggplant
½ teaspoon salt
6-8 shallots (*bawang merah*), or 1 medium or brown onion, very finely sliced
½-1 fresh green chilli, very finely chopped
1-2 tablespoons plain yoghurt

It took me quite some time to work out the measurements for this recipe, for the Indian friend who showed me this dish was seldom satisfied with her initial attempts and kept adding to it.

Grill the eggplants in their skins until well-browned on all sides and soft. Remove skins and mash the pulp thoroughly. Add all other ingredients and stir. The mixture should be a thick purée, not too sloppy. Serve with *chapati* or *puri*.

INDIAN

SOUTHERN INDIAN CABBAGE (picture page 118)

2 tablespoons oil
1 teaspoon brown mustard seed
1-2 fresh green chillies, sliced
4-6 shallots (*bawang merah*), or 1 small red or brown onion, very finely sliced
2 sprigs curry leaves (*karuvapillai*)
1 teaspoon blackgram *dhal* (*ulundoo*)
500 g (1 lb) cabbage, coarsely shredded
¼ teaspoon sugar
1 teaspoon salt
¼ cup water
3 tablespoons freshly grated coconut

Of all the cabbage dishes I have ever tasted, this is my favourite. Although desiccated coconut moistened with a little water could be substituted for fresh coconut, it lacks the true flavour and I feel it is well worth the trouble of buying fresh coconut, even if you have to grate it yourself.

Heat oil in a *kuali* and put in mustard seed. As soon as it starts popping, add chillies, shallots, curry leaves and *dhal* (the *dhal* should be husked, but do not soak before using in this or other vegetable recipes). Fry, stirring frequently, for 3-4 minutes. Add cabbage and fry, stirring to mix thoroughly, for 1 minute. Add sugar, salt and water. Cover *kuali* and simmer gently for about 10 minutes until the cabbage is almost soft. Remove lid, increase heat, and cook rapidly to evaporate any liquid. Stir in coconut and serve at room temperature.

INDIAN

CAULIFLOWER MASALA

500 g (1 lb) cauliflower
3 tablespoons *ghee* or oil
½ teaspoon brown mustard seed
½ teaspoon cummin
pinch fenugreek
½ teaspoon turmeric powder
3 slices fresh ginger, very finely chopped
2 cloves garlic, finely chopped
1 medium onion, finely sliced
1 large tomato, chopped
1 fresh green chilli, sliced
½ teaspoon salt
few grindings black pepper

This dish is similar to the cauliflower served by Singapore's most popular Sikh restaurant — a quick and easy dish, because none of the whole spice seeds need to be ground.

Separate cauliflower into flowerets and set aside.

Heat *ghee* or oil and fry mustard seed until it starts popping. Add cummin, fenugreek, turmeric, ginger, garlic and onion. Cook gently, stirring frequently, for 3-4 minutes until onion turns golden. Add cauliflower and fry for a couple of minutes, stirring well to coat it with the spices. Add tomato, chilli, salt and pepper and cook gently until the tomato softens. Cover pan and cook gently, stirring from time to time, until cauliflower is tender.

INDIAN

OKRA BHAJI

375 g (12 oz) okra (ladies' fingers)
60 g (2 oz) *ghee* or butter
1 medium onion, finely sliced
½ teaspoon turmeric powder
½ teaspoon salt
few grindings black pepper

Be sure that the okra (ladies' fingers) are small, fresh and crisp. Tiny zucchini can also be cooked in this way, although this vegetable is not used in Singapore or India.

Wash okra. Remove stalk end and cut each okra diagonally into 3 or 4 pieces. Heat *ghee* or butter and gently fry onion until pale golden. Add okra, stir thoroughly, and sprinkle with the turmeric. Cook for 1 minute, then add salt and pepper. Cover the pan and cook over very low heat, stirring from time to time, until okra is tender.

INDIAN

PAKHORA
BATTER-DIPPED VEGETABLES

Batter:
2 cups chickpea flour (*besan*)
1 teaspoon baking powder
½-1 teaspoon chilli powder
1 teaspoon salt
1 egg, lightly beaten
juice ½ lemon
1 fresh green chilli, seeded and very
    finely chopped
warm water to mix

Vegetables: use a mixture of any of the
    following
5 mm (¼ in) thick slices of eggplant,
    potato, or sweet potato
small pieces of cauliflower
onion rings
small whole okra (ladies' fingers)
whole silver beet or spinach leaves
green beans
rings of green capsicum

oil for deep frying

To make batter, mix all dry ingredients then add egg, lemon juice and sufficient warm water to make a thick batter.
    Wash and dry the vegetables. Heat oil in a large *kuali*. Dip the vegetables one at a time into the batter and deep fry, a few at a time, until just turning golden. Remove and drain. Allow time for the oil to reheat before adding the next batch of vegetables.
    Just before serving, heat the oil until it is very hot and fry the vegetables a second time for 30 seconds until brown on both sides. Although this second frying is not essential, it makes the *pakhora* more crisp.

INDIAN

CUCUMBER WITH YOGHURT

1 cucumber, peeled and sliced
1 teaspoon salt
1 tablespoon cold water
½ cup yoghurt
2 shallots (*bawang merah*), or ¼
    medium red or brown onion, very
    finely sliced
2 teaspoons finely chopped mint or fresh
    coriander leaves
few seedless raisins or sultanas
    (optional)
¼ teaspoon *garam masala* (see glossary)

Sprinkle sliced cucumber with salt and water and stand in the refrigerator for 30 minutes. Drain and squeeze out moisture. Combine with yoghurt, shallots, mint and raisins. Put in a serving dish with *garam masala* sprinkled on top.

INDIAN

TOMATO AND CUCUMBER SALAD (picture page 159)

1 small or ½ large cucumber
2-3 ripe tomatoes
1-2 shallots (bawang merah), or ¼
    medium red or brown onion, finely
    sliced
2 tablespoons white or brown vinegar
salt to taste
1 tablespoon mint or fresh coriander
    leaves, chopped

Peel cucumber and cut into 5 mm (¼ in) dice. Cut tomatoes into same size as cucumber and put vegetables into a glass or china bowl with vinegar and salt. Cover and stand in refrigerator for about 1 hour, stirring a couple of times. Mix in chopped mint or coriander just before serving.

Although the use of red wine vinegar is unorthodox, I find it improves this salad.

INDIAN

ONION AND TOMATO SALAD

2 large red or brown onions, very finely
    sliced
2 tablespoons lemon juice
½ teaspoon salt
½ teaspoon sugar
1 tomato, sliced
½ fresh green chilli, seeded and sliced
    (optional)
1 tablespoon chopped fresh coriander
    leaves

Combine onions with lemon juice and salt and set aside for at least 1 hour. Just before serving, add all other ingredients, toss thoroughly and serve.

SRI LANKAN

BRINJAL CURRY
EGGPLANT CURRY

4 small or 2 medium eggplants, total
    weight about 375 g (12 oz)
1 teaspoon salt
¼ teaspoon turmeric powder
½ cup oil
1 medium onion, sliced
1 clove garlic, finely chopped
1 teaspoon coriander
½ teaspoon cummin
¼ teaspoon fennel
¼ teaspoon brown mustard seed
pinch fenugreek
½ teaspoon chilli powder
1 cup coconut milk (see page 44)
½ teaspoon salt
2 teaspoons vinegar

Cut eggplant across in slices. Sprinkle with salt and turmeric and fry in hot oil for 2 minutes on either side. Roast the coriander, cummin, fennel, mustard seed and fenugreek in a dry pan until dark brown, then grind finely. Add chilli powder and enough cold water to make a stiff paste.

Heat 2 tablespoons oil and fry onion and garlic until soft. Add spice paste and fry 2-3 minutes, adding a little more oil if the mixture threatens to stick to the pan. Put in coconut milk and bring to the boil, stirring constantly. Simmer for a few minutes until the coconut milk thickens. Put in the fried eggplant and salt and simmer for 3-5 minutes. Add vinegar, cook a moment longer, then serve.

Seafood

The fish section of any Singapore market in the morning is a stunning sight. There are giant red snapper and tiny transparent whitebait; murky black catfish swimming in a shallow tank; baskets of brilliant blue-spotted or black crabs, still alive, their pincers tied together to render them harmless; greenish-grey flat-headed lobsters; enormous piles of prawns, always sold raw or 'green'; small squid, covered with a mottled wine-coloured skin; metre-long Spanish mackerel and bonito, smooth and silver-grey; mounds of cockles, rectangular mussels, tiny clams and all kinds of strange shellfish.

Singaporeans insist that their fish should be fresh, and would never dream of buying ready filleted fish, for how can they possibly judge its freshness if they cannot examine the gills and eyes? Many fish shops in Western cities sell only frozen filleted fish, but if you want to eat fish as Singaporeans do, then hunt for a shop or market that sells whole fresh fish.

There are literally thousands of edible fish in the world. Many of those found around Singapore and in the waters of Southeast Asia are also caught in Australian waters; in the UK and the USA, other fish with similar characteristics can be substituted. The following list describes Singapore's most commonly used fish, gives equivalents or substitutes, and mentions the major ways in which each type of fish is cooked.

IKAN MERAH

Literally 'red fish', this name is given to the fish in the Lutjanidae. family. These fish are well flavoured and not too bony; they are cut into steaks or fillets for frying or curries, and can also be grilled or fried whole. Equivalent fish are any type of snapper, bream and morwong.

IKAN BAWAL

This is the pomfret, which ranges in colour from black (*bawal hitam*) through to silvery-white (*bawal puteh*). The white pomfret is the most expensive fish in the market, and is particularly highly regarded by the Chinese. The flesh is firm and white, and separates easily from the bones; it is excellent for steaming whole, when the soft lower fin and tail become particularly succulent. Suitable substitutes are flounder, plaice, dart, swallowtail and John Dory.

IKAN KEMBONG

One of the Scombridae family, which includes tunny, mackerel and swordfish, this is a small mackerel averaging 20 cm (8 in) in length. It is excellent fried whole, grilled or baked. Any small mackerel or bonito can be used in recipes calling for *ikan kembong*.

IKAN KERAPU

Various types of grouper (groper), sea perch and sea bass are included in this category. Some of these fish are brownish in colour, with darker brown stripes or with blueish-purple spots.

Chilli crab (recipe page 134)

They are excellent for frying and grilling whole, and are popular among the Chinese with sweet and sour sauce. Grouper are known as rock or coral cod in Australia.

IKAN KURAU

This has always been the most popular fish among Singapore's European community, and is one of the most expensive on the market. It is large, with sweet juicy flesh and very few bones. It is normally cut into steaks for frying, grilling or for curry. Threadfin, tassel fish, and all types of Australian salmon can be used where recipes call for *ikan kurau*.

IKAN PARANG

A long bony fish with good-tasting flesh, used mainly for fish balls, this is known in English as dorab or wolf herring.

IKAN SELAR

Small horse mackerel, usually around 15 cm (6 in) in length, popular for frying whole. Although small and a bit fiddly to eat, the flesh is very tasty. Use any type of horse mackerel, yellow-stripe, trevally or yellowtail.

IKAN TENGGIRI

The Spanish mackerel, usually around 50 cm (20 in) long, often grows up to twice that length. It is cut into steaks and used for frying and curries. It has few bones, fine firm flesh, and no scales. Use snook, Queensland kingfish, bonito or tunny.

CHINESE

HAR LOKE
KING PRAWNS FRIED IN SHELLS

500 g (1 lb) very large raw prawns, with head and shell intact
2 spring onions, tied in knots
½ teaspoon ginger juice (see page 58)
2 teaspoons light soya sauce
1 teaspoon thick black soya sauce
¼ teaspoon sesame oil
1 teaspoon Chinese rice wine or dry sherry
2 teaspoons sugar
2 tablespoons lard or oil
¼ cup water
pinch salt
pinch monosodium glutamate
1 fresh red chilli, sliced
fresh coriander leaves

Wash and dry prawns. Trim the long hairs but leave head and shells on. Mix prawns with spring onion, ginger juice, soya sauce, sesame oil, wine and sugar and leave to stand for at least 30 minutes.

Heat lard in a *kuali*. Drain prawns, reserving marinade, and stir-fry prawns quickly in the lard, stirring constantly, for 3 minutes. Add water, the reserved marinade, salt and monosodium glutamate and simmer for another 2-3 minutes. Serve garnished with coriander leaves and red chilli.

CHINESE

PRAWNS IN BLACK BEAN SAUCE

500 g (1 lb) medium-sized raw prawns
1 tablespoon salted black beans (*tau see*)
1 tablespoon lard or oil
1 tablespoon oyster sauce
1 tablespoon Chinese rice wine or dry sherry
½ teaspoon ginger juice (see page 58)
1 teaspoon sugar
1 tablespoon water

Peel the prawns. Rinse and dry. If using canned salted black beans, rinse under running water then mash roughly with a fork. If using dried salted black beans, soak in water for 5 minutes and drain before mashing.

Heat lard or oil until quite hot and stir-fry the prawns for 1-2 minutes until they turn pink. Add the black beans, oyster sauce, wine, ginger juice and sugar and simmer for a minute, stirring all the time. Add water and cook another minute or two until the prawns are done.

130

CHINESE

FRIED PRAWN BALLS

1 thick slice stale white bread
500 g (1 lb) raw prawns
60 g (2 oz) hard pork fat
4 whole water chestnuts
1 slice fresh ginger, very finely chopped
¾ teaspoon salt
1 egg, separated
oil for deep frying

Remove crusts from bread and sprinkle it with a couple of table-spoons of cold water. Leave to soak.

Shell the prawns and chop very finely together with the pork fat, using a cleaver, until the mixture becomes paste-like. Chop the water chestnuts finely and put in a bowl together with pork and prawn paste, ginger, salt and egg yolk. Add soaked bread and mix all ingredients together thoroughly. If desired, the mixture may be covered and refrigerated for several hours.

Just before the prawns balls are required, beat the egg white until fairly stiff and add to the mixture. To make the balls, first wet your hands with cold water then take a handful of the mixture and squeeze a small amount (about a heaped teaspoon) between the thumb and forefinger. Pull the ball off with a spoon and drop immediately into hot oil. Fry for 2-3 minutes, tossing the balls around in the oil frequently. Drain and serve as a snack or first course of a Chinese dinner. Eat with salt and pepper powder (recipe page 188).

MALAY

SAMBAL UDANG (picture page 133)
CHILLI-FRIED PRAWNS

500 g (1 lb) raw prawns
12-15 dried red chillies, soaked
10 shallots (*bawang merah*) or 1 large
    red or brown onion
3 cloves garlic
2 slices fresh ginger
½ teaspoon dried shrimp paste (*blacan*)
2 tablespoons oil
1 large red or brown onion, finely sliced
1 tomato, quartered
1 teaspoon sugar
1 teaspoon salt
1 heaped tablespoon dried tamarind,
    soaked in ½ cup water and strained

Unlike the following recipe for sambal goreng udang, *this dish does not have any coconut milk and has far less gravy.*

Peel the prawns and set aside. Grind the chillies, shallots, garlic, ginger and dried shrimp paste finely. Heat oil in a *kuali* and gently fry the ground ingredients for 3-5 minutes until they smell fragrant. Add the prawns and fry, stirring constantly, for a minute or two until they change colour. Add all other ingredients and simmer gently, uncovered, for 3-5 minutes until the prawns are cooked.

MALAY

SAMBAL GORENG UDANG
CHILLI-FRIED PRAWNS IN COCONUT MILK

500 g (1 lb) raw prawns
8-10 shallots (*bawang merah*) or 1½
    medium red or brown onions
8-12 fresh red chillies
2 slices *lengkuas* or substitute
4 candlenuts (*buah keras*) or
    macadamias
½ teaspoon dried shrimp paste (*blacan*)
2 tablespoons oil
1 cup coconut milk (see page 44)
½ teaspoon salt
¼ cup tamarind water (see page 63)
2 stalks lemon grass (*serai*), bruised, or
    substitute

Wash and peel the prawns. Dry and set aside

Grind shallots, chillies, *lengkuas*, candlenuts and dried shrimp paste finely. Heat oil, then gently fry the ground ingredients for 3-5 minutes, until cooked and fragrant. Add prawns and fry for 1 minute, stirring constantly. Put in coconut milk, salt, tamarind water and lemon grass and bring slowly to the boil, stirring. Simmer gently, uncovered, until the coconut milk thickens and the prawns are cooked.

Some cooks add a cake of fermented soya beans (*tempe*) cut into very fine dice when putting in the prawns.

NONYA

GULAI UDANG NANAS
SOUR PRAWNS AND PINEAPPLE

500 g (1 lb) medium-sized raw prawns
2 heaped teaspoons tamarind
½ cup warm water
2 tablespoons oil
1 cup water
3 slices under-ripe pineapple, peeled and
    cut in bite-sized pieces
½ teaspoon salt
sugar to taste (optional)

Spices:
4 slices *lengkuas* or substitute
4 candlenuts (*buah keras*) or
    macadamias
1 cm (½ in) fresh turmeric (*kunyit*) or
    ½ teaspoon turmeric powder
½ teaspoon dried shrimp paste (*blacan*)
3-4 fresh red chillies
10 shallots (*bawang merah*) or 1 large
    red or brown onion

Peel the prawns and set aside. Mix the tamarind with warm water. Allow to soak for 5 minutes, then squeeze and strain to obtain liquid. Discard pulp and stones. Grind the spices finely, adding a little of the oil if you are using an electric blender.

Heat oil in a heavy saucepan and gently fry the ground ingredients for about 5 minutes, stirring frequently. Add 1 cup water, pineapple and salt and bring to the boil. Simmer gently, uncovered, for 5-10 minutes until pineapple is soft. Add the tamarind liquid and simmer for another 2 minutes. Taste and add a little sugar if the gravy seems extremely sour, but remember that this dish should have a sour tang.

Add the prawns at the last minute and simmer for a couple of minutes until cooked. Take care not to overcook them or they will become tough.

INDIAN

PRAWN CURRY

500 g (1 lb) medium-sized raw prawns
1 tablespoon *ghee* or butter
1 medium red or brown onion, sliced
1 teaspoon turmeric powder
2 tablespoons *garam masala*
    (see glossary)
1 teaspoon chilli powder
2 large ripe tomatoes, skinned and
    chopped
1 cup water
2 teaspoons lime or lemon juice
½ teaspoon salt

One of the easiest and also most delicious prawn curry recipes that I know.

Peel the prawns and set aside. Heat *ghee* and gently fry sliced onion until soft and beginning to turn golden. Mix the turmeric, *garam masala* and chilli powder to a stiff paste with a little cold water and add to onions. Fry, stirring frequently, for 2-3 minutes.

Add tomato and cook until it becomes soft and pulpy. Add water and simmer, uncovered, for 10 minutes. Put in the prawns, lime juice and salt and simmer uncovered until the prawns are tender. This should take 8-10 minutes. Serve with rice or *chapati* to help mop up the gravy.

CHINESE

STUFFED FRIED CRABS

2 large raw or cooked crabs
3 heaped tablespoons fresh breadcrumbs
1 dried black mushroom, soaked and
    shredded
1 spring onion, finely chopped
1 scant tablespoon finely chopped celery
½ teaspoon salt
white pepper
few drops sesame oil
1 egg, lightly beaten
1 tablespoon flour
oil for deep frying

If using raw crabs, boil in plenty of water for 10 minutes. When crabs are cooked, carefully remove the back shell and keep aside. Extract all the meat from the body, legs and claws of the crab, taking care to discard all the little bits of bony tissue.

Flake the crabmeat finely and mix with seasonings and egg. Divide the mixture and push firmly into each of the crab shells. Sprinkle the top with a little flour.

Heat plenty of oil in a *kuali* and fry the stuffed crab, floured side facing down, for a minute or two until golden brown. Serve with chilli sauce.

Sambal udang (recipe page 131).

CHINESE

CHILLI CRAB (picture page 128)

3 raw crabs, live, weighing about 500 g
   (1 lb) each
2 slices fresh ginger
3-4 fresh red chillies
3 tablespoons oil
1 scant tablespoon salted soya beans
   (*taucheo*), lightly pounded
1 tablespoon sugar
¾ cup water
4 tablespoons tomato sauce

Although a lot of Chinese touches are evident here, chilli crab is a true Singaporean dish. Many versions exist, some using more tomato sauce than others, some adding vinegar, some insisting on garlic while others omit it. This version was taught me by a friend's Chinese cook who also taught me how to deal with live crabs the squeamish way. I could never bring myself to insert a skewer under the back flap of a live crab, but Ah Moi suggested putting the live crabs into the freezer section of the refrigerator for 10 minutes to stun or immobilise them before cutting them up with a cleaver.

Chop crabs in half lengthwise and remove back shells. Discard the spongey grey matter. Remove claws from body and beat with the blunt side of a cleaver to crack in several places. Cut each side of the crab body into 2 or 3 pieces, each with legs still attached. Crack legs lightly. Wash crab thoroughly and drain.

Pound the ginger and chillies then fry gently in oil in a *kuali* for 2-3 minutes. Add salted soya beans and fry for another minute, stirring. Put in crab pieces and stir-fry over high heat until crab pieces turn red. Lower heat, add sugar, water and tomato sauce. Cover pan and simmer for about 5 minutes, stirring from time to time.

NONYA

SOTONG GAREM ASAM
SQUID IN TAMARIND SAUCE

250 g (8 oz) small squid (*sotong*) not
   more than 8 cm (3 in) long
2 heaped tablespoons dried tamarind
½ cup warm water
¼ teaspoon salt
2 tablespoons oil

Wash the squid and remove the reddish-brown skin but leave the heads intact.

Soak the tamarind in warm water for about 5 minutes then squeeze with the fingers and strain through a sieve. Mix in salt, then rub the squid with this liquid.

Just before cooking, pierce the black sacs just behind the eyes of the squid with a skewer. Heat a *kuali* without any oil and put in the squid. Cook over medium heat until all the liquid has come out of the squid and evaporated. Turn the squid over once or twice during this process. Add the oil and fry the squid for 1 minute, then serve.

MALAY

SAMBAL SOTONG
CHILLI-FRIED SQUID

250 g (8 oz) squid (*sotong*)
1 teaspoon dried shrimp paste (*blacan*)
6 dried red chillies, soaked
1 tablespoon oil
1 medium red or brown onion, finely
   sliced
¼ cup tamarind water (see page 63)
½ teaspoon salt
1-2 teaspoons palm sugar (*gula Melaka*)
   or brown sugar
1 stalk lemon grass (*serai*), bruised, or
   substitute

Wash the squid and peel off the reddish-brown skin. Discard transparent spine. Cut out black sac just behind the eyes and discard. Cut the body of the squid into 4 cm (1½ in) squares and lightly score a diamond pattern with the point of a sharp knife.

Grind the dried shrimp paste and chillies. Heat oil and gently fry sliced onion until soft. Add pounded ingredients and fry a further 3-4 minutes, stirring frequently. Put in tamarind water, salt, sugar and lemon grass and simmer for 3-4 minutes. Add squid and cook, uncovered, for 3-5 minutes. Do not overcook the squid or it will become tough.

MALAY

SOTONG BERISI SAMBAL
SQUID WITH SPICY STUFFING

6-8 medium squid (*sotong*)
125 g (4 oz) peeled raw prawns
1 dried red chilli, soaked
2 shallots (*bawang merah*) or ¼ medium
    red or brown onion
1 tablespoon oil

Gravy:
½ teaspoon dried shrimp paste (*blacan*)
6 dried red chillies, soaked
2 slices *lengkuas* or substitute
6-8 shallots (*bawang merah*) or 1
    medium red or brown onion
1 clove garlic
2 tablespoons oil
¼ cup tamarind water (see page 63)
1 stalk lemon grass (*serai*), bruised, or
    substitute
1 cup thick coconut milk (see page 44)
½ teaspoon salt

Wash the squid and peel off the reddish-brown skin. Discard the transparent spine but keep the head. Grind the chilli and shallots, then fry gently in oil for a couple of minutes. Add the prawns and fry, stirring frequently, for 3-4 minutes. Divide the fried mixture and stuff into each of the cleaned squid. Put the heads back on the top of each squid and fasten with a toothpick. You may need to make holes for the toothpick with a skewer or you'll finish up breaking a lot of toothpicks before getting them to penetrate the squid.

To make gravy, grind dried shrimp paste, soaked dried chillies, *lengkuas*, shallots and garlic, then fry gently in oil for 3-4 minutes. Add the tamarind water, lemon grass, coconut milk and salt and simmer, stirring constantly, until the gravy thickens. Put in the stuffed squid and simmer gently, with the *kuali* or pan uncovered, for about 5 minutes until the squid are cooked.

CHINESE

YEE SANG
CANTONESE NEW YEAR SALAD

150 g (5 oz) fish fillets (*ikan parang* or
    other herring, if possible)
250 g (8 oz) carrot
125 g (4 oz) giant white radish (*lobak*)
125 g (4 oz) sweet potato
3-4 fragrant lime leaves (*daun limau
    perut*) or young citrus leaves
3 thin slices fresh ginger, finely shredded
1 tablespoon preserved pickled red
    ginger, finely shredded
1 tablespoon candied melon rind or
    orange peel
2 heaped tablespoons shredded mixed
    pickles: leeks (*kew tow*), green
    papaya (*kwa yeng*) and melon
    (*kat peng*)

Sauce:
2 teaspoons sugar
¼ teaspoon five-spice powder
dash monosodium glutamate
½ teaspoon salt
1½ tablespoons Chinese lime juice
    (*limau kesturi*), or lime or lemon juice
2 tablespoons dry-roasted crushed
    peanuts
2 teaspoons lightly toasted sesame seeds

This unusual salad, which contains raw fish — an ingredient more commonly associated with Japanese rather than Chinese food — is traditionally eaten between the seventh and fifteenth days of the New Year. It makes a light, refreshing change from the rich food normally over-indulged in during New Year feasting, but is excellent at any time of the year. Any Cantonese provision shop should be able to give you the correct pickle mixture if you explain that it is for yee sang.

Rinse fish fillets in salty water, then hang to dry for about 4 hours. Chill until firm, then cut into very thin slices. Grate carrot, white radish and sweet potato into long, very thin shreds (less than half the thickness of a matchstick), then mix with shredded lime leaves. Put onto a plate with all other salad ingredients, including fish.

It is considered essential for good luck in the coming year for everyone eating the salad to help stir it, so final preparation is done at the table. Have all the individual sauce items ready, then put first five ingredients into a large bowl or deep platter. Stir to dissolve, then put in peanuts and sesame seeds, and add the salad ingredients a little at a time. Everyone should help stir the salad with his or her chopsticks. Serve immediately after mixing.

CHINESE

FISH IN TAUCHEO SAUCE (picture opposite)

500 g (1 lb) white fish fillets or steaks
½ cup oil
2 slices fresh ginger
1 clove garlic
1 fresh red chilli, seeds removed
1 medium red or brown onion, sliced
2 teaspoons salted soya beans (taucheo),
    lightly pounded
1 teaspoon sugar
1 teaspoon light soya sauce
½ cup water
¼ teaspoon salt

Dry fish thoroughly. Heat oil in a *kuali* until very hot and fry fish, a few pieces at a time, for just 1 minute on each side. Remove and drain. Pour off all but 1 tablespoon of oil.

Pound ginger, garlic and chilli together. Heat oil and fry sliced onion for 2 minutes, then add pounded mixture and stir fry for 2-3 minutes, taking care not to let it turn brown. Add soya beans and stir-fry for 1 minute. Put in sugar, soya sauce, water and salt and simmer for 2 minutes. Add fish and simmer gently until cooked, turning from time to time. The liquid should be reduced to just a couple of tablespoonsful of thick gravy.

CHINESE

FRIED FISH WITH HOT SWEET SOUR SAUCE

Sauce:
4-6 fresh red chillies
4 cloves garlic
3 slices fresh ginger
2 tablespoons oil
4 large ripe tomatoes, skinned and
    chopped
2 tablespoons tomato sauce
½ cup water
2 tablespoons vinegar
2 tablespoons light soya sauce
2 tablespoons sugar
1 teaspoon salt
2 heaped teaspoons cornflour
2 tablespoons water

500 g (1 lb) white fish fillets
salt and pepper
1 egg, lightly beaten
3 tablespoons plain flour
oil for deep frying
fresh coriander leaves to garnish

Chinese sweet and sour sauce has long been a universal favourite. This version reflects its Singapore origins with the addition of hot red chillies.

First prepare the sauce. Pound the chillies, garlic and ginger together until fine. Heat oil in a saucepan and gently fry the pounded mixture for 3-4 minutes. Add the tomatoes and cook gently, stirring frequently, until they are reduced to a pulp. Add all other ingredients except cornflour and water and bring gently to the boil. Simmer for a couple of minutes, then thicken with cornflour mixed with water.

Dry the fish fillets. Sprinkle with salt and pepper, dip in egg then in flour. Shake off excess flour and fry in plenty of hot oil. Serve fish with sauce poured over and garnish with coriander.

CHINESE

FISH BALLS

500 g (1 lb) soft-fleshed white fish fillets
    such as *ikan parang* (wolf herring),
    ikan tenggiri (Spanish mackerel) or, if
    these fish not available, bream or
    snapper
½ teaspoon salt
4-6 tablespoons cold water
pinch monosodium glutamate
white pepper
1 teaspoon cornflour

Home-made fish balls are infinitely superior to the commercial variety, which contain too much flour. If you have a blender or food processor, they can be made in just a few minutes.

Holding the fish fillets firmly at one end, scrape with a spoon to remove the flesh from the skin. Put flesh through a mincer or chop finely with a cleaver. Mix salt and water. Pound the fish flesh, a little at a time, in a mortar, adding salty water from time to time until the flesh is firm and smooth. Add all other ingredients and mix thoroughly.

If using a food processor, put 2.5 cm (1 in) cubes of fish (skin and bones discarded) in the machine. Process until finely mashed. Add salt, monosodium glutamate, pepper, cornflour

Fish in taucheo sauce (recipe this page).

and 4 tablespoons water and mix until well blended.

To shape the fish balls, take a handful of the mixture and squeeze the flesh through the thumb and forefinger, scraping a sizeable lump off with a spoon — the fish balls should be around 2 cm (¾ in) in diameter. Keep the fish balls in salted water (1 teaspoon for every 2 cups cold water) until required.

The fish-ball mixture can also be stuffed into fresh red or green chillies, slit on one side, or into hollowed slices of bitter gourd (peria) or marrow for use in soup or steamboat.

STEAMED WHOLE FISH (picture page 141)

1 large or 2 small pomfret (bawal puteh) weighing total of 500 g (1 lb), or flounder, sole, John Dory or plaice
1 teaspoon salt
¼ teaspoon monosodium glutamate
¼ teaspoon sugar
white pepper
4 cm (1½ in) fresh ginger, finely shredded lengthwise
2 spring onions, finely chopped
2 dried black mushrooms, soaked and shredded
2 teaspoons melted lard, chicken fat or oil

Gravy:
about ½ cup stock or water
2 teaspoons peanut oil
¼ teaspoon sugar
¼ teaspoon salt
½ teaspoon sesame oil
1 teaspoon oyster sauce
white pepper
1 fresh red chilli, shredded
fresh coriander leaves

Clean fish and make two diagonal cuts on both sides. Rub with salt, monosodium glutamate, sugar and pepper. Leave to stand for 15 minutes.

Shred ginger and scatter half of it on a deep plate. Put seasoned fish on top. Cover with remaining ginger, spring onions, dried mushrooms and melted lard. Steam for 10-15 minutes. Test fish with a skewer to make sure it is cooked.

To make gravy, pour liquid from the plate in which the fish was steamed and add sufficient stock or water to make ½ cup. Heat peanut oil in a saucepan and add stock and all other ingredients. Simmer for a minute.

Put fish on a large serving platter, decorate with coriander and chilli. Sprinkle liberally with pepper and pour the gravy over.

GULAI IKAN PENANG
SOUR HOT FISH STEW

500 g (1 lb) small pomfret (bawal puteh) or any white fish fillets or steaks
2 stalks lemon grass (serai)
1 cm (½ in) fresh turmeric (kunyit) or ½ teaspoon turmeric powder
2.5 cm (1 in) lengkuas
10-15 dried red chillies, soaked
15-20 shallots (bawang merah) or 2 medium red or brown onions
½ teaspoon dried shrimp paste (blacan)
2 tablespoons oil
1 tablespoon tamarind
3 cups warm water
2-3 teaspoons sugar
1 teaspoon salt

This is a lovely sour, fragrant curry that should be made only if you can obtain fresh turmeric, lemon grass and lengkuas — the flavour of dried substitutes cannot compare.

Clean the fish and, if using pomfret, cut in half crosswise, keeping the heads on. Grind the lemon grass, turmeric, lengkuas, chillies, shallots and dried shrimp paste until fine. Heat oil in a saucepan and fry the pounded ingredients gently for about 5 minutes.

Soak tamarind in warm water for 10 minutes. Squeeze and strain, discarding pulp and seeds, and add liquid to saucepan with sugar and salt. Simmer uncovered for 5 minutes then add the fish. Simmer for 5-10 minutes until fish is tender.

NONYA

IKAN MASAK KUAH PEDAS
FISH IN HOT GRAVY

20 shallots (*bawang merah*) or 2 large
    red or brown onions
3 fresh red chillies
4 slices *lengkuas* or substitute
4 candlenuts (*buah keras*) or
    macadamias
1 cm (½ in) fresh turmeric (*kunyit*) or
    ½ teaspoon turmeric powder
½ teaspoon dried shrimp paste (*blacan*),
    grilled
2 cups water
1 teaspoon salt
1 stalk lemon grass (*serai*), bruised, or
    substitute
4 slices *asam gelugor* or ¼ cup tamarind
    water (see page 63)
500 g (1 lb) fish cutlets or thick fillets

Sambal:
4-6 fresh red chillies
½ teaspoon dried shrimp paste (*blacan*),
    grilled
pinch sugar
pinch monosodium glutamate
1 tablespoon melted lard
3 Chinese limes (*limau kesturi*), halved,
    or 3 half-ripe kumquats, or 1 lime or
    lemon cut in wedges

Make the *sambal* (which is combined with the cooked fish immediately before serving) by pounding the chillies and shrimp paste and combining with sugar, monosodium glutamate and lard. Squeeze lime juice into *sambal*, and also put in the skins. Mix well and set aside.

Grind the shallots, chillies, *lengkuas*, candlenuts, turmeric and dried shrimp paste finely. Put together with water, salt, lemon grass and *asam gelugor* or tamarind water in a saucepan and simmer gently for 30 minutes. Remove the lemon grass and pieces of *asam gelugor* then put in fish and simmer until cooked. Add *sambal*, stirring in well, just before serving.

NONYA

OTAK OTAK
SPICY LEAF-WRAPPED FISH CAKES

1 kg (2 lb) soft white fish (*ikan tenggiri*
    or Spanish mackerel is ideal)
1 tablespoon coriander
3 medium red or brown onions, grated
12 dried red chillies, soaked
4 cloves garlic
1 cm (½ in) fresh turmeric (*kunyit*) or
    ½ teaspoon turmeric powder
6 candlenuts (*buah keras*) or
    macadamias
2 stalks lemon grass (*serai*) or substitute
1 cup thick coconut milk (see page 44)
2 teaspoons very finely chopped *daun
    kesom*
1 tablespoon salt
1 tablespoon sugar
½ teaspoon white pepper
pieces of banana leaf or aluminium foil,
    15 cm (6 in) square

Whenever I went to the old Orchard Road Market in Singapore I used to look for the elderly Baba who sold these little leaf-wrapped packages of grilled fish paste seasoned with spice and chilli. Although otak otak *can be served with rice or even spread on bread or crackers, I always ate it straight from the package, then and there, in the market or back-lane coffee shops frequented by that hawker.*

Otak otak *can be prepared well in advance if you are having a barbecue, needing only a last-minute grilling, or they can be cooked and taken cold on a picnic.*

Scrape the fish flesh from the bones and skin with a spoon, then chop it very finely with a cleaver to make a paste. If you have a blender or food processor, cut skinned fish into 2.5 cm (1 in) cubes and blend until it becomes a paste.

Dry-roast and grind the coriander. Grind the onions, chillies, garlic, turmeric, candlenuts and lemon grass. Mix coriander and other ground ingredients with the fish, then gradually add the coconut milk, beating all the time, until it is absorbed. Add chopped leaves, salt, sugar and pepper.

Traditionally, *otak otak* is cooked in overlapping leaves of coconut palm, but it is easier to use banana leaf or, if that is not available, foil. Dip the pieces of banana leaf into boiling water for a minute or two to soften, then dry. Put about 2 heaped tablespoons of the fish mixture onto a piece of banana leaf and fold up into a packet. Fasten with toothpicks. Repeat until all the mixture is used. Grill over charcoal for about 5 minutes on either side.

MALAY

GULAI IKAN
FISH CURRY

500 g (1 lb) fish cutlets or thick fillets
1 teaspoon coriander
½ teaspoon cummin
8 shallots (*bawang merah*) or 1 medium red or brown onion
1 clove garlic
6-8 fresh red chillies
3 slices fresh ginger
5 slices *lengkuas* or substitute
2 cm (¾ in) fresh turmeric (*kunyit*) or 1 teaspoon turmeric powder
¾ teaspoon dried shrimp paste (*blacan*)
2 tablespoons oil
1 stalk lemon grass (*serai*), bruised, or substitute
1½ cups thin coconut milk (see page 44)
1 teaspoon salt
1 teaspoon sugar
¼ cup tamarind water (see page 63)
½ cup thick coconut milk (see page 44)

Unlike gulai ikan Penang, *this recipe requires coconut milk and dried spices.*

Wash and dry fish and set aside.

Grind coriander and cummin until fine. Grind together the shallots, garlic, chillies, ginger, *lengkuas*, turmeric and dried shrimp paste. Heat oil and gently fry all the ground ingredients for 2-3 minutes. Add the lemon grass and pour in thin coconut milk, a little at a time. Add salt and sugar. Simmer for 3-5 minutes, stirring frequently. Put in the tamarind water, stir, then add the fish and simmer gently, uncovered, until the fish is cooked. Add thick coconut milk and heat for 2-3 minutes.

MALAY

IKAN ASAM PEDAS
SOUR HOT FISH CURRY

8-12 dried red chillies, soaked
2 slices fresh ginger
6-8 shallots (*bawang merah*) or 1 medium red or brown onion
3 cloves garlic
½ teaspoon dried shrimp paste (*blacan*)
500 g (1 lb) fish cutlets about 2 cm (¾ in) thick; use Spanish mackerel (*ikan tenggiri*), flathead, tailor or similar fish
½ teaspoon salt
½ teaspoon turmeric powder
½ cup oil
1 large red or brown onion, sliced
¼ cup tamarind water (see page 63)
½ cup water
extra salt to taste
pinch sugar

Grind dried chillies, ginger, shallots, garlic and dried shrimp paste until fine, then set aside. Dry the fish cutlets and rub with salt and turmeric. Heat oil in a *kuali* until quite hot and fry the fish for a couple of minutes on either side until golden. Drain and keep aside.

Pour out all but 1 tablespoon of the oil and gently fry sliced onion until golden. Add ground ingredients to the fried onion and cook gently, stirring frequently, for 2-3 minutes. Pour in tamarind water and plain water, and simmer for 1 minute. Add salt and sugar to taste, then put in fried fish and continue cooking for another few minutes until fish is cooked through.

Steamed whole fish (recipe page 138).

MALAY

IKAN PANGGANG
BARBECUED WHOLE FISH

1 whole fish, about 1 kg (2 lb), such as
  sea perch, snapper, bream or grouper
  (*ikan merah* or *ikan kerapu*)
1 medium red or brown onion
1 clove garlic
1 slice *lengkuas* or substitute
2 stalks lemon grass (*serai*) or substitute
1-2 teaspoons chilli powder
4 tablespoons oil
½ cup thick coconut milk (see page 44)
juice of 1 Chinese lime (*limau kesturi*) or
  ½ lemon
1 teaspoon salt
1 teaspoon sugar
pinch turmeric powder
1 fragrant lime leaf (*daun limau perut*)
  or young citrus leaf (optional)

Although the fish can be cooked under a griller, it is infinitely better — and more authentic — if barbecued.

Clean and scale the fish. Pound the onion, garlic, *lengkuas*, and lemon grass until fine then mix in the chilli powder. Rub about ⅓ of this mixture over the fish, inside and out, and leave to stand while preparing the sauce.

Heat oil and gently fry the remaining pounded mixture for 3-5 minutes. Add coconut milk and all other ingredients and cook, stirring constantly, until the sauce thickens.

Cook the fish on a greased grill over a charcoal fire, basting frequently with the sauce. Serve on a platter with the remaining sauce poured over.

MALAY

IKAN MOOLIE
FISH IN COCONUT MILK

6-8 shallots (*bawang merah*) or 1
  medium red or brown onion
3 fresh red chillies
1 tablespoon oil
1 cup thin coconut milk (see page 44)
½ teaspoon turmeric powder
1 stalk lemon grass (*serai*), bruised, or
  substitute
1 slice *asam gelugor* or ¼ cup tamarind
  water (see page 63)
½ teaspoon salt
½ cup thick coconut milk (see page 44)

The correct Malay name for this dish is ikan lemak *(fish cooked in coconut milk); however, it is almost identical to the Indian fish* moolie *and is more commonly known by this name in Singapore. Regardless of the name, it is a mild, easy-to-make dish that is really delicious.*

Pound the shallots and chillies. Heat oil in a saucepan or *kuali* and gently fry pounded mixture for 3-4 minutes. Add the thin coconut milk, turmeric, lemon grass and *asam gelugor* or tamarind water, and bring slowly to the boil, stirring constantly. Simmer for a couple of minutes, then add fish and salt and cook gently until fish is done. Add the thick coconut milk. Stir carefully over low heat until the gravy thickens.

MALAY

IKAN GORENG
FRIED FISH

500 g (1 lb) fish steaks or fillets
1 tablespoon dried tamarind
½ cup warm water
1 teaspoon salt
½ teaspoon turmeric powder
oil for deep frying

A very simple but tasty way of preparing fish. Malay cooks usually soak fish briefly in tamarind water before using it to eliminate any 'fishy' smell.

Rinse fish and pat dry. Soak tamarind in warm water for 5 minutes, then mix with the fingers; do not strain liquid. Put fish in liquid. Leave to soak for about 2-3 minutes, turn pieces of fish, and soak another 2-3 minutes. Remove from liquid and dry thoroughly.

Mix salt and turmeric together and rub over the pieces of fish. Heat plenty of oil in a *kuali* or deep frying pan. When very hot, fry fish until cooked. Drain and serve with *sambal blacan* (recipe page 182).

MALAY

SAMBAL IKAN
SMALL FRIED FISH WITH SAMBAL STUFFING

6 small fish weighing about 125 g (4 oz)
    each; use *ikan selar* (horse mackerel),
    ikan kembong, mackerel or yellowtail
4 shallots (*bawang merah*) or ½ medium
    red or brown onion
4 fresh red chillies
1 slice *lengkuas* or substitute
1 clove garlic
¼ teaspoon dried shrimp paste (*blacan*)
4 candlenuts (*buah keras*) or
    macadamias
1 stalk lemon grass (*serai*) or substitute
1½ tablespoons oil
½ teaspoon sugar
½ teaspoon salt
extra oil for frying fish

Wash, clean and dry the fish. Leave whole, but slit on either side of the backbone making a pocket on each side.

Grind the shallots, chillies, *lengkuas*, garlic, dried shrimp paste, candlenuts and lemon grass until fine. Heat 1½ tablespoons oil and fry the ground ingredients for 2-3 minutes. Mix in sugar and salt. Divide the fried mixture into six and stuff into the pockets along the backbone of each fish.

Heat oil and fry the fish until cooked, turning to make sure each side is golden.

MALAY

TINNED TUNA SAMBAL

1 tin (about 250 g or 8 oz) tuna chunks
4-6 fresh red chillies
6 shallots (*bawang merah*) or 1 small red
    or brown onion
2 stalks lemon grass (*serai*) or substitute
4 candlenuts (*buah keras*) or
    macadamias
2 tablespoons oil
1 cup coconut milk (see page 44)
3 fragrant lime leaves (*daun limau perut*)
    or young citrus leaves
1-2 teaspoons lime or lemon juice
salt to taste

Drain oil from tuna. Put tuna in a bowl and set aside. Pound or grind chillies, shallots, lemon grass and candlenuts together to a fine paste. Heat oil in a *kuali* or saucepan and gently fry the ground ingredients, stirring from time to time, for 5 minutes. Add coconut milk and lime leaves. Bring to the boil, stirring constantly, then add tuna. Simmer gently for about 3 minutes, then add lime juice and salt. Serve with rice.

INDIAN

FISH FRIED IN BATTER

¾ cup chickpea flour (*besan*)
2 heaped teaspoons *garam masala* (see
    glossary)
½-1 teaspoon chilli powder
½ teaspoon salt
¾ cup water
1 tablespoon oil
1 egg white
500 g (1 lb) white fish fillets, skinned
1 teaspoon salt
1 tablespoon lime or lemon juice
oil for deep frying
1 fresh green chilli, sliced
raw onion rings

Mix the chickpea flour, *garam masala*, chilli powder and salt, then gradually add water. Leave to stand for 30 minutes. Beat in 1 tablespoon oil for a couple of minutes. Whip the egg white, then fold into the batter.

Rub fish with salt and lime juice and leave to stand 15 minutes. Dry the fish, then dip into batter and deep fry in plenty of hot oil until golden. Serve garnished with onion rings and chilli. Good with mango or fresh mint chutney.

FISH

INDIAN

FISH CUTLETS

375 g (12 oz) steamed fresh fish, or
   tinned fish
1 tablespoon oil
1 medium red or brown onion, finely
   chopped
1 cm (½ in) fresh ginger, very finely
   chopped
1-2 fresh green chillies, very finely
   chopped
500 g (1 lb) potatoes, boiled and mashed
½ teaspoon turmeric powder
1 teaspoon salt
½ teaspoon white pepper
2 eggs
1 teaspoon lime or lemon juice
1 tablespoon finely chopped fresh
   coriander leaves
1½ cups fine dried breadcrumbs
oil for shallow frying

These fish cakes — which are always called 'cutlets' in Singapore — are best made with a strongly flavoured fish such as Spanish mackerel (ikan tenggiri). Tinned fish such as tuna, mackerel or snook may be used instead of fresh fish.

Remove bones from fish, flake, and set aside. Heat oil and gently fry onion, ginger and chillies until soft but not browned. Combine fish, fried ingredients, potato turmeric, salt, pepper, 1 egg, lime juice and coriander leaves and mix well. Set aside until cold.

Shape fish mixture into balls about 5 cm (2 in) in diameter, then flatten into circles. Beat the remaining egg, then dip fish mixture into egg and breadcrumbs to coat. If possible, leave in the refrigerator for 30 minutes before frying in hot oil, a few moments on either side, until cutlets are golden brown.

INDIAN

FISH-HEAD CURRY

1 large fish head weighing 1.25-1.5 kg
   (2½-3 lb) — use red bream, snapper
   or similar fish
4 teaspoons salt
4 heaped tablespoons dried tamarind
1 cup warm water
4 tablespoons oil
1 teaspoon brown mustard seed
5 cups thin coconut milk (see page 44)
1½ tablespoons sugar
¼ teaspoon monosodium glutamate
3-4 sprigs curry leaves (karuvapillai)
2 medium red or brown onions,
   quartered
3 medium tomatoes, quartered
4-6 small okra, cut in 5 cm (2 in) lengths

Chilli paste:
15-20 dried red chillies, soaked
8-10 shallots (bawang merah) or 2 small
   red or brown onions
3 cloves garlic
4 cm (1½ in) piece fresh ginger

Spice paste:
2 tablespoons coriander
1 tablespoon cummin
1 tablespoon fennel
½ teaspoon fenugreek
1 teaspoon white peppercorns
1 teaspoon turmeric powder

Those of you who thought fish heads were good only for fish stock or the family cat may be surprised to learn that this part of the fish is very highly regarded in Singapore. Taste fish-head curry and you'll know why!

Rinse the fish head, then rub with 2 teaspoons salt and stand in the refrigerator while preparing other ingredients.

Grind together all the chilli paste ingredients, adding a little of the oil if using a food processor or electric blender. Set aside. Heat all the spice paste ingredients, except for turmeric, in a dry pan for 3-4 minutes, then grind to a fine powder. Add the turmeric and sufficient water to make a stiff paste. Set aside. Mix tamarind with warm water, stand for 10 minutes, then squeeze and strain to obtain tamarind water. Discard seeds and skin.

Heat oil in a large pan and fry brown mustard seed until it starts to pop, then add the chilli paste and fry gently for 3-4 minutes, stirring from time to time. Add the spice paste and continue frying gently for another 2-3 minutes. Add the coconut milk, a little at a time, then put in the tamarind water, sugar, monosodium glutamate, salt, curry leaves and onions. Bring to the boil, stirring all the time, then simmer uncovered for 5 minutes.

Rinse the fish head and add to the pan together with tomatoes and okra. Simmer for 10-15 minutes until the fish is tender. Serve with plenty of white rice.

INDIAN

SOUTHERN INDIAN FISH CURRY

2 tablespoons oil
½ teaspoon fenugreek
4 shallots (*bawang merah*), or ½
    medium red or brown onion, finely
    sliced
2 slices fresh ginger, very finely chopped
1-2 cloves garlic, very finely chopped
1-2 small eggplants, quartered
    lengthwise then cut in half crosswise
3 heaped tablespoons fish curry powder
    (see page 189)
½-1 teaspoon chilli powder
2 sprigs curry leaves (*karuvapillai*)
1-2 tomatoes, quartered
1 teaspoon salt
4 small okra (ladies' fingers)
¾ cup water
¼ cup tamarind water (see page 63)
500 g (1 lb) fish fillets or cutlets
1 cup coconut milk (see page 44)

Heat oil and gently fry fenugreek seed for 30 seconds. Add shallots, ginger and garlic and fry, stirring frequently, for 2-3 minutes. Add eggplant and fry for 2 minutes.

Mix fish curry powder and chilli powder to a stiff paste with a little cold water while eggplant is frying. Add spice paste and curry leaves to the pan and fry for a couple of minutes. Put in tomatoes, salt, whole okra and water. Bring to the boil, add tamarind water and simmer until the vegetables are half-cooked.

Add coconut milk, Stir and bring to the boil, then put in fish and simmer gently until it is cooked and the gravy thickens.

EURASIAN

GUIZADO DE PEIXE
PORTUGUESE-STYLE FISH STEW

6 ripe tomatoes, peeled and chopped
1-2 medium red or brown onions, sliced
4-6 fresh green chillies, sliced
1 cup water
1 tablespoon tomato paste
1 tablespoon vinegar or lime juice
1 teaspoon salt
60 g (2 oz) butter
500 g (1 lb) fish steaks (such as *ikan
    tenggiri* or Spanish mackerel)

Put all ingredients except fish into an earthenware or other casserole. Bring to the boil and simmer for 5 minutes. Add the fish and continue cooking, uncovered, until the fish is tender and the gravy somewhat thickened. Serve with white rice.

Poultry

Until relatively recently, poultry was quite inexpensive in Singapore, and certainly cheaper than good quality meat. Even though prices have risen, chicken is still a firm favourite with all Singaporeans, while duck is a 'must' for all Chinese feasts.

Frozen chicken is very rarely used by Singaporeans. Although it is acceptable for Malay and Indian curries, fresh chicken must be used for Chinese dishes. When you become accustomed to the flavour and texture of fresh chicken, you'll agree that it's well worth the trouble of hunting it down. Many Singaporeans (my next-door neighbour included) even raise their own poultry specially for the kitchen; after being given the home-grown product to try ('no awful hormones added,' my neighbour reassured me), I had to agree that it was perfection.

To cut chicken, a heavy Chinese cleaver is essential (most Chinese stores overseas stock them). For curry, chicken is usually cut the following way: remove the legs and cut each in two at the joint; remove the wings and cut each in two at the joint; cut the breast portion in half lengthwise, then into two pieces crosswise; cut the back into two or three pieces crosswise.

For Chinese dishes, chicken is cut in a similar fashion, although in smaller pieces so that they do not need further cutting before being eaten.

CHINESE

SALT-BAKED CHICKEN (picture opposite)

1 fresh chicken, weighing about 1.2 kg (2½ lb)
2 teaspoons ginger juice (see page 58)
2 teaspoons Chinese rice wine or dry sherry
2 teaspoons peanut oil
3 spring onions, including green tops, chopped
4 large sheets greaseproof paper
3 kg (6 lb) coarse salt

Rub inside of chicken with ginger juice and rice wine, then rub the skin with oil. Stuff spring onion inside the chicken and wrap it with two layers of greaseproof paper (make sure you are greaseproof paper, not the shiny waxed-surface paper).

Heat salt in a *kuali* for about 10 minutes until very hot. Remove half the salt. Bury chicken breast-side down in remaining salt, then completely cover with the salt just removed. Cover the *kuali* and cook over very low heat for 1 hour. Alternatively, cook chicken buried in salt in a covered casserole in a moderate oven for 1 hour.

Remove chicken from salt, discard wrapping paper, and cut up. Put on a serving dish. Serve with Chinese peanut-oil sauce (recipe page 183).

Salt-baked chicken (recipe this page).

HAINANESE CHICKEN RICE

1 whole fresh chicken, weighing about
    1 kg (2 lb)
1 teaspoon Chinese rice wine or dry
    sherry
1½ tablespoons light soya sauce
2 slices fresh ginger
1 clove garlic, slightly bruised
1 spring onion, chopped
1 teaspoon sesame oil
½ teaspoon salt

The chicken for this dish must be fresh. Although a very simple recipe, the result is excellent.

Rub chicken inside with rice wine and ½ tablespoon light soya sauce, and stuff with ginger, garlic and spring onion. Bring a saucepanful of water to the boil, put in the chicken, and leave the pan on the stove but turn off the heat. Leave to stand for 1 hour.

After the first 5 minutes of standing, lift up chicken, drain the water from the stomach cavity, and put chicken back in the pan. Repeat this process 2 or 3 times during the cooking period to make sure the chicken cooks inside as well as outside. After 30 minutes, turn on the heat to bring the water almost to boiling point, then turn heat off. The chicken, never being allowed to boil, will be very tender and juicy. At the end of the hour, remove chicken and rub with remaining soya sauce combined with sesame oil and salt, then cut into bite-sized pieces.

Serve with rice cooked according to directions on page 85, but using chicken stock instead of water. Add a small lump of pork fat (about 2.5 cm or 1 in square) or 1 teaspoon oil to the water when boiling. A side-dish of chilli and ginger *sambal* (recipe page 181), a small plate of sliced fresh cucumber, and a bowl of chicken soup should also be served.

The stock in which the chicken has simmered can be reduced by boiling, or the flavour improved by the addition of a chicken stock cube. The soup is usually served with a few green vegetable leaves or a little chopped spring onion floating on top.

CRISPY SKIN CHICKEN

1 fresh chicken, weighing about 1.2 kg
    (2½ lb)
1 teaspoon salt
1 teaspoon five-spice powder
1 cup water
2 spring onions, roughly chopped
2 points star anise or 2.5 cm (1 in) stick
    cinnamon
2 tablespoons liquid honey
1 tablespoon white vinegar
oil for deep frying (optional)

To be strictly authentic, this chicken should be deep fried whole. If you are reluctant to use the large amount of oil required, the chicken can be roasted in the oven with perfectly satisfactory results.

Wipe chicken dry and rub inside and out with salt mixed with five-spice powder. Set aside for 15 minutes. Combine water, spring onion and star anise or cinnamon in a *kuali*, bring to the boil and simmer for 5 minutes. Remove spring onion and star anise or cinnamon and put inside the chicken. Add honey and vinegar to seasoned water, and stir to dissolve.

Hold the neck of the chicken firmly in one hand and use a ladle to baste the chicken with the liquid. Continue basting for at least 1 minute, pouring liquid down inside the cavity of the chicken as well as over the outside. Let excess liquid drip off the chicken, and then tie it securely and hang to dry in an airy place. Leave for 4-5 hours and make sure the chicken is thoroughly dry, as this is crucial to the crispness of the skin.

If you wish to fry the chicken, put about 8 cups of oil in a *kuali* and heat. When very hot, put in the chicken and cook, turning every few minutes, for about 10 minutes. Remove from oil, drain, chop with a cleaver. Serve with spiced salt (recipe page 188).

If preferred, roast the chicken in a hot oven (200°C/400°F /Gas No.6) for about 40 minutes.

CLAYPOT CHICKEN

½ chicken or 750 g (1½ lb) chicken
    pieces
4 dried black mushrooms, soaked and
    stems removed
1½ cups long-grain rice
2 cups water
4 thin slices fresh ginger
2 Chinese sausages (*lap cheong*), cut
    diagonally in 4 cm (1½ in) pieces

Marinade:
2 tablespoons oyster sauce
1 tablespoon thick black soya sauce
1 teaspoon Chinese rice wine or dry
    sherry
1 teaspoon cornflour
½ teaspoon sesame oil
½ teaspoon sugar
½ teaspoon salt

An example of typical Cantonese home cooking, this dish is easily prepared. It should be cooked in a special grey earthenware casserole (see page 68) which seems to give an extra flavour, although any casserole can be substituted.

Cut chicken into 12 pieces. Mix marinade ingredients together. Add chicken and mushrooms and leave to soak while preparing rice.

Wash rice thoroughly and put in a clay pot or other casserole. Add water, cover, and bring to the boil. Cook rapidly until all the water has evaporated and small 'craters' appear on the surface of the rice.

Take chicken and mushrooms out of the marinade and place together with ginger and pieces of sausage on the top of the rice. Cover clay pot securely and cook over very low heat for about 45 minutes, until chicken is tender. Serve directly from clay pot, together with a light soup (for example, chicken stock with a few pieces of green vegetable).

SPICED CHICKEN WINGS

1 kg (2 lb) chicken wings
1 tablespoon thick black soya sauce
1 tablespoon light soya sauce
4 cm (1½ in) fresh ginger, smashed
2-3 cloves garlic, smashed
1 tablespoon Chinese rice wine or dry
    sherry
1 tablespoon liquid honey
1 teaspoon five-spice powder

Chicken wings, so often ignored by Westerners, are regarded as a delicacy by the Chinese. Deep-frozen chicken wings are often sold in 2 kg (4 lb) bags; I find it convenient to marinate them all, then re-freeze them in smaller bags so that whenever I need something for a quick and easy meal, I just thaw out the spiced wings and grill or deep fry them.

Thaw chicken wings if deep-frozen. Mix all other ingredients together in a large bowl. Add chicken and marinate for at least 2 hours. The chicken wings can then be deep-frozen or brushed with oil and grilled, or, if preferred, deep fried in hot oil. Very good barbecued, too.

SILVER AND JADE CHICKEN

1 chicken, about 1 kg (2 lb)
5-6 cups chicken stock (see page 77)
4 slices fresh ginger
2 spring onions
3 slices raw ham (ham steaks) or canned
    Yunnan ham, 3 mm (⅛ in) thick
½ teaspoon light soya sauce
1 teaspoon cornflour
1 tablespoon chicken stock
250 g (8 oz) broccoli spears or Chinese
    broccoli (*kai lan*)
1 teaspoon oil

The appearance of this dish, with the white chicken and deep-pink ham surrounded by vivid green broccoli, gives it this poetic name. It is essential that fresh, not frozen, chicken be used.

Put 1 slice of ginger and 1 spring onion inside the chicken and put it into a pan just big enough to hold it. Pour over enough chicken stock to just cover the bird. Put in remaining ginger and spring onion and bring to the boil. Simmer for only 15 minutes, then turn off heat and allow chicken to stand in the liquid for 1 hour. This is sufficient to cook it through completely.

Cut ham into pieces 5 cm (2 in) by 2.5 cm (1 in). Measure ½ cup of the stock in which the chicken was cooked and bring to the boil in a saucepan with soya sauce. Thicken with cornflour

POULTRY

mixed with 1 tablespoon chicken stock.

Cut the chicken into bite-sized pieces, and remove bones but leave on skin. Arrange the chicken and ham in overlapping pieces on a deep serving dish. Pour over the thickened stock and cover dish with foil and keep warm in a heated oven. Alternatively, the dish can be placed in a steamer to keep warm.

Simmer the broccoli, until just tender, in a little of the stock with oil added. Arrange around the chicken and ham, and serve.

CHINESE

CHEE POW KAI
PAPER-WRAPPED CHICKEN

1 fresh chicken, weighing about 1.2 kg
  (2½ lb)
3 tablespoons light soya sauce
3 tablespoons Chinese rice wine or dry
  sherry
1 tablespoon ginger juice (see page 58)
2 teaspoons oyster sauce
½ teaspoon monosodium glutamate
½ teaspoon salt
½ teaspoon sugar
½ teaspoon sesame oil
20 pieces greaseproof paper, each 20 cm
  (8 in) square
oil for deep frying

This recipe was given to me by the Chia family, whose charming open-air pavilion, the Union Farm Eating House, in a semi-rural area of Singapore, specialises in this excellent dish.

Cut chicken into about 20 pieces. Mix all ingredients (except paper and oil for frying) and add chicken. Stir well and marinate the chicken for at least 2 hours, stirring from time to time.

Drain chicken pieces. Wrap each in a square of greaseproof paper (make sure you do not use the shiny waxed paper), tucking in the end envelope-style. Heat plenty of oil in a *kuali*. When it is very hot, fry the packets of chicken, a few at a time, for just 5 minutes. Stir the pieces and turn frequently while frying.

Serve chicken, still in paper wrapper, on a large platter. Each person unwraps his own pieces during the meal. Don't forget to provide finger bowls and a plate for the discarded paper.

CHINESE

DICED CHICKEN WITH DRIED CHILLIES (picture opposite)

500 g (1 lb) raw chicken breast
4 points star anise
10 black peppercorns
12 large dried red chillies
1 teaspoon sugar
1 teaspoon light soya sauce
½ teaspoon white vinegar
½ teaspoon Chinese rice wine or dry
  sherry
½ teaspoon monosodium glutamate
  (optional)
2 teaspoons cornflour
4 tablespoons water
6 tablespoons oil
1 clove garlic, smashed
1 slice fresh ginger, very finely chopped
2 spring onions, cut into 2.5 cm (1 in)
  lengths
few drops sesame oil

This recipe comes from the Golden Phoenix Restaurant, and is an excellent example of the delicious Szechuan food they serve. It is not, despite the presence of chillies, particularly hot.

Cut chicken into 1 cm (½ in) cubes. Pound or grind star anise and pepper until fine. Remove stalks from chillies, break into 4 cm (1½ in) lengths and shake to discard most of the seeds so that the chicken will not be too hot. Blend together sugar, soya sauce, vinegar, wine, monosodium glutamate, cornflour and water. Set aside.

Heat oil in a *kuali* until very hot. Fry chicken for 2 minutes, stirring frequently. Remove chicken from pan and pour off half the oil. Fry the chillies over high heat, stirring constantly until dark brown and crisp. Remove from the pan. Allow oil to cool a little then gently fry ground spices, garlic and ginger for 1 minute. Add blended mixture and spring onions and cook for 30 seconds. Put chicken and chillies back in *kuali* and stir over medium heat for about 1 minute until chicken is thoroughly coated with sauce. Sprinkle with sesame oil and serve immediately.

150

Diced chicken with dried chillies (recipe this page).

POULTRY

CHINESE

TEOCHEW SPICED DUCK

1 duck, weighing about 2 kg (4 lb)
2 teaspoons five-spice powder
½ teaspoon salt
4 tablespoons thick black soya sauce
2 tablespoons light soya sauce
5 slices *lengkuas* or substitute
2 tablespoons sugar
3 cups water
4 cloves garlic, skins left on, lightly
  bruised
2.5 cm (1 in) stick cinnamon

Remove fatty deposits from just inside the tail end of the duck. Wipe duck dry. Combine five-spice powder, salt, and both lots of soya sauce. Rub duck inside and out with the mixture and stand for 2 hours, turning occasionally and basting all over with the marinade. Stuff duck with slices of *lengkuas* just before cooking.

Put sugar in a *kuali* with a little water and cook until it turns golden brown. Add 3 cups water, garlic, cinnamon and the marinade from the duck. Put in duck, cover *kuali*, and simmer gently for about 1¼ hours until the duck is tender. Turn duck from time to time to ensure that it cooks evenly.

Cut duck into serving pieces when cool. Serve pieces at room temperature, arranged on a platter with some of the cooking liquid poured over. If liked, serve with individual sauce bowls containing a little very finely chopped garlic mixed with equal parts of water and white vinegar.

CHINESE

PEKING DUCK

1 fresh duck weighing about 2 kg (4 lb)
2½ cups water
3 tablespoons liquid honey
4 slices fresh ginger
2 points star anise
2 coriander seeds
22 spring onions
1 cucumber

Pancakes:
2 cups plain flour
about 1 cup boiling water
2 tablespoons sesame oil

Sauce:
3 tablespoons *hoisin* sauce
2 tablespoons water
1 teaspoon sesame oil
1 teaspoon sugar

An impressive meal to serve when entertaining. One duck, together with pancakes and garnishes, is adequate for 4-6 people; follow with a simple stir-fried vegetable and soup.

Wash and dry the duck inside and out, then hang to dry in a cool airy place for several hours. Put water in a *kuali* and add honey, ginger, star anise, coriander, and 2 of the spring onions, roughly chopped. Bring to the boil and simmer 5 minutes. Hold the duck by the neck over the *kuali* and use a ladle to baste it with the liquid, pouring it inside and outside the duck for at least 1 minute. Hang the duck up to drain and dry for at least 2 hours. Strain basting liquid, take out spices, ginger and onion, and keep to put inside duck when roasting.

While the duck is drying, prepare the pancakes. Sift flour into a bowl and add water gradually, Mix into a dough with a wooden spoon, then knead dough on a floured board for at least 5 minutes, until it is smooth. Cover with a damp cloth and leave for 15 minutes. Roll dough until it is about 5 mm (¼ in) thick, then cut into small discs about 8 cm (3 in) in diameter. Brush the tops of two discs with sesame oil, then place one piece on top of the other, greased sides facing. Roll carefully with a rolling pin until the pancake is about 15 cm (6 in) in diameter.

Cook the pancakes in a hot heavy ungreased pan for about 1 minute or until bubbles appear on the surface and brown spots form underneath. Turn and cook another minute on the other side. When the pancakes are starting to cool, separate slowly (the sesame oil makes the greased sides come apart easily). When all the pancakes are cooked, stack them up and wrap in foil. They can be placed in the oven to heat for about 10 minutes, just as the duck is finishing cooking.

To make the sauce, bring ingredients gently to the boil and simmer for a couple of minutes. Cool and put into individual sauce bowls.

Cut the remaining 20 spring onions into brushes. Cut each onion 10 cm (4 in) long, discarding green top. Make several cuts about 2.5 cm (1 in) long at both ends of the onion. Put in iced water and keep in the refrigerator until serving time, when the cut ends will have curled up. Peel and cut the cucumber into lengthwise strips about 1 cm (½ in) thick and 10 cm (4 in) long. Put in iced water in the refrigerator.

To cook the duck, first make sure it is absolutely dry. Stuff the inside with the reserved spices, ginger and onion, and place the duck, breast side up, on a rack in a roasting pan. Cook at 200°C/400°F/Gas No.6 for 1 hour.

To serve Peking duck, put bowls of sauce, pancakes, spring onion brushes and cucumber sticks on the table. Cut the duck up, putting the skin on one side of the plate and the flesh on the other, and serve. Each diner takes a pancake, uses the onion brush to smear the inside with sauce, puts in the onion, a cucumber stick, a piece of crisp skin and a piece of duck meat and rolls up the pancake.

The giblets and neck of the duck can be used to make duck and salted cabbage soup (recipe page 78). After carving the duck, add the carcass to the soup and simmer for a few minutes to add extra flavour.

NONYA

AYAM TEMPRA
CHICKEN COOKED WITH SOYA SAUCE AND LIME JUICE

1 fresh chicken, weighing about 1.2 kg
  (2½ lb), or 1 kg (2 lb) chicken pieces
4 tablespoons oil
4 medium red or brown onions, sliced
2-3 fresh red chillies, sliced
2 tablespoons sugar
4 tablespoons thick black soya sauce
½ teaspoon salt
4 tablespoons Chinese lime juice (*limau kesturi*) or lemon juice
1 cup water

If using whole chicken, cut into small pieces. Heat oil and gently fry sliced onion and chilli for 2 minutes, then add chicken and fry a further 10 minutes, stirring from time to time. Sprinkle sugar over chicken and fry for 1 minute, then add all other ingredients and simmer gently, uncovered, until the chicken is tender and the sauce has thickened.

NONYA

AYAM SIYOW
CHICKEN IN TAMARIND SAUCE

1 fresh chicken, weighing about 1.2 kg
  (2½ lb)
4 tablespoons oil

Marinade:
2 tablespoons coriander
6 tablespoons dried tamarind
2 cups warm water
3 tablespoons sugar
1½ tablespoons thick black soya sauce
2 teaspoons salt
1 teaspoon white pepper

This old Nonya dish was always prepared for the Chinese New Year period, when all markets and shops are closed. The tamarind acts as a preservative, so the marinated chicken can be kept for up to four days without refrigeration.

Cut chicken into quarters. To prepare marinade, gently roast the coriander seeds in a dry pan until fragrant. Pound or grind until fine. Combine tamarind with warm water and leave to stand for 10 minutes. Squeeze firmly with the fingers, and strain tamarind juice through a sieve, discarding seeds and skin. Add all other marinade ingredients and mix well. Put chicken in marinade and stand for at least 8 hours, turning pieces over from time to time.

To cook the chicken, put together with marinade into a *kuali* and simmer gently, uncovered, until chicken is tender. Remove chicken pieces and drain thoroughly. Continue simmering the marinade for a few more minutes until it is thick, then pour into a saucepan and keep warm. Clean out the *kuali*, put in a little oil and fry the chicken until brown all over. Cut chicken into smaller pieces and put in a serving dish, with the warm sauce poured over.

NONYA

AYAM LEMAK (picture opposite)
CHICKEN IN RICH COCONUT GRAVY

1 whole chicken, weighing about 1.2 kg (2½ lb)
1 cm (½ in) fresh turmeric (*kunyit*) or ½ teaspoon turmeric powder
5 cm (2 in) fresh ginger
16 shallots (*bawang merah*) or 2 medium red or brown onions
2 cloves garlic
3 stalks lemon grass (*serai*) or substitute
6-8 fresh red chillies
2 slices *lengkuas* or substitute
3 tablespoons oil
3 cups thick coconut milk (see page 44)
1 *pandan* leaf
1 teaspoon salt

Cut chicken into about 14 pieces. Pound the fresh turmeric to obtain juice, or mix turmeric powder with a little water to make a paste. Rub chicken with turmeric and set aside.

Grind ginger, shallots, garlic, lemon grass, chillies and *lengkuas* until fine. Heat oil in a large *kuali* or deep pan and gently fry the ground ingredients for about 5 minutes. Add the chicken pieces and fry for 5 minutes, stirring frequently so chicken is thoroughly coated with spices. Add the coconut milk, *pandan* leaf and salt. Stir constantly until the coconut milk comes to the boil, then simmer, uncovered, until the chicken is tender and gravy has thickened.

MALAY

OPOR AYAM
MILD CHICKEN CURRY

1 whole chicken, weighing about 1.5 kg (3 lb)
2½ cups thin coconut milk (see page 44)
1 stalk lemon grass (*serai*), bruised, or substitute
1 thick slice *lengkuas*, bruised, or substitute
2 *daun salam* or bay leaves
2 fragrant lime leaves (*daun limau perut*) or young citrus leaves
1 teaspoon palm sugar (*gula Melaka*) or brown sugar
1 teaspoon salt
½ cup thick coconut milk (see page 44)
lime or lemon juice
fried onion flakes (see page 188)

Spice paste:
3 teaspoons coriander
¾ teaspoon cummin
¼ teaspoon fennel
4 candlenuts (*buah keras*) or macadamias
8 shallots (*bawang merah*) or 1 medium red or brown onion
2 cloves garlic
1 cm (½ in) fresh ginger
½ teaspoon white pepper powder

This dish, which is Indonesian in origin, is ideal for people who do not like hot food, for it does not contain any chillies. Because the pale colour is an important feature of this dish, cook it in an enamel or earthenware pan so that the coconut milk will not discolour. Some Singapore cooks fry the spices first, while others leave out this step — I prefer not to fry them.

Cut chicken into about 14 pieces.

Prepare spice paste. Heat coriander, cummin and fennel in a dry pan for 2-3 minutes, then pound or grind finely. Add candlenuts, shallots, garlic and ginger and grind to make a paste. Mix in pepper.

Put spice paste in a pan and add thin coconut milk, a little at a time, stirring to mix well. Add lemon grass, *lengkuas*, leaves, sugar and salt. Simmer for a couple of minutes, then put in chicken pieces and cook, uncovered, until the chicken is tender. Add thick coconut milk and heat for 2-3 minutes. Just before serving, add lime or lemon juice to taste and garnish with fried onion flakes.

Ayam lemak (recipe this page), roti jala (recipe page 102) and sambal blacan (recipe page 182).

MALAY

AYAM KORMA
MILD CHICKEN CURRY

1 whole chicken, weighing about 1.2 kg
    (2½ lb)
2 tablespoons *ghee* or oil
3 medium red or brown onions, finely
    sliced
3 cloves garlic, finely chopped
2.5 m (1 in) fresh ginger, very finely
    chopped
2 tablespoons coriander
1 tablespoon cummin
2 teaspoons fennel
2 teaspoons white peppercorns
4 cloves
2.5 cm (1 in) stick cinnamon
½ teaspoon turmeric powder
1 teaspoon salt
2 cups thin coconut milk (see page 44)
½ cup thick coconut milk (see page 44)

Cut chicken in 12-14 pieces. Heat *ghee* or oil and fry onions, garlic and ginger until golden. Heat coriander, cummin, fennel and peppercorns in a dry pan, then grind until fine. Add to the fried ingredients, together with cloves, cinnamon and turmeric, and continue frying gently for 2-3 minutes. Add chicken and salt and cook, stirring constantly until chicken is well coated with spices. Add thin coconut milk and simmer, uncovered, until chicken is tender. Add thick coconut milk and heat for 2-3 minutes.

MALAY

GULAI AYAM
CHICKEN CURRY

1 whole chicken, weighing about 1.2 kg
    (2½ lb)
3 tablespoons oil
1½ cups thin coconut milk (see page 44)
2 stalks lemon grass (*serai*), bruised, or
    substitute
½ cup thick coconut milk (see page 44)

Spice paste:
12-15 shallots (*bawang merah*) or 2
    medium red or brown onions
8-12 dried red chilies, soaked
2.5 cm (1 in) fresh ginger
2 cloves garlic
4 candlenuts (*buah keras*) or
    macadamias
1 tablespoon coriander
2 teaspoons cummin
1 teaspoon fennel
2.5 cm (1 in) stick cinnamon
¼ teaspoon freshly grated nutmeg
½ teaspoon turmeric powder

Cut chicken into 12-14 pieces. Pound or grind shallots, chillies, ginger, garlic and candlenuts until fine, and set aside. Heat coriander, cummin, fennel and cinnamon in a dry pan, then grind together finely. Add nutmeg and turmeric and set dry spices aside.

Heat oil in a *kuali* and gently fry shallot and chilli paste for 3-4 minutes. Add ground dry spices and fry, stirring occasionally, for another 3 minutes. Put in chicken pieces and cook, stirring frequently, until chicken is well coated with spices. Add thin coconut milk, salt and lemon grass. Simmer uncovered, stirring from time to time, until chicken is tender and the gravy has thickened. Add thick coconut milk and heat for 2-3 minutes.

MALAY

CHICKEN CURRY CAPTAIN

1 kg (2 lb) chicken pieces
2-3 cloves garlic
1 teaspoon black peppercorns
1 cm (½ in) fresh turmeric (*kunyit*) or
   ½ teaspoon tumeric powder
1 teaspoon salt
1 cup thick coconut milk (see page 44)
fried onion flakes (see page 188)
fried garlic slices
1 fresh red chilli, sliced
1 small lime or ½ lemon

This is a very mild dish created for Western tastes, supposedly by a Chinese cook who told his captain that the evening meal was going to be 'Curry, Captain'.

Dry the chicken pieces. Grind the garlic, pepper and turmeric together, then mix with salt. Rub the paste into the chicken and allow to stand for about 15 minutes.

Put the coconut milk into a *kuali* and bring to the boil, stirring constantly. Add chicken and simmer uncovered, stirring from time to time, until the liquid has almost completely dried up.

Serve in a bowl, garnished with onion flakes, garlic and chilli. Squeeze over the lime or lemon juice.

MALAY

AYAM GORENG JAWA
JAVANESE FRIED CHICKEN

1 chicken, weighing about 1 kg (2 lb)
2 teaspoons coriander
1 teaspoon turmeric powder
1½ teaspoons salt
8 shallots (*bawang merah*) or 1 medium
   red or brown onion
1 clove garlic
1-2 fresh red chillies
2 slices *lengkuas* or substitute
1 stalk lemon grass (*serai*) or substitute
1½ cups coconut milk (see page 44)
1 teaspoon palm sugar (*gula Melaka*) or
   brown sugar

Cut the chicken into serving pieces. Grind the coriander and mix with turmeric and salt. Rub this mixture into the chicken and set it aside.

Grind the shallots, garlic, chillies, *lengkuas* and lemon grass in a mortar and pestle, or put them in a blender with a little of the coconut milk until finely ground.

Put the ground mixture, coconut milk and sugar into a *kuali* and bring to the boil, stirring constantly. Simmer for a couple of minutes then add the chicken and cook, uncovered, for 20-30 minutes until the chicken is tender and the sauce almost completely evaporated. It will be necessary to turn the chicken pieces as they cook to ensure even cooking. The chicken can be left in the *kuali* to soak in the remaining spicy liquid until just before it is required, or it can be kept in the refrigerator for a day.

To finish the chicken, heat plenty of oil in a *kuali* and deep fry the pieces, a few at a time, for 2-3 minutes until golden brown. Serve with a chilli *sambal* which has plenty of lime or lemon juice squeezed over.

MALAY

AYAM GORENG
FRIED CHICKEN

1 whole fresh chicken, weighing about
   1.2 kg (2½ lb), or 1 kg (2 lb) chicken
   pieces
2 teaspoons salt
2 teaspoons turmeric powder
oil for deep frying

One of the easiest yet nicest ways of cooking chicken.

If using a whole chicken, cut into about 10-12 pieces. Combine salt and turmeric and rub all over the chicken pieces. Leave aside for 5 minutes. Heat oil in a *kuali* and when very hot, deep fry the chicken, a few pieces at a time, for about 3-4 minutes. Allow cooked chicken pieces to drain. When all the chicken has been cooked, raise the heat and when oil is smoking hot, put back the chicken, a few pieces at a time, and cook for 1 minute until crisp and a rich golden brown. Drain and serve immediately with a chilli *sambal*.

MALAY

AYAM PANGGANG
SPICY BARBECUED CHICKEN

1 whole fresh chicken, weighing about 1.5 kg (3 lb)
8-10 shallots (*bawang merah*) or 1 medium red or brown onion
1 cm (½ in) fresh ginger
10 fresh red chillies
1 tablespoon coriander, freshly ground
1 teaspoon cummin, freshly ground
1½ cups thick coconut milk (see page 44)
1 stalk lemon grass (*serai*), bruised, or substitute
1 teaspoon salt
1 fragrant lime leaf (*daun limau perut*) or young citrus leaf (optional)
1 lime or lemon, quartered

Wash chicken, dry, and cut in half lengthwise. Grind together shallots, ginger and chillies, then mix in freshly ground spices. Rub this mixture into the chicken and let it stand while preparing gravy. Put coconut milk, lemon grass, salt and lime leaf into a *kuali* and bring to the boil, stirring constantly. Simmer for 2 minutes, then put in chicken halves and simmer uncovered, turning several times, until chicken is tender. The cooked chicken can be stored in a refrigerator for up to 24 hours before barbecueing.

Heat barbecue or grill, and oil the metal grid. Barbecue or grill the chicken halves for about 5 minutes on either side until golden brown. Squeeze over the lime or lemon juice when serving. Cut into smaller pieces before serving if desired.

INDIAN

TANDOORI CHICKEN (picture opposite)

1 fresh chicken, weighing about 1 kg (2 lb)
1 tablespoon melted *ghee* or butter

Marinade 1:
1 teaspoon salt
½ teaspoon turmeric powder
½ teaspoon chilli powder
¼ teaspoon white pepper powder
pinch cloves
1 teaspoon crushed garlic
1½ tablespoons lemon juice

Marinade 2:
4 tablespoons plain yoghurt
1 heaped tablespoon fresh coriander leaves, pounded
1 heaped tablespoon mint leaves, pounded
1 tablespoon cummin, finely ground
½ teaspoon salt
1 teaspoon crushed fresh ginger
1 teaspoon white vinegar
¼ teaspoon cinnamon powder
⅓ teaspoon cardamom powder
few drops orange food colouring (optional)

This dish gets its name from the clay oven or tandoor *in which the chicken should be cooked. A rotisserie or gas or electric oven will do a fairly good job, but I find the closest I can get to the flavour of a genuine tandoor-cooked chicken is to use a charcoal barbecue. This recipe was given to me by Wadhu Sakhrani, the charming owner of one of Singapore's best restaurants, the Omar Khayyam.*

Remove feet, head and skin from the chicken and make deep cuts in the thighs and breast. Combine all ingredients for Marinade 1 and rub well into the chicken. Leave in the refrigerator for about 3 hours.

Combine ingredients for Marinade 2 and rub evenly all over the chicken, making sure some of the marinade penetrates the slits. Leave in the refrigerator for at least 6 hours.

Brush barbecue grill with *ghee* or butter and cook chicken over hot coals, brushing from time to time. Cook until chicken is done and has turned a rich reddish-gold. If cooking chicken in a rotisserie or oven, roast for about 45 minutes at 200°C/400°F/ Gas No.6.

Serve chicken with tomato and cucumber salad, wedges of fresh lime or lemon, and mint chutney (recipe page 186).

Tandoori chicken (recipe this page), tomato and cucumber salad (recipe page 127), fresh mint chutney (recipe page 186) and naan (recipe page 101).

SOUTHERN INDIAN CHICKEN CURRY

1 whole chicken, weighing about 1.5 kg
    (3 lb), or 1.2 kg (2½ lb) chicken
    pieces
12-16 dried red chillies, soaked
2.5 cm (1 in) fresh ginger
2 cloves garlic
8 shallots (*bawang merah*) or 1 medium
    red or brown onion
2 tablespoons oil
2 teaspoons coriander, freshly ground
1 teaspoon cummin, freshly ground
pinch fenugreek
1 teaspoon turmeric powder
1½ cups thin coconut milk (see page 44)
2 sprigs curry leaves (*karuvapillai*)
1 stalk lemon grass (*serai*), bruised, or
    substitute
1 teaspoon salt
½ cup thick coconut milk (see page 44)
lime or lemon juice

Wash chicken, wipe dry, and cut into about 14 pieces. Grind or pound together chillies, ginger, garlic and shallots. Heat oil in a *kuali* or saucepan and gently fry the ground paste for 3 minutes. Add coriander, cummin, fenugreek seeds and turmeric and fry another 2 minutes. Put in chicken pieces and stir-fry for about 5 minutes until well coated with spice paste. Add thin coconut milk, curry leaves, lemon grass and salt. Simmer uncovered until chicken is tender, then add thick coconut milk and cook for another 2-3 minutes. Just before serving, add lime or lemon juice to taste.

MILD CHICKEN CURRY

1 medium chicken or 1.2 kg (2½ lb)
    chicken pieces
1 teaspoon turmeric powder
2 teaspoons *garam masala* (see glossary)
1 teaspoon chilli powder
1 teaspoon salt
2 tablespoons *ghee* or butter
1 medium onion, grated
2.5 cm (1 in) fresh ginger, very finely
    chopped
3 cloves garlic, very finely chopped
¼ teaspoon freshly ground black pepper
2.5 cm (1 in) cinnamon stick
3 whole cardamom pods, bruised
1 cup plain yoghurt
fresh coriander leaves

This north Indian dish is very easy to prepare, for it does not require freshly ground spices and uses yoghurt rather than coconut milk.

Cut chicken into serving pieces. Mix turmeric, *garam masala*, chilli powder and salt together and rub into chicken pieces. Set aside.

Heat *ghee* or butter and fry onion, ginger and garlic gently for 3-4 minutes. Add pepper, cinnamon and cardamom and fry for another 2 minutes. Add yoghurt, stir well and simmer for 2 minutes, then put in chicken pieces. Cover pan and cook gently until chicken is tender, stirring from time to time to prevent sticking. If there is still a lot of sauce left when chicken is cooked, remove lid and simmer to evaporate most of the sauce. Serve chicken garnished with fresh coriander leaves.

INDIAN

CHICKEN LIVER CURRY

500 g (1 lb) chicken livers, or mixture of
    liver and gizzards
1 cm (½ in) fresh ginger
2 cloves garlic
2 tablespoons *ghee* or oil
1 large onion, finely chopped
4 cm (1½ in) stick cinnamon
1 tablespoon meat curry powder (see
    page 189)
¼ - ½ teaspoon chilli powder
3 ripe tomatoes, peeled and chopped
2 tablespoons plain yoghurt
½ teaspoon salt

Wash chicken livers and cut in half. If using gizzard, cut in 5 mm (¼ in) slices.

Pound or grate ginger and garlic and set aside. Heat *ghee* in a pan and gently fry onion for 2-3 minutes. Add ginger and garlic and cook for another 2 minutes, stirring frequently. Put in cinnamon stick and fry for 1 minute. Mix curry and chilli powders together with enough water to make a stiff paste and add to pan. Fry for a couple of minutes, then add tomatoes and cook until slightly softened. Add yoghurt and simmer for 1 minute, then put in salt and gizzard (if using). Cover pan, and simmer for 10 minutes.

Finally, put in the chicken livers and simmer, with the pan covered, for 10 minutes. Serve with white rice.

SRI LANKAN

RICH CHICKEN CURRY

1 whole chicken, weighing about 1.2 kg
    (2½ lb)
2 teaspoons turmeric powder
2 teaspoons white vinegar
1 teaspoon salt
2 tablespoons *ghee* or oil
3 sprigs curry leaves (*karuvapillai*)
1 teaspoon brown mustard seed
1 large onion, finely sliced
2.5 cm (1 in) fresh ginger, finely
    chopped
3-4 cloves garlic, smashed and chopped
1 stalk lemon grass (*serai*), bruised, or
    substitute
3 cardamom pods, lightly crushed
2 teaspoons lime or lemon juice
1 cup evaporated milk
½ cup warm water
lime or lemon juice

Spices for roasting:
8-10 whole dried red chillies
2 teaspoons coriander
1 teaspoon cummin
½ teaspoon fennel
¼ teaspoon fenugreek

The curries of Sri Lanka (Ceylon) have a distinctively different flavour that is the result of roasting the spices until they are dark brown before grinding. Tinned evaporated milk soured with lime juice is often used instead of coconut milk by Sri Lankan and Indian cooks in Singapore.

Cut chicken into about 14 pieces. Combine turmeric, vinegar and salt, rub into chicken pieces, and set aside.

Put spices for roasting into a dry pan and cook over low heat, stirring frequently, until the spice seeds turn dark brown and the chillies have become crisp. Allow to cool, then grind to a powder with a coffee grinder or mortar and pestle. Set aside.

Heat *ghee* or oil in a earthenware pot or casserole and fry curry leaves and mustard seed until seeds begin to pop. Add onion, ginger and garlic and cook gently until golden. Put in chicken pieces, stir well, and cover the pan. Cook over low heat, stirring from time to time, for 20 minutes. Add lemon grass, cardamom, lime juice mixed with evaporated milk, warm water and ground roasted spices. Simmer uncovered, stirring from time to time, until the chicken is tender and the sauce has reduced considerably. Sprinkle with lime juice to taste just before serving.

Meat

Although the Chinese have some excellent beef dishes, pork is by far the most popular meat. Nonya cooks, too, love pork, although they generally cook it with Malay spices and sometimes with coconut milk. Pork is forbidden to Malay and Indian Muslims, who make up for its absence with flavourful mutton or lamb dishes. Hindus do not, of course, eat beef, but Malays have several beef dishes in their repertoire.

Regardless of their ethnic origin, Singaporeans never eat vast quantities of meat like their Western counterparts. The quantity of meat specified in the following recipes, especially in Chinese dishes where it is often combined with vegetables, may seem rather small, but do not increase it, because the correct proportions must be maintained. Remember, too, that a Chinese dish containing meat will not be the sole source of protein at the meal, since fish, poultry or beancurd will also be served.

CHINESE

BEEF RIBS WITH BLACK BEANS

750 g (1½ lb) beef ribs
1 tablespoon salted black beans *(tau see)*
2 cloves garlic, crushed
2 teaspoons light soya sauce
1 teaspoon Chinese rice wine or dry
   sherry
1 tablespoon oil
½ teaspoon sugar

Cut ribs into pieces 5 cm (2 in) long and 2.5 cm (1 in) wide. If using dried salted beans, soak in water for 5 minutes, then squeeze out excess water; if using canned black beans, rinse and drain. Mash black beans and combine with garlic, soya sauce and wine. Heat oil in a pan and fry the ribs until brown, then add all other ingredients and continue frying for 2-3 minutes, stirring all the time. Add sufficient water to just cover the ribs. Cover pan and simmer until meat is tender.

CHINESE

BRAISED ANISEED BEEF

500 g (1 lb) shin beef, in one piece
½ cup light soya sauce
2 slices fresh ginger
1 whole star anise
5 cm (2 in) stick cinnamon
1 teaspoon Chinese rice wine or dry
   sherry
1 teaspoon sesame oil

This dish is served cold, so it is ideal when you are entertaining because it can be prepared well in advance.

Put meat into a saucepan which is just big enough to hold it. Cover meat with cold water and bring to the boil. Carefully scoop off and discard all the scum that floats to the surface, then add all ingredients except sesame oil. Simmer meat gently until very tender, then add sesame oil. Leave meat to cool in the cooking liquid. Cut into 5 mm (¼ in) thick slices just before serving, and pour the cooking liquid over.

Chinese beef steak (recipe page 165).

CLAYPOT BEEF

750 g (1½ lb) lean brisket beef, in one
    piece
3 tablespoons oil
4 dried black mushrooms, soaked, stems
    removed, caps quartered
6 shallots (*bawang merah*), left whole,
    or 1 small red or brown onion, sliced
4 cloves garlic
3 slices fresh ginger
1 tablespoon oyster sauce
1 tablespoon thick black soya sauce
1 tablespoon light soya sauce
½ teaspoon monosodium glutamate
few leaves of green vegetable (*chye sim*,
    spinach, etc.)
white pepper

Seasoning:
2 slices fresh ginger
2 teaspoons sugar
1 teaspoon salt
½ teaspoon Chinese rice wine or dry
    sherry
2 whole star anise
1 teaspoon black peppercorns
2 strips dried or fresh orange peel

Put beef into boiling water to cover and simmer for 5 minutes. Rinse with cold water, then cut beef into pieces 1 cm (½ in) thick and 4 cm (1½ in) square. Heat 2 tablespoons oil and fry pieces of beef for 2 minutes on each side. Put beef in a bowl with all seasoning ingredients and steam for 1½-2 hours until beef is tender.

Heat 1 tablespoon oil in a clay pot or casserole and gently fry mushrooms, whole shallots or sliced onions, garlic (left whole) and ginger for 2-3 minutes. Add beef and strained steaming liquid. Put in oyster sauce, both lots of soya sauce and monosodium glutamate. Cover pot and simmer for 10 minutes.

Boil leafy green vegetable in plenty of water with a dash of oil for 1 minute. Drain and add to clay pot. Sprinkle liberally with pepper and serve with rice.

BEEF WITH CELERY AND BUTTON MUSHROOMS

250 g (8 oz) rump steak, very finely
    sliced
1½ cups oil
1 slice fresh ginger, very finely chopped
2 cloves garlic, smashed and chopped
4-5 large stalks celery, cut diagonally in
    1 cm (½ in) slices
1 cup canned button mushrooms, halved
    if large
2 teaspoons oyster sauce
1 fresh red chilli, cut in very fine length-
    wise strips

Marinade:
1 tablespoon cornflour
1 teaspoon bicarbonate of soda
2 tablespoons water
1 tablespoon peanut oil
1 teaspoon thick black soya sauce
1 teaspoon light soya sauce
1 teaspoon sesame oil
1 teaspoon salt
½ teaspoon sugar
¼ teaspoon monosodium glutamate
¼ teaspoon white pepper powder

Combine all marinade ingredients in a bowl. Add beef, stir well, then leave to marinate for about 30 minutes. Heat oil in a *kuali* until very hot. Drain beef thoroughly then deep fry in hot oil for just 30 seconds. Remove and drain on paper towel.

Pour out all but 2 tablespoons of oil. Fry ginger and garlic gently for 30 seconds. Raise heat and add celery. Stir-fry for 2 minutes, then put in button mushrooms and stir-fry for 1 minute. Lower heat slightly, cover the *kuali*, and cook until celery is just cooked but still crisp. Remove lid, add beef and oyster sauce, and stir-fry over high heat for 30 seconds. Put into a serving bowl or on a platter. Decorate with chilli and serve immediately.

CHINESE BEEF STEAK (picture page 162)

500 g (1 lb) rump steak, cut 1 cm (½ in)
   thick
2 tablespoons oil
1 clove garlic, finely chopped

Marinade:
1 tablespoon light soya sauce
1 tablespoon HP sauce
2 tablespoons peanut oil
1 teaspoon Chinese rice wine or dry
   sherry
½ teaspoon sesame oil
1 teaspoon bicarbonate of soda
1 tablespoon cornflour
1 egg, beaten

Gravy:
¾ cup water
1 tablespoon Worcestershire sauce
1 tablespoon tomato sauce
1 teaspoon oyster sauce
1 teaspoon sugar
½ teaspoon salt
pinch monosodium glutamate

The ingenuity of the Chinese cook, who combines both Chinese and Western seasonings in this dish, produces an excellent result.

Cut meat into squares of about 4 cm (1½ in). Combine all marinade ingredients and soak meat for 8 hours, stirring occasionally. Remove meat from marinade and drain. Heat oil in a large frying pan and cook garlic until it turns golden. Discard garlic, raise heat, and quickly fry meat for 2 minutes on each side.

Heat gravy ingredients and pour over browned meat. Cover pan and simmer gently until meat is tender and gravy reduced.

CHAR SIEW
RED BARBECUED PORK

500 g (1 lb) pork fillet or boneless loin,
   in one piece
2 cloves garlic, crushed
1 tablespoon liquid honey
1 tablespoon light soya sauce
2 teaspoons Chinese rice wine or dry
   sherry
1 teaspoon tomato sauce
½ teaspoon five-spice powder
pinch powdered ginger
red food colouring (optional)

You'll see long red strips of pork hanging up inside Chinese delicatessen shops and markets all over the world, for this is a favourite way of cooking meat for use as an hors d'oeuvre, as a garnish for many noodle dishes, or as a quick, simple meal when accompanied by rice.

Cut pork lengthwise into strips about 4 cm (1½ in) thick. Combine all other ingredients. Soak pork in this marinade for at least 2 hours, turning from time to time. Put pork strips on a greased rack set over a pan of water and roast for 45 minutes at 230°C/450°F/Gas No. 8, basting with the marinade every 15 minutes. Allow to cool. Cut into thin slices when serving.

TAU YU BAK
PORK IN SOYA SAUCE

500 g (1 lb) pork
2 teaspoons oil
4 cloves garlic, smashed and chopped
1 tablespoon sugar
4 tablespoons thick black soya sauce
1 cup water
1 cm (½ in) stick cinnamon
¼ teaspoon five-spice powder
2-3 hardboiled eggs, shelled (optional)

A very easy dish. Although belly pork is normally used, if you prefer a less fatty cut try pork shoulder or loin with just a little fat on it.

Cut pork into cubes about 4 cm (1½ in) square. Heat oil and fry garlic gently for 15 seconds. Raise heat and add pork. Fry, stirring constantly, to seal the meat, then lower heat slightly and sprinkle in the sugar. Cook for 1 minute then add all other ingredients (except eggs) and simmer until pork is tender. If using eggs, add during the last 5 minutes of cooking.

MINCED PORK WITH CUCUMBERS

1 large or 2 small cucumbers
1 tablespoon pork lard or oil
375 g (12 oz) lean minced pork
½ teaspoon salt
1 slice fresh ginger, very finely chopped
1 clove garlic, smashed and chopped
1 teaspoon salted soya beans (taucheo), crushed
2 teaspoons light soya sauce
1 teaspoon Chinese rice wine or dry sherry
½ cup chicken stock (see page 77)
1 heaped teaspoon cornflour
few drops sesame oil

Cut 1 cm (½ in) off top of cucumber and rub the top portion over the cut surface of the rest of the cucumber in a circular motion for about 30 seconds. A white 'scum' will accumulate on both cut surfaces. Discard the cut top portion. Cut another 1 cm (½ in) off the top of the rest of the cucumber and discard this also. This will remove the bitterness. Cut cucumber into four lengthwise and discard seeds, then dice flesh finely.

Heat lard and stir-fry pork over high heat for 2 minutes. Sprinkle over salt, lower heat slightly and add ginger, garlic and salted soya beans. Stir-fry for 2 minutes, then add soya sauce, rice wine, stock and cucumber and simmer for 2 minutes. Mix cornflour with a little water and add to pan. Stir to thicken sauce. Serve immediately, sprinkled with a few drops of sesame oil.

RICH BRAISED PORK IN BLACK SAUCE

500 g (1 lb) streaky belly pork, skin left on
2 tablespoons thick black soya sauce
white pepper
oil for deep frying
2.5 cm (1 in) stick cinnamon
1 tablespoon sweet red sauce (tim cheong) or barbecue sauce
2 tablespoons light soya sauce
¼ teaspoon monosodium glutamate
1 tablespoon sugar
¼ teaspoon mustard powder
½ teaspoon salt
1 cup water

Choose a piece of pork that is not too fatty, and cut into 4 cm (1½ in) pieces. Sprinkle with 1 tablespoon of thick black soya sauce and a liberal dash of white pepper and leave to marinate for 1-2 hours.

Heat oil in a pan and fry the pork pieces for 3-5 minutes, until browned. Put pork in a saucepan with all other ingredients and simmer gently until pork is very tender. Serve with white rice.

STEWED PORK LEG

1 pork leg, weighing about 1 kg (2 lb)
125 g (4 oz) dried beancurd twists (taufu kee)
½ cup oil
3-4 cloves garlic, very finely chopped
1 tablespoon salted soya beans (taucheo), lightly mashed
2 slices fresh ginger
4 dried black mushrooms, soaked, liquid reserved
1 heaped teaspoon fermented red beancurd (nam yee)
2 tablespoons light soya sauce
2 tablespoons thick black soya sauce

A real home-style dish, this was taught to me by Madam Fu, an elderly Cantonese lady. Pigs sold in Singapore are generally fairly small; the front leg of the pig is preferred for dishes such as this, and the upper part of the leg, minus the trotter, weighs only about 1 kg (2 lb.)

Wipe the pork leg and set aside. Wipe beancurd twists clean with a cloth and cut with scissors into 5 cm (2 in) lengths. Heat oil in a kuali and fry the cut pieces, a few at a time, until they puff up and turn golden. Set aside. Pour out all but 1 tablespoon of oil and gently fry the garlic until golden. Add salted soya beans and fry, stirring constantly, for 1 minute. Add pork, ginger, mushrooms and fermented red beancurd and fry for 5 minutes, stirring to mix well. Transfer all ingredients to a saucepan or casserole just big enough to hold pork. Add both lots of soya sauce, the mushroom soaking liquid, and just enough water to cover the pork. Cover and simmer until pork is tender.

CHINESE

BRAISED PORK RIBS

500 g (1 lb) meaty pork ribs
oil for deep frying
1 medium red or brown onion, finely
   chopped
2 cloves garlic, smashed and chopped
2 slices fresh ginger, very finely chopped
½ fresh red chilli, sliced (optional)
2 spring onions, cut in 2.5 cm (1 in)
   lengths
1 or 2 dried black mushrooms, soaked
   and shredded
1 tablespoon salted soya beans
   (taucheo), mashed lightly
1 teaspoon Chinese rice wine or dry
   sherry

Marinade:
½ teaspoon salt
¼ teaspoon monosodium glutamate
½ teaspoon sugar
1 teaspoon light soya sauce
1 teaspoon thick black soya sauce
½ teaspoon sesame oil
sprinkle white pepper
2 teaspoons cornflour

Gravy:
½ cup water
1 teaspoon sugar
½ teaspoon light soya sauce
½ teaspoon thick black soya sauce
few drops sesame oil
white pepper

Have ribs cut into 4 cm (1½ in)) pieces. Combine marinade ingredients and rub into pork ribs. Leave aside for 30 minutes. Drain ribs and deep fry in hot oil for just 1 minute. Remove and drain.

Pour out all but 1½ tablespoons oil and gently fry onion, garlic, ginger and chilli for 3-4 minutes, then add the ribs and all other ingredients (except wine). Stir-fry for 1 minute, then add the wine and cook for another minute. Combine all gravy ingredients and add to the ribs. Cover the pan and simmer until the ribs are cooked. Remove the lid, stir, and continue cooking until the sauce is almost completely dried up. Serve with white rice.

CHINESE

MA PO TAUFU
HOT BEANCURD WITH PORK

3-4 large squares soft beancurd (tauhu
   or taufu), weighing a total of about
   750 g (1½ lb)
1½ tablespoons oil
4 cloves garlic, smashed and chopped
3 dried black mushrooms, soaked and
   shredded
250 g (8 oz) minced lean pork
1½-2 tablespoons hot bean paste
½ cup beef stock (see page 77)
1 tablespoon dark soya sauce
1 tablespoon light soya sauce
pinch monosodium glutamate
2 teaspoons cornflour
2 tablespoons water
1 teaspoon sesame oil
1-2 spring onions, finely chopped

Cut beancurd into 2 cm (¾ in) cubes and put in a colander to drain. Heat oil and gently fry garlic for 15 seconds, then add mushrooms and stir-fry for another 15 seconds. Put in pork, raise heat a little, and stir-fry for 3 minutes. Add bean paste and stir-fry for 30 seconds, then pour in stock, both lots of soya sauce and sprinkle with monosodium glutamate. Cook for 2 minutes, then add cornflour combined with water. Stir and add beancurd pieces. Cook, stirring gently for 1 minute, then serve immediately sprinkled with sesame oil and spring onions.

STEAMED PORK AND YAM SLICES

500 g (1 lb) belly pork, in one piece
2 teaspoons thick black soya sauce
1 cup oil
2 cloves garlic, smashed and chopped
250 g (8 oz) taro yam, peeled
8-10 lettuce leaves

Gravy:
6 tablespoons pork stock (see method)
1 tablespoon light soya sauce
1 teaspoon thick black soya sauce
1 teaspoon cornflour
¼ teaspoon monosodium glutamate
1 teaspoon sugar
1 teaspoon sesame oil
2 teaspoons salted soya beans (taucheo),
    mashed
¼ teaspoon white pepper

Simmer pork in water to cover for 20 minutes. Reserve stock. Rub meat with 2 teaspoons black soya sauce and set aside. Heat oil and fry garlic until golden. Discard garlic. Fry pork in garlic-flavoured oil, skin side up, for 3 minutes. Turn and fry the other side for 2 minutes. Drain and allow to cool, then cut into slices about 1 cm (½ in) thick. Cut yam into slices 5 mm (¼ in) thick and fry in hot oil for 2-3 minutes. Drain.

Combine all gravy ingredients, put in a pan and simmer for 5 minutes. Rub into pork and yam slices, then put in a bowl, alternating pork and yam. Cover bowl and put in a steamer. Cook for 1¾-2 hours, until pork and yam are tender. Plunge lettuce leaves in boiling water with a dash of oil added. Drain and arrange on a large serving platter. Put alternate slices of pork and yam on top of the lettuce and serve.

STEAMBOAT (picture page 171)

Stock:
6-8 cups light stock, made with chicken
    and beef stock cubes
2 teaspoons Chinese rice wine or dry
    sherry
2 teaspoons sesame oil
sprinkle of white pepper
fried onion flakes (see page 188)

Meat and fish:
250 g (8 oz) lean pork, finely sliced
250 g (8 oz) rump steak, finely sliced
250 g (8 oz) raw prawns, peeled
1-2 white fish steaks or fillets, cubed
200 g (6½ oz) fish balls
1 chicken breast, sliced
2 chicken livers, sliced

Vegetables:
leafy green vegetables such as lettuce,
    Chinese celery cabbage,
    chrysanthemum leaves, watercress,
    silver beet
bunch of spring onions, cleaned and cut
    in 15 cm (6 in) lengths
fresh red or green chillies, stuffed with
    fish-ball mixture
slices of bitter gourd, stuffed with fish-
    ball mixture
8 dried black mushrooms, soaked
2-3 cakes hard beancurd (taukwa),
    cubed

This dish, which originated in northern China, is named after the utensil in which it is cooked — a type of fondue with a funnel up the centre. Food is cooked in the 'moat' containing boiling stock, traditionally kept hot by a charcoal fire. Electric steamboats, any other type of fondue, a deep saucepan placed over a burner, or even a large electric rice cooker can be used instead of a charcoal-fired steamboat.

Steamboat is a 'fun' meal where diners cook their own food at the table, a great icebreaker if you're entertaining people you don't know well. It can be prepared well in advance, another boon when entertaining. Bite-sized portions of meat, fish and vegetables are laid on the table, and dipped into the boiling stock for a few moments, then eaten with a variety of sauces. As the dinner progresses, the stock reduces and becomes wonderfully rich and tasty. It is then poured over rice vermicelli into which an egg is broken. The ingredients given in this recipe are merely a guide to some of the possibilities, and can be varied according to your taste and imagination. The quantities given here are sufficient for 8 people.

Prepare the stock by boiling together all stock ingredients except onion flakes for 3 minutes. Put into a steamboat or other utensil and sprinkle with onion flakes.

Arrange the meat and fish, and the vegetables, attractively on large platters and place on the table. If preparing in advanced don't tear or cut the vegetables, and keep ingredients tightly covered in the refrigerator.

Soak the Chinese rice vermicelli in hot water for 5 minutes, then divide between 8 soup bowls and place on the table. Put eggs in a bowl and set on the table. Place prepared sauces in individual sauce bowls and put beside each diner.

To cook the food, each person lowers a few morsels into the boiling stock and leaves them for a minute or two, then removes

Additional items:
16 hardboiled quails' eggs (optional)
250 g (8 oz) Chinese rice vermicelli
  (*beehoon*)
8 eggs

Sauces:
soya sauce with sesame seeds
  (see page 183)
soya sauce with ginger (see page 183)
bottled chilli sauce
bottled plum sauce
hot mustard

them with a small wire mesh ladle or pair of chopsticks. When all the meat, fish, quails' eggs and vegetables have been finished, and the stock has reduced and enriched, pour it over the noodles in the soup bowls and break in a whole egg, stirring to cook it. This rich soup brings the meal to an end.

NONYA

HATI BABI
PIG'S LIVER BALLS

250 g (8 oz) lean minced pork
½ teaspoon five-spice powder
¼ teaspoon white pepper
1 egg, lightly beaten
1 teaspoon cornflour
200 g (6½ oz) pig's liver
250 g (8 oz) pig's caul

Marinade:
1 medium red or brown onion, grated
¼ cup tamarind water (see page 63)
1 teaspoon coriander, freshly ground
1 teaspoon malt vinegar
1 teaspoon salt
¼ teaspoon sugar

Seasoned pork and pig's liver are wrapped in caul, the lacy membrane which lines the pig's stomach, then gently fried or grilled to make a delicious sausage reminiscent of French crépinette. I had trouble locating pig's liver while in Australia, for my suburban butcher swore it wasn't fit for human consumption and was fed 'to the dogs'. However, I soon discovered it at a Chinese delicatessen. If you cannot obtain pig's caul, the seasoned meat can be shaped into patties, dipped in flour, and fried in a little oil.

Combine minced pork with five-spice powder, pepper, egg and cornflour. Slice liver thinly and prick all over. Soak liver in marinade for 1 hour, then simmer gently in the marinade until almost all the liquid evaporates, leaving only 1 tablespoon of thick gravy. Chop liver coarsely and add together with the marinade to the pork mixture, stirring to mix well.

Soak pig's caul for 5 minutes in a large basin of warm water with 1 tablespoon vinegar added. Spread caul out gently on a table top and cut into pieces about 13 cm (5 in) square. Put a heaped tablespoon of the pork mixture into the centre of each piece of caul and roll up to form a sausage or a round cake. Cook under a griller for about 15 minutes, turning to cook both sides, or shallow fry in a little oil.

NONYA

BABI LEMAK
PORK IN COCONUT MILK

10-15 shallots (*bawang merah*) or 2
  medium red or brown onions
8 dried red chillies, soaked
4 candlenuts (*buah keras*) or
  macadamias
½ teaspoon dried shrimp paste (*blacan*)
2 tablespoons oil
500 g (1 lb) lean pork, cubed
1 cup water
salt to taste
1 cup thick coconut milk (see page 44)
1 tablespoon sugar
2 tablespoons Chinese lime juice (*limau*
  ***kesturi*) or lemon juice**

This dish illustrates perfectly the blending of two cuisines, with a Chinese ingredient (pork) cooked Malay-style in coconut milk and seasonings.

Grind shallots, chillies, candlenuts and dried shrimp paste together until fine. Heat oil in a *kuali* and gently fry the ground ingredients, stirring frequently, for 3-4 minutes. Add pork and cook until it changes colour and is well coated with spice paste. Add water and salt, cover *kuali*, and simmer gently until pork is just tender.

Remove lid and add coconut milk. Simmer uncovered for 10-15 minutes, stirring from time to time. Just before serving, add sugar and lime juice. Check and adjust seasonings to taste.

NONYA

SAMBAL BABI
SPICY PORK

500 g (1 lb) lean pork
8 shallots (*bawang merah*) or 1 medium
   red or brown onion
6-8 dried red chillies, soaked
1 teaspoon dried shrimp paste (*blacan*)
2 tablespoons oil
¼ cup tamarind water (see page 63)
1 teaspoon sugar
½ teaspoon salt

Cut meat into pieces about 1 cm (½ in) thick, 5 cm (2 in) long and 1 cm (½ in) wide. Pound or grind shallots, chillies and shrimp paste together until fine. Heat oil in a *kuali* and gently fry the ground ingredients, stirring occasionally, for 4-5 minutes. Add pork and stir-fry until it changes colour and is well coated with spices. Add tamarind water, sugar and salt, and enough cold water to almost cover the meat. Simmer uncovered, stirring frequently, until meat is tender and the sauce has reduced and thickened.

NONYA

SATAY BABI
PORK SATAY

25-30 bamboo *satay* skewers
500 g (1 lb) boneless pork loin
1 stalk lemon grass (*serai*) or substitute
8 shallots (*bawang merah*) or 1 medium
   red or brown onion
2 teaspoons coriander
½ teaspoon turmeric powder
1 teaspoon salt
2 teaspoons brown sugar
4 tablespoons oil

Sauce:
1 quantity *satay* sauce (see page 184)
¾ cup canned crushed pineapple

Be sure to cut the pieces of meat as directed: satay *is not* kebab; *large chunks of meat will not absorb the seasonings properly, take longer to cook, and are difficult to eat as a snack.*

Soak the bamboo *satay* skewers in cold water for an hour or so to make them less likely to burn during grilling. Cut pork into pieces 2 cm (¾ in) square and 1 cm (½ in) thick.
   Slice lemon grass finely then grind or pound together with shallots to make a paste. Heat coriander then grind to a powder and mix with shallot paste, turmeric, salt, sugar and 1 tablespoon oil. Put in pork pieces and stir to coat with the mixture. Leave for at least 2 hours.
   Make *satay* sauce according to directions. Finely chop the crushed pineapple, making sure there are no large pieces, and mix into sauce.
   Thread 4 or 5 pieces of pork onto each skewer. Brush with oil and cook over charcoal or under a griller until cooked. Serve with sauce, pieces of raw onion, and cucumber chunks.

MALAY

SATAY
SPICED GRILLED MEAT ON SKEWERS

1 kg (2 lb) chicken breast, leg lamb, or
   rump steak
1 tablespoon coriander
1 teaspoon cummin
½ teaspoon fennel
8-10 shallots (*bawang merah*), or 1½
   medium red or brown onions
2 cloves garlic
1 stalk lemon grass (*serai*) or substitute
2 slices *lengkuas* or substitute
1 cm (½ in) fresh ginger
1½ teaspoons salt
1 teaspoon turmeric powder
2 teaspoons brown sugar
¼ cup tamarind water (see page 63)
4 tablespoons oil
50-60 bamboo *satay* skewers

Cut chicken or meat into pieces 2 cm (¾ in) square and 1 cm (½ in) thick. Heat coriander, cummin and fennel in a dry pan then grind and set aside. Pound or grind shallots, garlic, lemon grass, *lengkuas* and ginger together until fine, then combine in a bowl with ground spices and all other ingredients except oil. Add meat and leave to marinate for at least 6 hours.
   Thread meat onto bamboo skewers which have been soaked in cold water for 1 hour. Brush both sides of meat with oil and cook over charcoal or under a griller until golden brown. Serve with *satay* sauce (recipe page 184), chunks of cucumber, pieces of raw onion, and steamed compressed rice cakes (*ketupat*) (recipe page 88).

Steamboat (recipe page 168).

SAMBAL GORENG HATI
LIVER IN COCONUT CHILLI SAUCE

500 g (1 lb) liver (chicken liver, lamb's
    fry or calves' liver)
2 tablespoons oil
1½ cups coconut milk (see page 44)
¼ cup tamarind water (see page 63)
1 teaspoon salt
1 teaspoon sugar
1 stalk lemon grass (serai), bruised, or
    substitute

Spice paste:
3 candlenuts (buah keras) or
    macadamias
6-8 shallots (bawang merah) or 1
    medium red or brown onion
2 cloves garlic
8-10 dried red chillies, soaked
1 thick slice lengkuas or substitute
1 teaspoon dried shrimp paste (blacan)

Wash and slice the liver. If using chicken livers, leave whole. Grind the spice paste ingredients together until fine. Heat oil and fry the spice paste gently for 3-4 minutes, then add liver and continue cooking for another 2 minutes. Add coconut milk, tamarind water, salt, sugar and lemon grass and simmer uncovered until the liver is cooked and the gravy has thickened.

GULAI KAMBING
MUTTON CURRY

16 shallots (bawang merah) or 2 medium
    red or brown onions
2 cloves garlic
2.5 cm (1 in) fresh ginger
6 dried red chillies, soaked
3 tablespoons oil
500 g (1 lb) mutton cut from leg
1½ cups water
1 teaspoon salt
½ cup thick coconut milk (see page 44)
¼ cup tamarind water (see page 63)

Spice paste:
1 tablespoon coriander
2 teaspoons cummin
1 teaspoon fennel
2.5 cm (1 in) stick cinnamon
4 cloves
¼ teaspoon black peppercorns
small chunk nutmeg (about ⅛ whole
    nut)
½ teaspoon turmeric powder

A marvellously full-bodied curry that needs the rich flavour of mutton for best results, although hogget can be substituted.

Heat ingredients for spice paste, except turmeric powder, in a dry pan for 2-3 minutes, then grind finely in a coffee grinder or with a mortar and pestle. Add turmeric and sufficient cold water to make a stiff paste. Set aside.

Pound or grind shallots, garlic, ginger and chillies together. Heat oil in a kuali and stir-fry pounded mixture gently for 3-5 minutes. Add spice paste and cook for another 3 minutes, stirring frequently.

Cut mutton into pieces about 5 cm (2 in) square and 1 cm (½ in) thick. Add to kuali and cook, stirring constantly, until thoroughly covered with the spice mixture. Put in water and salt, cover kuali and simmer until meat is just tender. Remove lid and simmer to evaporate liquid until about ½ cup remains. Add thick coconut milk and tamarind water. Simmer gently, stirring frequently with the kuali uncovered for another 15 minutes.

Some Malay cooks add quartered potatoes to the mutton about 20 minutes before the end of cooking time.

MALAY

RENDANG DAGING (picture page 174)
BEEF IN SPICY COCONUT GRAVY

500 g (1 lb) topside beef
6-8 shallots (*bawang merah*) or 1
    medium red or brown onion
3 slices *lengkuas* or substitute
2.5 cm (1 in) fresh ginger
16-20 dried red chillies, soaked
2 stalks lemon grass (*serai*) or substitute
1 clove garlic
6 tablespoons freshly grated coconut or
    4 tablespoons desiccated coconut
2½ tablespoons oil
2½ cups coconut milk (see page 44)
1 leaf fresh turmeric, very finely
    shredded (optional)
1 teaspoon salt
1 teaspoon sugar

Cut the beef into pieces about 5 cm (2 in) square and 1 cm (½ in) thick. Grind the shallots, *lengkuas*, ginger, chillies, lemon grass and garlic together until fine. Gently fry the grated coconut in a dry pan, stirring constantly, until golden brown. Allow to cool slightly, then pound to a paste.

Heat oil in a *kuali* and gently fry the ground shallot mixture for 4-5 minutes. Add pounded coconut and fry for another minute, then put in beef and stir-fry until it changes colour. Add all other ingredients and stir, lifting the coconut milk and pouring it back into the *kuali* until it comes to the boil. Reduce heat and simmer, uncovered, until the meat is tender. If the sauce threatens to dry out before the meat is cooked, add a little hot water.

The sauce should finally reduce so that all that remains is a very thick coating on the meat. The oil will come out of the coconut milk and the meat will start to fry in it.

MALAY

DAGING PEAJA
MALAY BEEF STEW

500 g (1 lb) topside beef
8-10 shallots (*bawang merah*), or 1½
    medium red or brown onions, finely
    sliced
1 thick slice fresh ginger, very finely
    chopped
1-2 cloves garlic, smashed and chopped
3 tablespoons oil
3 tablespoons meat curry powder (see
    page 189)
1 tablespoon water
¼ cup tamarind water (see page 63)
1 stalk lemon grass (*serai*), bruised, or
    substitute
¼ whole nutmeg, grated
1 teaspoon fenugreek
4 medium potatoes, peeled and
    quartered

Cut beef into slices 1 cm (½ in) thick and about 4 cm (1½ in) square. Fry shallots, ginger and garlic gently in oil in a *kuali* until golden. Mix curry powder with water to form a paste, then add to *kuali* and fry, stirring constantly, for 2 minutes. Add beef and continue frying until it changes colour and is well coated with spices. Put in just enough water to cover the meat, and add tamarind water, lemon grass, nutmeg and fenugreek seeds. Cover and simmer until meat is just tender, then add potatoes and continue simmering until the potatoes are soft and the gravy has thickened.

INDIAN

MUTTON MYSORE

500 g (1 lb) lean mutton or lamb
2 cloves garlic
1 heaped teaspoon finely chopped mint
1 teaspoon salt
1-2 teaspoons chilli powder
½ teaspoon cummin powder
½ teaspoon turmeric powder
1 teaspoon vinegar
1 teaspoon sugar
1 teaspoon light soya sauce
2 tablespoons *ghee* or butter

This Singaporean version contains Chinese soya sauce — something you wouldn't find in Mysore.

Cut the meat into pieces about 1 cm (½ in) thick.

Pound garlic with chopped mint and salt, then combine pounded mixture with spices, vinegar, sugar and soya sauce. Rub well into the meat and leave to stand for 30 minutes.

Heat *ghee* or butter gently in a heavy pan and add the meat. Do not add any water. Cover the pan and cook over very low heat, stirring from time to time, until the meat is tender. Remove the lid to allow any moisture to evaporate, and continue cooking until the meat fries to a rich brown colour.

INDIAN

DHANSAK
PARSI MEAT, LENTIL AND VEGETABLE STEW

500 g (1 lb) mixed *dhal*, using roughly
    equal amounts of yellow lentils, red
    lentils, green mung peas and
    chickpeas
1 kg (2 lb) lean lamb, cut into large
    pieces
1 or 2 small eggplants, peeled and
    chopped into large chunks
thick slice of pumpkin, peeled
2 large potatoes, peeled and quartered
1 large onion, chopped
small bunch spinach, washed and
    roughly chopped
4 spring onions, chopped
small bunch mint
small bunch fresh coriander leaves or
    watercress
1 large green pepper, roughly chopped
2 teaspoons fenugreek
2 teaspoons coriander powder
1 tablespoon salt
60 g (2 oz) butter
5-6 cups water

Final addition:
4-6 cloves garlic
30 g (1 oz) butter
1-2 teaspoons chilli powder
2 teaspoons cummin

Wash the *dhal* and put into a large saucepan with the meat. Add all other ingredients, stir well, and bring to the boil slowly. Simmer gently, stirring from time to time, until the meat is tender. If contents threaten to dry out, add a little hot water.

Remove pieces of meat and keep aside. Mash *dhal* and vegetables (which should be quite mushy by this stage) and return meat to the resulting purée. The *dhanksak* can now be set aside, or even deep frozen, until needed.

Just before serving the *dhanksak*, prepare the final addition. Peel and mash garlic and put into a saucepan together with butter, chilli and cummin seeds. Fry gently for 2-3 minutes, then add to the meat and lentil purée. Heat and serve with onion *sambal* (recipe page 183), lemon slices and *puri* (recipe page 101).

INDIAN

ROGAN JOSH
NORTH INDIAN LAMB CURRY

60 g (2 oz) *ghee* or butter
2 medium red or brown onions, grated
½ cup plain yoghurt
2 medium tomatoes, skinned and
    chopped
500 g (1 lb) leg lamb, cut into cubes
1 teaspoon salt
½ cup water

Spice paste:
1 tablespoon coriander
1 teaspoon white poppy seeds (optional)
1 teaspoon cummin
4 cardamom pods
12 black peppercorns
small chunk nutmeg (about ⅛ of a nut)
2 heaped tablespoons desiccated coconut
10 almonds (15 if not using poppy seeds)
2.5 cm (1 in) fresh ginger
6 cloves garlic
1-2 teaspoons chilli powder
½ teaspoon turmeric powder

Prepare spice paste first. Fry coriander, poppy seeds, cummin, cardamom, peppercorns and nutmeg in a dry pan over low heat until they smell fragrant. Set aside. Cook the coconut in the same manner, stirring frequently, until it turns golden. Grind cooked spices and coconut together finely. Grind almonds, ginger and garlic together, then mix with the ground spice and coconut mixture, adding chilli and turmeric powder.

Heat *ghee* in a *kuali* or deep pan and gently fry grated onion for 2-3 minutes. Add the spice paste and continue frying gently for another 3-5 minutes. Slowly add the yoghurt, stirring constantly, then add the tomatoes and cook for 5 minutes. Put in the lamb and salt and continue cooking until the meat changes colour. Add water, cover the pan, and cook over low heat, stirring occasionally, until the meat is tender and the liquid reduced to a thick sauce.

Clockwise from left: rendang daging (recipe page 173), nasi kunyit (recipe page 88), tempe goreng (recipe page 192), sambal telur (recipe page 192) and urap (recipe page 120).

INDIAN

SPICED MUTTON CHOPS

500 g (1 lb) lean mutton chops
4 medium-sized ripe tomatoes,
   quartered
1 cm (½ in) fresh ginger, very finely
   chopped
6 shallots (*bawang merah*), or 1 small
   red or brown onion, finely chopped
3 cloves garlic, smashed
1 fresh green chilli, halved
2 teaspoons meat curry powder
   (see page 189)
½-1 teaspoon chilli powder
1 teaspoon salt
black pepper to taste
ghee or butter for frying

This recipe is the closest I can get to the superbly flavoured chops cooked in Ujagar Singh's famous Sikh restaurant, just down a lane near the Armenian Church in Singapore.

Put the chops, together with all other ingredients except *ghee*, in a heavy pan with a firm-fitting lid. Add just enough water to prevent chops from sticking and simmer, stirring from time to time, until chops are tender and the liquid has dried up.

Remove chops from pan and scrape off any tomato skins that may be adhering to them. Leave to cool. The chops can be wrapped and stored in the deep freeze at this stage.

Just before serving the chops, heat a little *ghee* in a frying pan until very hot and fry the chops for a few minutes on both sides. Serve with mint chutney, and garnish with lime or lemon wedges.

INDIAN

MUTTON CUTLETS

500 g (1 lb) minced mutton or lamb
4-6 shallots (*bawang merah*), or 1 small
   red or brown onion
2 slices fresh ginger
1-2 fresh green chillies
6-8 curry leaves (*karuvapillai*)
pinch each of cloves, cinnamon, and
   turmeric
1 egg, lightly beaten
½ teaspoon salt
6 tablespoons fresh breadcrumbs, or 1
   large boiled potato, mashed
oil for shallow frying

To coat the cutlets:
1 egg, lightly beaten
breadcrumbs

Break the minced meat up with a fork. Chop shallots, ginger and chillies finely. Shred or crumble the curry leaves, then mix all seasonings and chopped ingredients with the meat. Add egg, salt and breadcrumbs or potato and blend thoroughly.

Shape the mixture into egg-sized balls. Flatten, then dip in beaten egg and coat with breadcrumbs. Fry until golden brown. Serve with chilli sauce or spicy chutney.

INDIAN

KOFTA
DEEP-FRIED MEAT BALLS

500 g (1 lb) very finely minced lamb or
   beef
1 medium red or brown onion
1 clove garlic
1 slice fresh ginger
1 fresh green chilli
1 heaped tablespoon finely chopped
   fresh coriander or nunt leaves
2 teaspoons *garam masala*
   (see glossary)
2 heaped tablespoons plain yoghurt
1 teaspoon salt
oil for deep frying

Put meat into a deep bowl. Chop onion, garlic, ginger and chilli together until very fine, then mix with the meat. Add coriander or mint leaves, *garam masala*, yoghurt and salt and mix well. Leave to stand for at least 30 minutes to allow yoghurt to tenderise the meat.

Put plenty of oil into a *kuali* or deep frying pan and heat. Shape meat into balls about 2.5 cm (1 in) and deep fry until golden brown. Do not overcook. Drain and serve with rice and chutney, or as a savoury snack.

Gammon curry (recipe page 178).

KEEMA
SPICY MINCED MEAT

500 g (1 lb) minced lean lamb or beef
2 tablespoons *ghee* or butter
1 large onion, chopped
2 slices fresh ginger, very finely chopped
1 clove garlic, smashed and chopped
4 cm (1½ in) stick cinnamon
6 cloves
4 cardamom pods, slit and bruised
½ teaspoon turmeric powder
½ teaspoon chilli powder
1 large tomato, chopped
3 tablespoons plain yoghurt
1 teaspoon salt
2 teaspoons *garam masala* (see glossary)
1 cup frozen green peas (optional)

Break mince up with a fork. Heat *ghee* and gently fry onion, ginger, garlic and whole spices for 3-4 minutes. Add turmeric and chilli powder, fry for a few seconds, then put in meat and stir-fry until it changes colour. Cover pan and cook for 10 minutes. Add tomato, yoghurt, salt and *garam masala* and cook for another 5 minutes. If using frozen peas, add now and continue cooking until both meat and peas are tender.

VINDALOO
SPICED MEAT

500 g (1 lb) pork
1 heaped tablespoon cummin
1 tablespoon brown mustard seed
1 teaspoon black peppercorns
2 cardamom pods
4 cloves
1 cm (½ in) stick cinnamon
4-6 cloves garlic
4 cm (1½ in) fresh ginger
16 dried red chillies, soaked
½ teaspoon turmeric powder
1 teaspoon salt
1 teaspoon sugar
½ cup white vinegar
½ cup oil

Cut meat into pieces about 5 cm (2 in) square and 2 cm (¾ in) thick. Grind cummin, mustard seed, peppercorns, cardamom, cloves and cinnamon and set aside. Grind garlic, ginger and chillies. Combine all ingredients except oil and leave to stand in a glass or porcelain bowl for at least 4 hours.

Heat oil in a pan (do not use aluminium) until moderately hot. Drain meat, keeping marinade aside. Fry meat until it changes colour, then add marinade. Cover pan and cook over very low heat, stirring occassionally, until meat is tender.

GAMMON CURRY (picture page 177)

500 g (1 lb) gammon
1 tablespoon cummin
10 dried red chillies, soaked
3 tablespoons olive oil
¾ cup red wine vinegar
¼ teaspoon fenugreek
½ teaspoon brown mustard seed
1 sprig curry leaves (*karuvapillai*)
½ cup prunes
8 green olives
sugar to taste (optional)

This recipe, given to me by a Eurasian friend who is an excellent cook, sounds really bizarre. Who ever heard of mixing olives, prunes, chilli and southern Indian seasonings all in the one dish! Let me reassure you that the result is superb, and that if you're serving more than four people, you'll need to double the quantities given here for the curry is bound to disappear quickly.

Cut gammon into cubes of about 3 cm (1¼ in), leaving on any skin. Taste a small piece of gammon, and if it is very salty, soak in cold water for about 15 minutes.

Heat cummin seeds in a dry saucepan then grind to a powder. Pound or grind the soaked chillies and mix with cummin. Heat 1 tablespoon of olive oil and gently fry the chilli-cummin mixture for 3-4 minutes. Mix fried spices with vinegar and put into a glass or china bowl. Add meat, stir well, and leave to marinate for 2 hours.

Heat remaining 2 tablespoons olive oil (in an earthenware casserole if possible) and gently fry the fenugreek, mustard seed and curry leaves for about 1 minute, taking care the fenugreek seeds do not turn brown. Add the drained meat (keeping the marinade aside) and fry gently, stirring frequently, until the meat changes colour and the juices have dried up. Add marinade and sufficient cold water to just cover the meat. Cover casserole and simmer gently until meat is tender. Add prunes and olives and cook a further 10 minutes. Taste and add sugar if desired. Serve with white rice.

EURASIAN

FENG
MIXED MEAT CURRY

250 g (8 oz) boiled ox tongue
250 g (8 oz) topside beef
250 g (8 oz) boiled ox tripe
250 g (8 oz) belly pork with skin
250 g (8 oz) pig's liver
1 pig's kidney or 2 lamb kidneys
2 tablespoons olive oil
2.5 cm (1 in) stick cinnamon
1 whole star anise
4 cloves
1 teaspoon salt
¼ teaspoon freshly grated nutmeg
3-4 medium potatoes, peeled and cut into quarters
2 medium red or brown onions, cut into 1 cm (½ in) cubes
½-1 cup red wine vinegar
1 tablespoon chopped 'local' celery to garnish

Marinade:
4 tablespoons coriander
1 tablespoon black peppercorns
2 tablespoons cummin
1 tablespoon fennel
½ teaspoon turmeric powder
20 shallots (bawang merah) or 2 large red or brown onions
2.5 cm (1 in) fresh ginger
8-10 cloves garlic
3 tablespoons sweet sherry

Feng, a festive dish that is a must with the Eurasian community at Christmas, is surprisingly similar to the Goan sorpotel (a pork and liver curry) and the Sri Lankan Burger or Eurasian favourite, lampries, which uses four different types of meat cooked together in a curry. This recipe was kindly given to me by Mrs Joan Frois.

Cut tongue, topside beef, tripe and belly pork into 1 cm (½ in) dice. Drop liver and kidney into boiling water for 1 minute to firm slightly, then cut into 1 cm (½ in) dice.

Prepare the marinade by roasting coriander, peppercorns, cummin and fennel in a dry pan until they turn light brown. Grind with a mortar and pestle or in an electric coffee grinder to make a powder and add turmeric. Grind shallots, ginger and garlic until fine (add a little of the sherry if using a blender or food processor) then mix with spice powder and rest of sherry. Combine meat with marinade and leave in a covered bowl in the refrigerator for 1-2 hours.

Heat oil in an earthenware or enamelled casserole and fry cinnamon, star anise and cloves for 2 minutes. Add all the meats and fry until the moisture dries up. Add salt, nutmeg, and sufficient cold water to just cover the meat, and simmer for about 45 minutes. Add potatoes, cook a further 10 minutes, then put in cubed onions, wine vinegar to taste, and cook another 5-10 minutes until potatoes are soft. Sprinkle with chopped celery and serve with *pilau*.

Condiments, Snacks & Accompaniments

Spicy (and often hot) side-dishes, dips, sauces, chutneys and other condiments are an integral part of most Singapore meals. Many different types of *sambals* or chilli-based side-dishes are prepared, of which the most famous is the Malay *sambal blacan*, a potent combination of fresh red chillies, dried shrimp paste (*blacan*) and juice from the small round 'local' or Chinese lime (*limau kesturi*). A love of *sambal blacan* is universal in Singapore, and I've known people from each of the ethnic groups here who've bemoaned the absence of their favourite condiment during overseas trips.

Singapore snack foods are imaginative and tasty, so it's not surprising that local people always seem to be eating — especially as many of these snacks are sold at roadside stalls or by itinerant hawkers.

CHINESE

CHILLI AND GINGER SAMBAL

10 fresh red chillies, seeds removed
1-2 cloves garlic
5 cm (2 in) fresh ginger
2 teaspoons chicken stock
juice from Chinese limes (*limau kesturi*)
   or lemon to taste
salt to taste

Serve with Hainanese chicken rice or any other dish as desired. Scoop the chicken stock from the top of the liquid in which chicken was cooked, obtaining as much fat as possible.

Pound or grind red chillies together with garlic and ginger. Add chicken stock, lime juice and salt to taste. Will keep in covered container in the refrigerator for a few days, but is best served fresh.

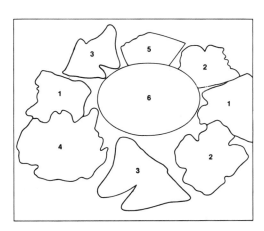

1 Small spring rolls (recipe page 190), **2** *prawn toast (recipe page 189),* **3** *samosa (recipe page 194),* **4** *deep-fried wun tun (recipe page 191),* **5** *ikan bilis goreng (recipe page 192),* **6** *wun tun sauce.*

SAMBAL BLACAN (picture page 155)
CHILLI AND SHRIMP PASTE SAMBAL

4-6 fresh red chillies
pinch of salt
1 teaspoon dried shrimp paste (*blacan*)
1-2 teaspoons Chinese lime juice (*limau kesturi*) or lemon juice

This condiment is as essential to many Singaporeans as salt is to Westerners, and has no doubt astonished customs officials all over the world when they've discovered it secreted in the luggage of travelling Singaporeans. It is very pungent, and probably an acquired taste, but, believe me, one well worth acquiring. Keeps several days if stored in the refrigerator in an airtight container.

Cut chillies into 3 or 4 pieces, then pound with salt until finely ground. Flatten the dried shrimp paste to about 5 mm (¼ in) thick and cook under a griller or in a dry pan, turning so that both sides cook thoroughly. This will take 3-5 minutes and is important as it removes the 'raw' taste of the shrimp paste.

Add cooked shrimp paste to the mortar or blender and pound or blend until it is thoroughly mixed with the chilli. Add lime or lemon juice to taste.

SAMBAL UDANG KERING
DRIED PRAWN SAMBAL

¾ cup dried prawns
4-6 fresh red chillies
8 shallots (*bawang merah*) or 1 medium red or brown onion
2 tablespoons oil
salt to taste
2-4 teaspoons Chinese lime juice (*limau kesturi*) or lemon juice

Also popular with the Straits Chinese, who call it sambal hay bee, this is served as an accompaniment to rice meals, as a sandwich spread, or as a filling for savoury pancakes. Will keep on the shelf for several weeks if stored in an airtight container.

Soak prawns in warm water for 10 minutes. Drain and pick over, discarding any hard pieces of shell. Pound prawns until finely shredded, or put in food processor or blender for about 1 minute. Gently fry shredded prawns in a dry pan, stirring frequently, for about 5 minutes. Set aside.

Pound chillies and shallots together to make a paste. Heat oil in a *kuali* and gently fry pounded mixture for 2-3 minutes, then add shredded prawns and fry over very low heat, stirring from time to time, until dry and crisp. This will take about 15 minutes.

Add salt and lime or lemon juice to taste. Allow to cool, then store in an airtight container.

CUCUMBER AND PINEAPPLE SAMBAL

1 small to medium cucumber
1 cup chopped pineapple (fresh or tinned)
2 shallots (*bawang merah*), or ¼ medium red or brown onion, finely sliced
1 fresh red chilli, sliced
1 tablespoon white vinegar, or more to taste
½ teaspoon salt
2 teaspoons sugar (optional)

Peel most of the skin from the cucumber, then cut into small pieces. Combine with all other ingredients and mix well. If using tinned pineapple, omit the sugar. Cover and leave to stand for at least 30 minutes before serving as a side-dish with rice.

INDIAN

ONION SAMBAL

2 medium red or brown onions, finely
    sliced across
1 teaspoon salt
2 tablespoons lemon juice
sprinkle of chilli powder (optional)

Mix sliced onions and salt. Cover and stand in refrigerator for 1 hour, then squeeze onion and discard liquid. Toss onion with lemon juice and chilli powder and serve. Salting the onion removes much of the sharp taste, making this a pleasantly mild *sambal*.

SRI LANKAN

CHILLI AND ONION SAMBAL

8-10 dried red chillies, soaked
1 tablespoon dried prawns, soaked and
    pounded
4 shallots (*bawang merah*), or ½
    medium red or brown onion,
    chopped
pinch salt
1-2 teaspoons lemon juice, or more to
    taste

This accompaniment is to the Sri Lankans what sambal blacan is to Malays — an almost indispensable condiment that spikes rice or other bland foods.

Using a mortar and pestle if possible, pound the chillies until well ground. Add pounded or shredded dried prawns (a blender does the job of shredding prawns in a few seconds). Continue pounding until fine, then add shallots and pound to make a paste. Add salt and lemon juice to taste.

CHINESE

SOYA SAUCE WITH SESAME SEEDS

2 tablespoons sesame seeds
6 tablespoons light soya sauce
1 tablespoon white vinegar
1 slice ginger, very finely chopped
1 spring onion, very finely chopped

Toast sesame seeds lightly in a dry pan, stirring constantly, until they turn golden. Crush with a mortar and pestle or in a blender and mix with all other ingredients. Serve as a dipping sauce with steamboat.

CHINESE

SOYA SAUCE WITH GINGER

4 cm (1½ in) fresh ginger
6 tablespoons light soya sauce

Chop ginger then extract juice by pounding and squeezing with a cloth, or by putting in a garlic press. Mix ginger juice with soya sauce and serve with steamboat.

CHINESE

PEANUT-OIL SAUCE

2.5 cm (1 in) fresh ginger
1 spring onion, very finely chopped
3 tablespoons finest quality peanut oil
¼ teaspoon sesame oil
1 tablespoon oyster sauce

Chop ginger as finely as possible, then mix with all other ingredients and put into individual sauce bowls. Serve with salt-baked chicken.

MALAY

SATAY SAUCE

8 dried chillies, soaked
8 shallots (bawang merah) or 1 medium
    red or brown onion
1 clove garlic
4 candlenuts (buah keras) or
    macadamias
1 stalk lemon grass (serai) or substitute
½ cup raw peanuts, or ½ cup crunchy
    peanut butter
2 tablespoons oil
1 cup coconut milk (see page 44)
2 teaspoons tamarind soaked in ¼ cup
    water
1 teaspoon brown sugar
salt to taste

The rich spicy peanut sauce served with satay *provides the finishing touch to make this an irresistible dish. Double the amounts given below and freeze half, re-heating gently at a later date if you wish to cut down on work.*

Pound chillies, shallots, garlic, candlenuts and lemon grass together until fine. Lightly roast peanuts in the oven or in a dry frying pan and pound coarsely.
    Heat oil in a saucepan and gently fry the ground items (except peanuts) for 5 minutes, stirring from time to time. Add coconut milk and bring slowly to the boil, stirring continuously. Add tamarind water, brown sugar, peanuts or peanut butter and salt. Simmer gently for a couple of minutes. Thin sauce with a little boiled water if desired and serve at room temperature.

MALAY

GADO GADO SAUCE

8 fresh red chillies
1 teaspoon dried shrimp paste (blacan)
2 tablespoons oil
8 shallots (bawang merah), or 1 medium
    red or brown onion, finely sliced
1½ cups coconut milk (see page 44)
½ cup peanuts, roasted and coarsely
    crushed, or ½ cup crunchy peanut
    butter
1-2 teaspoons palm sugar (gula Melaka)
    or brown sugar
¼ cup tamarind water (see page 63)
salt to taste

Pound chillies and dried shrimp paste together until finely ground. Heat oil in a saucepan and fry shallots gently until soft. Add pounded mixture and fry, stirring from time to time, for 4-5 minutes. Add coconut milk, a little at a time, then put in all other ingredients and simmer for about 3 minutes until the sauce thickens. Cool and serve with *gado gado* salad.

INDIAN

FRESH COCONUT CHUTNEY (picture page 118)

1 heaped cup freshly grated coconut
¼-½ fresh green chilli
1 small slice fresh ginger
¼ clove garlic
½ teaspoon salt
2 tablespoons water

Fried mixture:
1 tablespoon oil
½ teaspoon brown mustard seed
2 shallots (bawang merah), or
    ¼ medium red or brown onion,
    ½ finely sliced
1 sprig curry leaves (karuvapillai)
½ teaspoon blackgram dhal (ulundoo)
½ dried red chilli, sliced

Pound or blend the coconut, chilli, ginger, garlic and salt, gradually adding water to form a thick paste.
    Heat oil and fry the mustard seed for a few seconds before adding all other ingredients to be fried. Cook for another couple of minutes, stirring constantly, then take off heat and mix in the pounded coconut paste. Blend well and turn into a serving dish. This chutney is usually eaten with *dosay*.

Acar (foreground, recipe page 187) and salt fish pickle (recipe page 188).

FRESH CORIANDER CHUTNEY

1 cup firmly packed fresh coriander
    leaves
8 shallots (*bawang merah*) or 1 medium
    red or brown onion
1-2 fresh green chillies
1 slice fresh ginger, finely chopped
1 tablespoon freshly grated or desiccated
    coconut
1 teaspoon salt
1 teaspoon sugar
¼ cup tamarind water (see page 63) or
    2-3 tablespoons malt vinegar

Put coriander, roughly chopped onions, chillies, ginger and coconut in the jar of an electric blender or food processor and blend until fine. Add salt, sugar and liquid, a little at a time, blending until well mixed. Store covered in the refrigerator until needed.

FRESH MINT CHUTNEY (picture page 159)

1 cup firmly packed fresh mint leaves
8 shallots (*bawang merah*) or 1 medium
    red or brown onion
1-2 fresh green chillies
1 teaspoon salt
1 teaspoon sugar
¼ cup tamarind water (see page 63) or
    2-3 tablespoons malt vinegar

Put mint in the jar of a blender or food processor. Chop shallots and chillies coarsely and put with mint. Blend until fine, then add salt, sugar and liquid, a little at a time, blending until well mixed. Store covered in the refrigerator until needed.

MANGO CHUTNEY

6-8 unripe green mangoes, weighing a
    total of about 750 g (1½ lb)
1 tablespoon salt
10 dried red chillies
30 g (1 oz) fresh ginger
4 cloves garlic
3 tablespoons oil
1 teaspoon brown mustard seed
¾ cup malt vinegar
1 cup brown sugar
½ teaspoon turmeric powder
1 heaped tablespoon raisins

Generally, Indians prefer to serve fresh chutneys with their meals, and slices of green mango are often simply tossed with salt and chilli and served immediately. However, when large numbers of unripe green mango are available, chutneys such as this one, which can be kept for several months, are prepared.

Peel the mangoes and cut into thick slices. The mangoes should be sufficiently unripe for you to be able to cut through the still-soft stone. If, however, you have underestimated the maturity of the mangoes, don't worry. Cut around the stone, slicing the flesh, and cook the stone in the chutney. Sprinkle mango with salt and leave aside.

Pull off the stalk end of the chillies and shake out most of the seeds. If you do not want a rather hot chutney, reduce the number of chillies to 6 or 7. Break each chilli into 3 or 4 pieces and soak in hot water until softened. Peel ginger and garlic, then grind together with soaked chillies to get a paste, adding a little of the oil if using a blender or food processor.

Heat oil in a saucepan and put in the mustard seed. When it starts popping, cover the pan for a moment or two to stop the seeds going all over the kitchen, then put in the ground mixture and fry, stirring all the time, for a couple of minutes. Add vinegar, sugar and turmeric. Bring to the boil then simmer uncovered for 10 minutes.

Put in the mangoes, together with any liquid which may have

run off them, and simmer for about 15 minutes until the mangoes become transparent. Add the raisins, remove pan from heat, then pack chutney into sterilised glass jars with airtight lids. Cover only when cold, and store in a cupboard. When removing chutney to serve in a smaller dish at the table, use a wooden or plastic spoon.

CHINESE

PICKLED GREEN CHILLIES

10 fresh green chillies, sliced crosswise
½ cup boiling water
½ cup white vinegar

You'll find a jar or side-dish of these green chillies on almost every coffee shop or restaurant table in Singapore. They are usually doused with light soya sauce and eaten with noodles and rice dishes.

Put chillies in a screwtop jar. Combine boiling water and vinegar and pour over the chillies. Cool, then cover jar and leave chillies to stand in cupboard for about 3 days before using. Will keep for about 3 weeks on the shelf, and much longer if refrigerated.

MALAY

ACAR (picture page 185)
VEGETABLE PICKLE

2 cucumbers
1 large carrot
10-12 shallots (*bawang merah*) or small pickling onions
6-8 small cloves garlic
4 cm (1½ in) fresh ginger
3 fresh red chillies
6 tablespoons oil
3 teaspoons sugar
½ teaspoon salt
pinch monosodium glutamate
3 tablespoons white vinegar

Spice paste:
6 dried red chillies, soaked
4 shallots (*bawang merah*) or ½ medium red or brown onion
2.5 cm (1 in) fresh ginger
1 cm (½ in) fresh turmeric, or 1 teaspoon turmeric powder
1 tablespoon dried prawns, soaked
2 candlenuts (*buah keras*) or macadamias, soaked in cold water for 5 minutes

Do not peel cucumbers, but cut into four lengthwise and discard seeds. Cut into pieces 5 cm (2 in) long, then cut into narrow strips. Scrub carrot, then cut into matchstick pieces about 5 cm (2 in) long. Peel shallots and garlic, and leave whole. Peel ginger and cut lengthwise into very fine shreds. Cut slits up both sides of each chilli to within about 1 cm (½ in) of the top. Soak cucumber in salty water to cover for about 10 minutes. Soak carrot strips in plain water.

Grind spice paste ingredients together, or put in food processor, adding a little of the oil until a fine paste results. Heat oil and gently fry spice paste for 3 minutes. Add sugar, stir, then add shredded ginger, shallots and garlic. Stir-fry for a couple of minutes then add salt and monosodium glutamate. Stir, then add vinegar and stir again.

Add drained carrots and cook gently for 3-4 minutes, stirring from time to time. Add drained cucumber and slit red chillies and stir-fry for 4-5 minutes. Remove from pan and allow to cool. Serve at room temperature as a side-dish with rice. Will keep refrigerated for at least 1 week.

INDIAN

LIME PICKLE

1 pickled lime (commercially bottled variety), chopped
¼ medium red or brown onion, finely sliced
1 green chilli, finely sliced

Combine all ingredients and serve as a condiment with Indian or Sri Lankan food. Only a very small amount, say a teaspoonful per person, is needed.

EURASIAN
SALT FISH PICKLE (picture page 185)

300 g (6½ oz) salted dried fish (*ikan
  kurau, mergui,* or cod)
2½ tablespoons coriander
1 tablespoon cummin
2 teaspoons black peppercorns
½ teaspoon white peppercorns
½ teaspoon turmeric powder
10 dried red chillies, soaked
8 shallots (*bawang merah*) or 1 medium
  red or brown onion
4-6 cloves garlic
1 cup malt vinegar, or more
¼ cup sugar

Wash dried fish and cut into pieces about 5 cm (2 in) square. Leave to dry in the sun for 1-2 days, or dry in a very low oven.

Heat coriander, cummin and both lots of peppercorns gently in a dry pan then grind to a fine powder in a coffee grinder or mortar and pestle. Add turmeric and set aside.

Grind chillies, shallots and garlic to a paste, adding just a little of the vinegar if using a blender or food processor. Mix with dried spices and sugar, stirring to dissolve sugar. Put fish into a stoneware jar, pour over the vinegar mixture, adding more vinegar if necessary to cover fish, and cover with a weighted wooden lid. Leave in a cool cupboard for at least 7 days.

When requiring salt fish pickle, remove a few pieces and dry on a paper towel. Heat equal parts of olive and peanut oils and fry the fish over very low heat for about 5 minutes on each side. The pickle will keep for several weeks. Serve as a side-dish with rice.

CHINESE
SALT AND PEPPER POWDER

4 teaspoons salt
1 teaspoon black peppercorns

Put salt and peppercorns in a pan and cook over moderate heat, stirring constantly, until the salt begins to turn golden. Remove from pan immediately and crush with a mortar and pestle or in an electric coffee grinder until fine. Put in individual sauce bowls and serve with roasted poultry or deep-fried prawns.

CHINESE
SPICED SALT

3 teaspoons salt
½ teaspoon five-spice powder

Combine salt and spice and put in individual sauce bowls. Serve with crispy skin chicken.

FRIED ONION FLAKES

shallots, large onions or dried chopped
  onion
oil for deep frying

A garnish of finely sliced, crisp-fried shallots is used by all Singaporeans, regardless of ethnic origin, in many dishes. This can be made from large onions if shallots are not available, or from commercially prepared dried chopped onion.

If using shallots, peel and slice finely. If using large onions, cut in quarters lengthwise then slice very finely crosswise. Dry sliced shallots or onions with paper towel and put in sun to dry for about an hour, if possible. Heat oil in a *kuali* and deep fry sliced shallots or sliced onions over moderate heat, stirring frequently, until golden brown. If using dried chopped onion, merely drop into the oil and fry, stirring until golden brown. Remove fried onions quickly, taking care they do not burn, and drain on paper towel. When cool and dry, store in an airtight jar. Do not add salt or they will become soggy.

SPICE POWDERS
MEAT CURRY POWDER

300 g (10 oz) coriander
75 g (2½ oz) cummin
75 g (2½ oz) fennel
75 g (2½ oz) dried red chillies
45 g (1½ oz) black peppercorns
15 g (½ oz) cinnamon sticks
10 whole cardamom pods
10 whole cloves
45 g (1½ oz) turmeric powder

FISH CURRY POWDER

300 g (10 oz) coriander
75 g (2½ oz) fennel
75 g (2½ oz) dried red chillies
45 g (1½ oz) cummin
30 g (1 oz) fenugreek
30 g (1 oz) black peppercorns
45 g (1½ oz) turmeric powder

The art of spicing is highly individual and creative, and no Singapore cook worth her chilli powder would dream of using the one spice mixture or curry powder on its own for every type of dish from fish to fowl, meat to vegetables. However, certain basic combinations of spices are sometimes used as the starting point in making a spiced or 'curry' dish, with extra whole spices and other seasonings being added during cooking, depending upon the main ingredient.

Most local cooks use two types of curry powder: one which goes well with meat and the other which enhances the flavour of fish and other seafood. As ready-mixed commercial curry powders are sometimes adulterated with rice flour (as, indeed, is turmeric, so make sure the brand you buy is really bright yellow), Singapore cooks take their own whole spices to a mill. They literally stand over the man as he grinds the spices for them to ensure the purity of their curry powder!

A tip on storing curry powder. If you do not use it frequently and wish to store it for more than three months, try keeping it in an airtight container in the deep-freeze section of the refrigerator. It will not set solid, and will remain fresh almost indefinitely.

Pick over the spice seeds and discard any stalks, grit and other foreign matter. Put in a bowl, rinse with water, pour off water and drain in a very fine mesh sieve. Dry spices in the sun or a warm place, preferably on a flat cane tray, for 2-3 days. If you are buying cleaned and bottled spices, this procedure should not be necessary, but in Singapore, spices are sold from huge sacks and are therefore often very dusty.

Heat a dry pan (a *kuali* is ideal) and gently fry, one item at a time, the coriander, cummin, fennel, peppercorns, fenugreek (if using), and whole dried chillies until they become light golden-brown and give off a pleasant fragrance. Allow to cool slightly, then grind, a little at a time, in an electric coffee grinder until very fine. Break the fried chillies into several pieces, discarding the stalk end, before grinding. Grind other whole spices such as cinnamon, cardamon and cloves. Combine all ground spices, then add the turmeric powder, stirring to blend well. Store in airtight containers when cold.

CHINESE

PRAWN TOAST (picture page 180)

250 g (8 oz) raw prawns
50 g (1½ oz) hard pork fat
4 water chestnuts, finely chopped
1 teaspoon Chinese rice wine or dry
   sherry
¾ teaspoon salt
¼ teaspoon sugar
dash of white pepper
1 egg, lightly beaten
1 heaped tablespoon cornflour
loaf of sliced white sandwich bread
oil for deep frying

Using a cleaver, chop peeled prawns and pork fat together until you get a fine paste. If you have a food processor, cut pork fat into small squares and put in machine for a few seconds, then add prawns and blend for another few seconds. Add all other ingredients, except bread, and blend well.

Remove crust from bread and cut into circles or small squares. Spread a mound of prawn paste on top of each piece of bread. Heat oil and deep fry the pieces of prawn toast, for 2-3 minutes, turning over once during cooking so that both sides turn golden brown. If liked, a hardboiled quail's egg can be pressed into the centre of each prawn toast just before deep frying. Serve hot as a snack or as an *hors d'oeuvre*.

CHINESE

LOBAH
DEEP-FRIED PORK AND PRAWN ROLLS

375 g (12 oz) lean pork
250 g (8 oz) raw prawns
1 small carrot, grated
4 shallots (*bawang merah*), or ½
    medium red or brown onion, finely
    chopped
2-3 spring onions, finely chopped
6 water chestnuts, finely chopped
½ teaspoon salt
dash of white pepper
pinch monosodium glutamate
1 egg, lightly beaten
1 heaped tablespoon cornflour
3 large dried beancurd sheets
oil for deep frying

Chop the pork and peeled prawns together with a cleaver or put in a blender or food processor until a fine paste results. Simmer carrot in 2 tablespoons of water for 2 minutes, then add to pork paste together with all other ingredients except beancurd sheets and oil. Mix thoroughly.

Wipe beancurd sheets with a damp cloth and cut into 15 cm (6 in) squares. Put a little of the mixture into the centre of each piece of beancurd and roll up firmly into a cigar shape, tucking in the sides. Deep fry in hot oil for about 4-5 minutes. Drain and serve with plum or chilli sauce.

CHINESE

SPRING ROLLS (picture page 180)

25 large or 50 small spring roll wrappers
1 tablespoon plain flour
water to mix flour to thick paste
oil for deep frying

Filling:
3 tablespoons oil
2 slices fresh ginger, finely chopped
250 g (8 oz) pork, shredded
125 g (4 oz) raw prawns, peeled and
    coarsely chopped
4 dried black mushrooms, soaked and
    shredded
250 g (8 oz) beansprouts
2¼ cups shredded bamboo shoot
6 water chestnuts, finely chopped
¾ cup shredded yam bean
    (*bangkwang*), or ¾ cup extra
    bamboo shoot
1 tablespoon light soya sauce
4 spring onions, including 15 cm (6 in)
    green tops, finely chopped
¼ teaspoon monosodium glutamate
salt and white pepper to taste

There are many different versions of this tasty savoury; fillings include vegetables such as beansprouts, yam bean (bangkwang), bamboo shoots, water chestnuts and cabbage, together with meat or seafood such as prawns, crabmeat, dried squid and seasonings. You can experiment according to taste and availability of ingredients. This recipe should make about 25 large or 40-50 small spring rolls. Spring rolls can be deep frozen if they are partially fried before storage.

To prepare the filling, heat 1 tablespoon oil in a *kuali* and stir-fry ginger for about 30 seconds. Add the pork and stir-fry for 2-3 minutes, then add prawns and mushroom and cook for another 2-3 minutes, stirring frequently. Remove mixture from *kuali* and set aside.

Add another tablespoon of oil to the *kuali* and stir-fry the beansprouts, bamboo shoot, and water chestnuts for 2-3 minutes until beansprouts just start to loose their crispness. Remove and set aside.

Put the remaining 1 tablespoon of oil in the *kuali* and stir-fry the yam bean until it softens, then sprinkle with soya sauce and cook for another minute or two before removing from *kuali*. Mix all the fried ingredients together and add spring onions, monosodium glutamate, salt and pepper. Leave to cool.

To assemble the spring rolls, gently peel off four wrappers at a time and lay on a table. Cover remaining wrappers with a damp cloth to prevent them drying out. Using the back of a spoon, smear a little of the flour and water paste onto the far end of each wrapper. Put about 1 heaped tablespoon of the filling on large wrappers, or 2 heaped teaspoons on small wrappers. Fold up by tucking over the nearest end first, then each side, then roll up to the far end and press firmly.

Heat plenty of oil in a *kuali* and deep fry the spring rolls, a few at a time, until golden brown, Drain and serve with bottled chilli sauce.

CHINESE

DEEP-FRIED WUN TUN (picture page 180)

wun tun dumplings (see page 77)
oil for deep frying

Sauce:
3 tablespoons apricot jam
1½ tablespoons white vinegar
1 tablespoon hot water

Prepare dumplings are directed. They can be stored in an airtight container until needed. Combine all ingredients for sauce, mixing well, and put in a bowl. Heat plenty of oil and deep fry the dumplings until golden brown. Drain and serve immediately with sauce for dipping.

NONYA

POPIAH

Egg wrappers:
scant cup of flour, sifted
1¼ cups cold water
½ teaspoon salt
5 eggs, lightly beaten

Cooked filling:
1 tablespoon oil
1 small onion, sliced
2 cloves garlic, finely chopped
1 tablespoon salted soya beans
    (*taucheo*), mashed
100 g (3½ oz) pork, shredded
100 g (3½ oz) raw prawns, shelled
250 g (8 oz) boiled bamboo shoot,
    grated
1 small yam bean (*bangkwang*),
    shredded, or 1 cup shredded water
    chestnuts
1 tablespoon light soya sauce

Fresh filling:
100 g (3½ oz) canned or fresh crabmeat
1-2 pieces hard beancurd (*taukwa*), deep
    fried and finely sliced
250 g (8 oz) beansprouts, blanched and
    drained
18 lettuce leaves ('local' or Romaine
    lettuce if possible)
½ cucumber, skin left on, shredded
2 hardboiled eggs, chopped
2 Chinese sausages (*lap cheong*),
    steamed and sliced (optional)

Sauces:
chilli paste made from 12 fresh red
    chillies, pounded
10 cloves garlic, pounded to a paste
    with a pinch of salt
4 tablespoons Chinese treacle sauce
    (thick black *tim cheong*), or sweet
    black soya sauce (*kicup manis*)

This is the Straits Chinese version of spring rolls. Although the list of ingredients looks formidable, popiah *are really quite easy to prepare and consist of egg wrappers, cooked and fresh fillings, and sauces.*

Popiah *ingredients are normally prepared in advance and set out on dishes on the table. Either the hostess can assemble the* popiah *on the spot, or each diner can help himself. The following amounts will make about 18* popiah.

To make the egg wrappers, put flour in a bowl, gradually add the cold water, then stir in salt and beaten eggs. Heat a lightly greased small frying pan about 20 cm (8 in) in diameter. Pour in a small amount of the egg mixture, swirl it around to cover the pan, and cook over medium heat until set. Turn over and cook on the other side. Be sure not to make the wrappers too thick, and keep stirring the batter before making each new wrapper. Stack wrappers on a plate.

Heat the oil for the cooked filling and fry the onion and garlic gently until soft and light gold in colour. Add the mashed salted soya beans and fry, stirring, for another couple of minutes. Put in the pork and fry for 1 minute, then add prawns and continue frying, stirring frequently, for 5 minutes. Add bamboo shoot, yam bean and soya sauce and stir thoroughly. Cover the pan and simmer ingredients for 30 minutes, checking occasionally that the mixture has not dried out completely. If this happens, add a tablespoon of cold water. Allow cooked mixture to cool in a bowl.

To assemble the *popiah*, lay an egg wrapper on a plate and smear it lightly with a little of each of the sauces. Then add a lettuce leaf, some of the cooked filling, a little crabmeat, beancurd, beansprouts, shredded cucumber, hardboiled egg and Chinese sausage. Roll up, tucking in both sides. The *popiah* can be sliced into 4 or 5 bite-sized pieces, or left whole if preferred.

MALAY

SAMBAL TELUR (picture page 174)
EGGS IN CHILLI SAUCE

6 hardboiled eggs
2 teaspoons dried tamarind
½ cup warm water
10 dried red chillies, soaked
2 fresh red chillies
8 shallots (*bawang merah*) or 1 medium
    red or brown onion
1 teaspoon dried shrimp paste (*blacan*)
1 clove garlic
2½ tablespoons oil
1 teaspoon salt
1 teaspoon sugar

Peel eggs and deep fry in hot oil for a couple of minutes, stirring so that they turn golden all over. Remove from oil and drain. Soak tamarind in water for 10 minutes, then squeeze and strain to obtain tamarind water. Set aside.

Pound or grind together both lots of chillies, shallots, shrimp paste and garlic. When they become a fine paste, heat oil in a pan and gently fry pounded ingredients, stirring frequently, for 4-5 minutes. Add tamarind water, sugar and salt and simmer for 1 minute. Put in eggs and simmer for 1 more minute, stirring so that eggs are well coated with sauce. Serve at room temperature. The eggs can be halved lengthwise before serving.

MALAY

TEMPE GORENG (picture page 174)
FRIED FERMENTED SOYA BEAN CAKES

4 fermented soya bean cakes (*tempe*)
1½ teaspoons coriander, freshly ground
2 cloves garlic, finely ground or put
    through garlic press
1 teaspoon salt
2 teaspoons water
oil for deep frying

Unwrap the *tempe*, and if liked, slice in half lengthwise to make very thin cakes. Cut *tempe* in half crosswise. Combine coriander, garlic and salt, then mix in water. Rub each piece of *tempe* with this mixture and leave to stand for 5 minutes.

Heat plenty of oil in a *kuali* and deep fry *tempe* pieces for 3-4 minutes until golden brown on both sides. Fry a little longer if you have not cut *tempe* in half lengthwise. Drain and serve as an accompaniment to rice, meat, fish and vegetables.

MALAY

IKAN BILIS GORENG (picture page 180)
FRIED DRIED WHITEBAIT WITH PEANUTS

2½ cups dried anchovies (*ikan bilis*)
¼ cup oil
8 shallots (*bawang merah*), or 1 medium
    red or brown onion, pounded or
    grated
½-1 teaspoon chilli powder
¼ teaspoon turmeric powder
2 teaspoons sugar
½ cup fried or roasted peanuts

This is served as an accompaniment at a main meal, or can be eaten as a snack with drinks. Many of the ikan bilis *sold outside Singapore are unsalted, so if you are using this type, add salt to taste.*

Unless you are using the very thin tiny variety of *ikan bilis* often known as 'silver fish' and about 2.5 cm (1 in) long, you will need to discard the head and dark intestinal tract of each fish. Make sure the *ikan bilis* are completely dry by putting them in the sun for an hour (watch for cats) or drying them in a very low oven for about 15 minutes.

Heat oil in a *kuali* and gently fry the *ikan bilis* until brown and crisp. Drain and set aside. Wipe out the pan and put in another tablespoon of oil. Gently fry the shallots, chilli powder and turmeric, stirring frequently, until golden and fragrant. Add *ikan bilis*, sugar and peanuts and fry for another minute or two, stirring constantly to amalgamate all ingredients. Allow to cool before serving.

INDIAN

CHILLI TAIRU (picture page 118)
CHILLIES PRESERVED IN YOGHURT

500 g (1 lb) fresh green chillies
2½ cups plain yoghurt (preferably
　home-made)
½ cup salt

It's no use pretending that this is not a time-consuming recipe, but if you enjoy a tangy accompaniment to Indian meals and can buy or grow a large quantity of green chillies, it's well worth attempting. I really missed chilli tairu while living in Australia, so went to the bother of following this receipe and was delighted with the result. So, too, were my friends with whom I shared them.

Make a 2.5 cm (1 in) slit in one side of each chilli, but do not remove the stems if still attached. Mix yoghurt and salt together in a glass or china bowl. Add chillies and stir carefully. Keep for 3 days in a dry place, stirring daily with a wooden spoon.

Remove chillies from yoghurt and dry in the sun for the whole day, returning them to the yoghurt at night. Repeat daily until all the yoghurt is absorbed — it will take 5-7 days. When yoghurt has been absorbed, dry chillies in the sun until they become crisp.

Store (they will last for several months) in an airtight container. When required as an accompaniment, fry in hot oil for a couple of minutes until crisp and light brown.

INDIAN

VADAY
DEEP-FRIED LENTIL SAVOURIES

1½ cups blackgram *dhal* (*ulundoo*)
2-3 fresh green chillies
1 medium red or brown onion
3 slices fresh ginger
1 sprig curry leaves (*karuvapillai*)
1 teaspoon salt
oil for deep frying

Soak the *dhal* in cold water overnight. Rub the skins from *dhal* if you have not been able to buy the husked variety. Drain. Grind to a paste with a mortar and pestle or in an electric blender.

Chop the chillies, onion, ginger and curry leaves very finely and mix with ground *dhal*. Add salt and stir thoroughly.

Oil your hands before shaping mixture into small balls. Place on an oiled plate while heating plenty of oil in a *kuali*. Fry the *vaday* a few at a time, turning around as they cook, until golden brown. This will take at least 5 minutes. Drain and serve as a snack.

If you are using an electric blender to grind the *dhal*, you will need to add 3-4 tablespoons of water to keep the blades turning. If the resulting mixture is too wet to handle, add a tablespoon or two of rice flour.

INDIAN

SAMOSA (picture page 180)
POTATO AND PEA SAVOURIES

12 spring roll wrappers
flour and water paste
oil for deep frying

Filling:
3 medium potatoes
2 tablespoons *ghee* or butter
1 medium red or brown onion, finely
   chopped
2 fresh green chillies, sliced
1 clove garlic, smashed and chopped
1 slice fresh ginger, very finely chopped
125 g (4 oz) frozen peas, thawed
1 teaspoon *garam masala* (see glossary)
½ teaspoon salt
1 tablespoon finely chopped fresh
   coriander or mint leaves
1 tablespoon lemon juice

Although these delightful little savouries are most commonly prepared with home-made pastry, I prefer to copy the short cut used by a well-known Singapore restaurant which wraps the filling in strips of spring roll wrapper.

Prepare the filling first. Boil the potatoes until cooked, then peel and dice into 1 cm (¼ in) cubes. Heat *ghee* and gently fry onion, chilli, garlic and ginger together for 2-3 minutes, until softened. Add potatoes and peas and cook gently, stirring from time to time, for another 2-3 minutes. Sprinkle with *garam masala*, salt, fresh coriander and lemon juice, then stir well and set aside to cool.

When filling is cool, cut each spring roll wrapper into three strips lengthwise. Cover with a damp cloth to prevent them from drying out while working. Place 1 heaped teaspoon of filling at the end of each strip and fold over diagonally. Continue folding back and forth, each time making a triangle. Seal the final flap of the last triangle with a little flour and water paste.

When all the *samosa* are ready, deep fry in very hot oil, a few at a time, until crisp and golden. As *samosa* are best eaten warm, you may like to prepare them ahead of time, frying until just turning golden, then keeping them aside for a quick second frying just before serving. Delicious with mint or coriander chutney (recipes page 186).

CURRY PUFFS

1 large packet flaky or puff pastry,
   weighing about 450 g (14 oz)
2 tablespoons oil
1 medium red or brown onion, finely
   chopped
2 slices fresh ginger, very finely chopped
2 heaped tablespoons meat curry
   powder (see page 189)
250 g (8 oz) minced lean lamb or beef
1 large ripe tomato, chopped
½ teaspoon salt, or more to taste
1 large potato, boiled and cut into 5 mm
   (¼ in) dice

The curry puff and kueh *man, often an Indian with a huge round metal container strapped to the back of his bicycle, is a popular figure in the* kampungs *and suburban areas of Singapore. His curry puffs are a favourite snack with everyone, regardless of ethnic origin. They can be made with short crust pastry and deep fried, but the following version, which uses flaky or puff pastry and is cooked in the oven, is lighter.*

Allow pastry to thaw to room temperature. Heat oil and gently fry onion and ginger, stirring from time to time, until soft. Mix curry powder with sufficient water to make a stiff paste, then add to onions and ginger. Fry for 3-4 minutes then add meat and fry until it changes colour. Add chopped tomato and sprinkle with salt, then cover the pan and simmer gently for 10 minutes, stirring from time to time. Add a tablespoonful or two of water during cooking if meat threatens to burn. Add diced potato and cook for another minute or two, taste and adjust seasonings, then leave to cool.

Roll pastry out very thinly and cut into about 14 squares measuring 8 cm (3 in). Wet two edges of each square with milk, then put in about a tablespoonful of the cold meat filling. Fold over to make a triangle, press the edges with a fork, and bake at 220°C/425°F/Gas No. 7 for 12-15 minutes, until puffed and golden brown. Serve warm.

Desserts, Cakes & Drinks

Cakes based on rice or tapioca flour and coconut milk, and heavy porridge-like dishes made from various beans and rice, are generally eaten as between-meal snacks (or even as a breakfast!) rather than as desserts in Singapore. However, this doesn't mean that you can't serve them as desserts, so long as you make sure that the food which precedes them is not too heavy. One ideal solution, if you like to finish your meal with something sweet (apart from fresh fruit) is to serve these desserts or cakes at the end of a light luncheon, or to eat them as a snack the way Singaporeans do.

CHINESE

TOFFEED APPLES

4 large green apples, peeled
oil for deep frying
bowl of cold water with ice cubes
greased serving platter

Batter:
1 cup plain flour
1 egg
¾ cup water

Syrup:
¾ cup sugar
3 tablespoons peanut oil
1 teaspoon sesame oil
3 tablespoons water
2 tablespoons sesame seeds

One of the few desserts prepared by Chinese cooks, this is a northern and western Chinese speciality particularly popular in Singapore's Chinese restaurants. Although it is not difficult to prepare, it is essential that everything should be laid out ready so that you can work quickly during the final cooking stage. Chinese pears (or any other variety of firm pear) are excellent prepared this way; so, too, are firm bananas.

Prepare the batter by sifting flour into a bowl and gradually adding egg and water to make a smooth consistency. Set aside.

Combine sugar, peanut and sesame oil and water in a pan. Boil until very hot and syrupy. Add sesame seeds and keep syrup warm.

Put oil in a *kuali* and while it is heating, cut each apple into 8 pieces. Have the syrup, bowl of iced water and serving platter near at hand. Dip a few pieces of apple at a time into the batter and deep fry in very hot oil for 1-2 minutes until golden. Remove from oil, drain for a second or two, then stir in the hot syrup until glazed. Dip immediately into the iced water to make the syrup set into a toffee-like coating, and put on the greased serving dish. Continue until all apple pieces are cooked and serve immediately.

CHINESE

ALMOND JELLY WITH LONGGANS

2 cups water
2½ teaspoons agar agar powder
1 cup evaporated milk
½ cup sugar
½ teaspoon almond essence, or to taste
1 large tin longgans or lychees

The favourite conclusion to most restaurant meals, this is easily prepared ahead of time. Tinned lychees can be used if preferred.

Put water in a saucepan and sprinkle the agar agar powder over the top. Bring slowly to the boil, then simmer gently for 5 minutes. Add the evaporated milk and sugar and stir gently until sugar is dissolved. Add almond essence, and taste to see if it is strong enough (different brands vary in strength). Pour into a large rectangular or square dish and leave to cool, then refrigerate for at least 1 hour.

Put the tin of fruit into the refrigerator at the same time as the almond jelly. At serving time, cut the jelly into diamond shapes. Put the longgans and juice into a large bowl, add the almond jelly pieces and stir very gently to mix.

NONYA

BUBOR PULOT HITAM (picture opposite)
BLACK RICE PUDDING

1½ cups glutinous black rice
8 cups water
3 tablespoons palm sugar (*gula Melaka*) or brown sugar
2-3 tablespoons white sugar
1 slice fresh ginger
6-8 dried longgans (optional)
1½ cups thick coconut milk (see page 44)
pinch salt

The marvellous fragrance and flavour of glutinous black rice makes this simple snack or dessert something out of the ordinary. The dried longgans (known as 'dragon's eyes') add a faintly smokey taste. If you leave them out, then you have the Malay version of this bubor.

Wash rice thoroughly and put in a large saucepan with water. Cover, bring to boil, and simmer for 30 minutes. Add both sugars, ginger, longgans (removed from shell) and simmer very gently stirring from time to time, until the rice is soft and swollen (or, as the Nonyas say, *kembang*, or 'flower-like'). It may be necessary to add water during cooking. The final consistency of the *bubor* should be that of a porridge.

Mix thick coconut milk (made with milk if using dessicated coconut) with a pinch of salt. Serve warm *bubor pulot hitam* in individual bowls with a little coconut milk poured over the top.

MALAY

BUBOR KACANG HIJAU
GREEN MUNG PEA PORRIDGE

1½ cups green mung peas
2½ cups water
1 slice fresh ginger
pinch salt
2 cups thin coconut milk (see page 44)
4 tablespoons palm sugar (*gula Melaka*) or brown sugar
white sugar to taste
½ cup thick coconut milk (see page 44)

Wash peas thoroughly and put into a large saucepan with water, ginger and salt. Bring to the boil and simmer, covered, for about 45 minutes until all the water has been absorbed and the peas have swelled.

Add thin coconut milk and palm sugar. Stir over low heat until sugar has dissolved, then cook uncovered for about 1 hour until the peas are very soft. If the *bubor* seems too thick, add a little more thin coconut milk or hot water. Taste, adding white sugar if desired. Put thick coconut milk mixed with a pinch of salt into a serving jug. Pour the *bubor* into small bowls and serve warm, topped with a spoonful or two of thick coconut milk.

Bubor pulot hitam (recipe this page).

MALAY

KUEH DADAR
PANCAKES WITH SWEET COCONUT FILLING

1½ cups plain flour
1 egg, well beaten
pinch salt
2¼-2½ cups milk
few drops green food colouring or 3
    pandan leaves, pounded for green
    juice

Filling:
1½ cups freshly grated coconut or 1¼
    cups desiccated coconut
½ cup roughly chopped palm sugar
    (*gula Melaka*) or 3 heaped
    tablespoons brown sugar
3 tablespoons water

Prepare the filling first. If using desiccated coconut, moisten with a little warm milk so that it swells up. Put palm or brown sugar in a small saucepan with the water and stir over low heat until dissolved. If using palm sugar, strain the syrup to remove any grit or dirt, clean the pan, and return syrup to pan. Add fresh or desiccated coconut to the syrup and stir over low heat for 1 minute. Remove from heat and allow to cool before stuffing pancakes.

To prepare pancakes, sift flour into a bowl and add egg and salt. Pour in the milk gradually, mixing well to avoid lumps. Add sufficient milk to make a thin batter, then add food colouring or *pandan* juice and allow to stand for 5 minutes. Grease a small frying pan, preferably non-stick, and fry the pancakes on both sides, taking care they do not become brown. Stack on a plate and, when cool, put in some of the coconut filling and roll up, tucking in the sides. Serve as a snack or, if liked, as a dessert after a light meal.

MALAY

KUEH NAGA SARI
BANANA BLANCMANGE CAKE

½ cup (100 g or 3½ oz) green
    mung pea flour (*tepong hoen kwe*) or
    arrowroot
4 cups coconut milk (see page 44)
¾ cup sugar
few drops vanilla essence
4-6 ripe bananas
approximately 20 pieces banana leaf
    cut into 16 cm (6½ in) squares, or
    aluminium foil

A superb ending to a hot, spicy meal, these cool, refreshing cakes are make from green mung pea flour (tepong hoen kwe) and served in their banana-leaf wrapper.

Mix flour and coconut milk together in a saucepan and bring slowly to the boil, stirring constantly. Cook until the mixture becomes very thick, smooth and shiny, then add sugar and vanilla and leave to cool slightly.

If using banana leaves, soak in boiling water for a few minutes to clean and soften. Cut the bananas in lengthwise pieces 1 cm (½ in) thick, then cut crosswise into pieces about 6 cm (2½ in) long. To assemble the cakes, put a heaped tablespoonful of the cooked coconut-milk mixture in the centre of the banana leaf or foil. Lay a piece of banana on top, then cover with another tablespoonful of coconut-milk mixture. Wrap the packet up, envelope style, and continue until all the mixture is used up. Set packets inside a steamer and steam for 15 minutes. Allow to cool, then put in the refrigerator to chill.

MALAY

PENGAT
FRUIT IN COCONUT MILK

2 cups thin coconut milk (see page 44)
1 *pandan* leaf (optional)
3 heaped tablespoons palm sugar (*gula
    Melaka*) or brown sugar
4 large bananas
4-5 pieces jackfruit (*nangka*) or 1
    medium sweet potato
½ cup thick coconut milk (see page 44)

A typical home-style dish, pengat is simply a sweet coconut-milk sauce in which cheap, readily available items are cooked: bananas, pieces of yam or sweet potato, chunks of fermented tapioca root (tape), pieces of jackfruit (nangka), slivers of young coconut flesh, and even cellophane noodles. Although normally served as a teatime snack, it makes a nice finish to a light luncheon or supper.

Put thin coconut milk, *pandan* leaf (scraped with a fork and tied into a knot) and sugar into a saucepan. Bring slowly to the boil, stirring constantly, and simmer for a few minutes until sugar is dissolved. If using palm sugar, strain coconut milk mixture into a bowl, rinse out saucepan, then return strained liquid and *pandan* leaf to saucepan.

Peel bananas and cut diagonally into 4 cm (1 ½ in) pieces. If using jackfruit, cut each piece into four and discard seeds. If using sweet potato, peel and dice into 1 cm (½ in) cubes, and boil in a little water for 5 minutes. Add bananas and jackfruit or boiled sweet potato to coconut milk and simmer uncovered for 5 minutes. Add thick coconut milk, bring to the boil, and simmer for a minute or two to thicken. Discard *pandan* leaf and serve warm.

MALAY

COCONUT ROSE AGAR AGAR

4 cups coconut milk (see page 44)
3 teaspoons agar agar powder
½ cup sugar
few drops rose essence
few drops cochineal or other red food
    colouring

Put coconut milk into a saucepan and sprinkle agar agar powder on top. Bring very slowly to the boil, stirring constantly with a wooden spoon. Simmer for 1 minute, then remove from heat and stir in sugar, rose essence to taste, and enough cochineal to give a light pink colour. Pour into a large mould rinsed out with cold water, or, if preferred, into several small moulds. Allow to cool, then refrigerate until needed. Unmould onto a serving platter.

MALAY

JEMPUT JEMPUT
FRIED BANANA CAKES

4 ripe bananas, mashed
1 tablespoon sugar, or to taste
¾ cup plain flour
pinch salt
1 tablespoon water
oil for deep frying

Mix bananas and sugar and taste to see if sufficiently sweet. Sift in flour and salt, and mix well. Add water if necessary to make a very thick batter. Heat oil. Using a tablespoon, drop heaped spoonfuls of batter into very hot oil and fry for about 3 minutes, turning to make sure they turn golden brown all over. Drain on paper towel and serve warm. A good way of using up over-ripe bananas.

MALAY

PISANG GORENG
CRUNCHY FRIED BANANAS

1 cup plain flour
½ cup rice flour
2 teaspoons baking powder
pinch salt
1 cup water
oil for deep frying
8-10 large ripe bananas

A popular snack sold everywhere in Singapore, especially by Chinese hawkers who muddle up their Malay and refer to it as goreng pisang! *Either way, the taste's delicious.*

Sift both lots of flour, baking powder and salt into a bowl. Stir in water gradually to make a smooth thick batter.

Heat oil until smoking hot. Dip peeled bananas into the batter to coat thoroughly, then deep fry, two or three at a time, until rich golden-brown in colour. Drain and serve warm.

MALAY

GULA MELAKA
SAGO DESSERT WITH PALM SUGAR AND COCONUT MILK

2 cups pearl sago
6-8 cups boiling water
1 tablespoon milk
1 cup thick coconut milk (see page 44)
pinch salt

Syrup:
250 g (8 oz) palm sugar (*gula Melaka*) or
    200 g (6½ oz) brown sugar with 2
    tablespoons treacle
1½ cups water
1 *pandan* leaf (optional)

Much loved by the colonial British, this is still a favourite dessert after an expansive curry tiffin.

Put sago in a sieve and pick over to remove any grit or foreign matter. Shake the sieve to dislodge any dust, but do not wash sago or it will become gluey. Fill a very large saucepan with boiling water, and when it is boiling rapidly, pour the sago into the pan in a thin stream, stirring all the time with a wooden spoon. Boil for about 10 minutes, stirring constantly, until balls of sago swell and become transparent. Pour sago into a large sieve and hold under running water to wash away the starch. Shake the sieve until all the liquid has gone. Stir in milk to give sago a white colour, then put the sago into one large or 8-10 small moulds. Cool, then refrigerate until needed.
    Put coconut milk in a jug and stir in salt. Store in refrigerator. To make syrup, put palm sugar or brown sugar and treacle in a pan. If using *pandan* leaf, scrape with a fork, tie into a bundle, and add with water to pan. Simmer until sugar has dissolved, then continue cooking until the syrup has reduced to about 1 cup. Sieve, then discard *pandan* leaf. Put syrup into a jug and leave to cool.
    When serving, unmould the sago and pour a little coconut milk and syrup over each individual serving.

PAPAYA AGAR AGAR (picture opposite)

4 cups water
3½ teaspoons agar agar powder
4 tablespoons sugar, or more to taste
1 medium-sized ripe papaya (pawpaw)
1½ tablespoons Chinese lime juice
    (*limau kesturi*) or lemon juice

I'm not sure of the origin of this dish, but I suspect it is a Western or Eurasian variation upon an agar agar theme. It makes a very decorative and refreshing change from plain fresh fruit at the end of a meal.

Put water into a saucepan and sprinkle agar agar powder on top. Bring to the boil, stirring constantly, then simmer for 5 minutes to completely dissolve the powder. Add sugar, stir to dissolve, then leave to cool.
    Peel the papaya, discard the seeds. Chop flesh into large chunks and pulverise in a blender or food processor to get a fine pulp. If you do not have a blender, press through a sieve or a food mill. When the agar agar liquid is cool but not yet starting to set, stir in papaya pulp and lime juice, mixing well. Taste and adjust sugar to suit your taste. Pour into a large decorative mould and refrigerate until serving. Unmould onto a large plate (glass looks very decorative), garnish with mint leaves if liked, and serve.

Papaya agar agar (recipe this page).

INDIAN

FIRNEE
INDIAN MILK DESSERT

3½ cups milk
4 tablespoons rice flour
1 tablespoon ground almonds (optional)
2½-3 tablespoons sugar
few drops rose essence
few drops cochineal or red food
    colouring
½ teaspoon freshly ground cardamom
    seeds or cardamom powder
10 almonds, blanched and slivered
6 unsalted pistachio nuts, slivered
    (optional)

Mix ½ cup cold milk with rice flour and ground almonds. Bring remaining milk slowly to the boil, then pour in the rice flour mixture. Cook over low heat, stirring all the time, until the mixture thickens. Simmer for 2 minutes, then add sugar and stir until dissolved. Flavour with rose essence and add red food colouring to make the mixture a very pale pink.

Pour into 6 small glass serving bowls. Scatter cardamom over the top of each bowl, then garnish with slivered nuts. Cool, then refrigerate until serving time.

INDIAN

PAYASAM

2 tablespoons sago
2½ cups water
1 tablespoon *ghee* or butter
2 tablespoons sultanas or small raisins
3 tablespoons raw cashews, halved and
    broken
1 cup yellow egg or 'Indian' vermicelli,
    broken in 2.5 cm (1 in) pieces
3 cardamom pods, split and bruised
1 large tin (410 g) evaporated milk
vanilla essence to taste
2-3 tablespoons sugar
yellow food colouring (optional)

This southern Indian dessert is a popular finish to vegetarian meals, and is usually served in a glass and drunk as well as spooned out. This version is slightly thicker and more like a conventional custard dessert. If you prefer it the genuine way, use only 1 tablespoon of sago.

Put the sago and water in a saucepan. Bring to the boil and simmer, stirring frequently, for about 5 minutes until the sago balls become transparent.

Gently heat the *ghee* and fry the sultanas and cashews until golden, taking care not to burn them. Drain and reserve, leaving *ghee* in the pan. Fry the broken vermicelli in the remaining *ghee* for a couple of minutes, turning it over constantly to allow it to absorb the *ghee*.

Put the vermicelli, cardamom and milk into the saucepan with the sago and water. Bring slowly to the boil, stirring, and simmer for 3 minutes. Add sultanas and cashews and cook for another few minutes until sago and vermicelli are soft. Add vanilla, sugar and food colouring and stir until dissolved. Serve at room temperature.

INDIAN

CARROT HALWA

500 g (1 lb) carrots, washed and finely
    grated
2½ cups milk
4 tablespoons instant powdered milk
1¼ cups sugar
2 tablespoons blanched slivered almonds
3 tablespoons *ghee* or butter
2 tablespoons raisins, soaked 5 minutes
    in warm water
few drops rose essence
6 cardamom pods, or ¼ teaspoon
    cardamom powder

This is rather a time-consuming dish, though very easy. It is so delicious that it's well worth making when you have other tasks to keep you near the kitchen.

Put carrots in a large heavy saucepan and add milk. Sprinkle powdered milk over the top and bring to the boil, stirring frequently. Simmer, stirring from time to time, until the liquid has reduced by half. Add sugar, all but 2 teaspoons of the almonds, *ghee*, raisins and rose essence. Stir well and keep cooking gently, stirring occasionally, until the mixture becomes dry and leaves the sides of the pan. (The cooking process takes about 1 hour.)

Grease a rectangular dish and put in the cooked mixture, pressing down well with the back of a spoon. Sprinkle with cardamom powder or, if using cardamom pods, slit them, remove the seeds, crush coarsely and sprinkle over *halwa*. Decorate the top with the reserved slivered almonds and press the top gently once more. Allow to cool, then cut into small squares or diamond shapes and serve. If liked, individual pieces of carrot *halwa* can be wrapped in cellophane paper as a gift.

CHINESE

SOYA BEAN MILK

1 cup dried soya beans
6 cups water
4 tablespoons sugar, or more to taste
2 *pandan* leaves (optional)
few drops almond essence

Very few Singaporeans bother to make this at home, for it can be bought in bottles or by the glass from hawkers all over the island. It is such an excellent drink that it's well worth making at home, especially if you have a blender or food processor.

Soak the soya beans overnight in cold water. Drain, rinse thoroughly, then grind to a fine paste with a mortar and pestle or in a blender or food processor. If using a machine, you may need to add a little water during grinding.

Put the ground beans into a large bowl. Bring water, sugar and *pandan* leaves to the boil, then pour gradually onto the ground soya beans. Pour the whole lot back into a saucepan and bring slowly to the boil, stirring frequently. Simmer very gently for 15 minutes, then strain through a sieve. Put back in the saucepan, bring slowly back to the boil, then remove from heat. Allow to cool, then remove *pandan* leaf and add almond essence to taste. Serve well chilled.

MALAY

ROSE SYRUP

1½ cups lightly crushed rock sugar
　　(500 g or 1 lb)
1½ cups granulated white sugar
4 cups water
few drops rose essence
¼-½ teaspoon cochineal or other red
　　food colouring

The most popular cordial among the Malays, rose syrup is just as delicious mixed with ice-cold milk as it is with water. Do try to obtain rock sugar if you can, as it greatly improves the flavour and consistency of the syrup.

Combine both types of sugar and water in a large saucepan. If you cannot obtain rock sugar, use 3 cups granulated sugar. Bring to the boil and simmer uncovered for 30 minutes. Strain through muslin and allow to cool, then add rose essence to taste and sufficient cochineal to colour the syrup bright red. To serve, combine to taste with ice-cold water or milk.

INDIAN

LASSI
ICED YOGHURT DRINK

2 heaped tablespoons plain yoghurt
　　(home-made if possible)
¾ cup iced water
large pinch of salt
ice cubes

The perfect accompaniment to a hot curry, lassi or a very similar drink is served right through India Afghanistan and Iran. This recipe is for 1 glass — multiply amounts by the number of glasses required.

Put yoghurt, water and salt into a blender and mix for a few seconds. If preferred, put yoghurt and salt into a bowl, beat with an eggbeater until smooth, then add the water and mix well. Serve in a glass with ice cubes.

Acknowledgements

When I first came to Singapore in 1969, all I knew about Singapore food was that I loved it. Since then, literally dozens of people have helped me learn more about the local food — friends, acquaintances, restaurant owners, market stallholders, professional cooks and enthusiastic gourmets (who form about ninety percent of the population), all of whom have generously shared their knowledge with me.

I owe particular thanks to my friend Fu Jok En, to her mother and to the rest of her family for treating my family as part of theirs over the years. Fatimah binte Abdullah, who has been my *amah* and friend since I first arrived in Singapore, has not only helped me explore the Malay culinary world but has helped clear up countless messy kitchens afterwards (how I missed her during my stay in Australia!) My friends Rani Sivamani and Mrs Tan were both most helpful in teaching me more about the Indian and Nonya cuisines.

Others who gave generously of their time and experience include my ex-colleague, Violet Oon; Mrs Joan Frois; Wadhu Sakhrani and Irene of the Omar Khayyam restaurant; José Parrett; Mrs Lee Geow Hai; Che Siti; Che Tonah; Madam Goh Eng Kiaw; Madhavi Krishnan; See Phui Yee; Lin Foo; Philip Little; S. Rasoo, my favourite spice merchant; and the Chia family of the Union Farm Eating House.

Colonel L.T. Firbank generously allowed me to reproduce three prints from his outstanding collection of early Singapore lithographs and etchings; the National Archives were helpful in giving me permission to reproduce several old photographs; and Lim Arts and Crafts of Holland Village Shopping Centre kindly lent a number of items for use in photography.

I sincerely thank Singapore Airlines for enabling Reg Morrison to come to Singapore to take photographs for this book. Reg is one of the world's most patient, understanding and enthusiastic food photographers. He also adores Singapore food, plays a mean game of *carrom* (an Asian board game), gets turned on by local markets, and added to our menagerie with a Peking robin and a baby rabbit from Chinatown — all of which made him fit perfectly into our household.

My mother, Moira Warren, deserves special thanks. Being presented with authentic, home-cooked Chinese food (and chopsticks to eat it with) in New Zealand more than twenty years ago no doubt had a shattering effect on me. I'm now the one who comes up with the exotic food whenever we get together, but I'm sure my mother is responsible for instilling in me a love of exciting food. Tiffany Hutton, my daughter, promises to continue the family interest in cooking, and was a willing kitchen assistant, taste-tester and general critic during the preparation of this book.

My bachelor friends, and particularly Hans Hoefer, deserve a big hug for their enthusiastic reactions at my dining table over the years. But most of all I must thank my husband and editor, Peter Hutton. He introduced me to Elizabeth David, but didn't mind when I switched continents. His support and encouragement throughout our professional relationship have been invaluable. Although always a painstaking editor, he has excelled himself with the effort he has put into the design, editing and packaging of this book. For once, words fail me.

Picture credits: pages 9, 17, 18, 22, 23, courtesy of Singapore National Archives and Records Centre; pages 14, 20, 21, courtesy of Colonel L.T. Firbank (photographer Winson Tan); page 28, Hans Hoefer (ApaPhotoAgency); all other photographs by Reg Morrison.

General Index

Recipe Index